The Fall and Rise of Small Businesses

The Fall and Rise of Small Businesses

Race, Government Aid, and Growth After the Pandemic

Robert W. Fairlie

The MIT Press
Cambridge, Massachusetts
London, England

The MIT Press
Massachusetts Institute of Technology
77 Massachusetts Avenue
Cambridge, MA 02139
mitpress.mit.edu

The MIT Press would like to thank the anonymous peer reviewers who provided comments on drafts of this book. The generous work of academic experts is essential for establishing the authority and quality of our publications. We acknowledge with gratitude the contributions of these otherwise uncredited readers.

This book was set in Stone Serif and Stone Sans by Westchester Publishing Services. Printed and bound in the United States of America.

Library of Congress Cataloging-in-Publication Data

Names: Fairlie, Robert W. author
Title: The fall and rise of small businesses : race, government aid, and growth after the pandemic / Robert W. Fairlie.
Description: Cambridge, Massachusetts : The MIT Press, [2026] | Includes bibliographical references and index.
Identifiers: LCCN 2026000055 (print) | LCCN 2026000056 (ebook) | ISBN 9780262054751 paperback | ISBN 9780262055215 pdf | ISBN 9780262055222 epub
Subjects: LCSH: Small business—United States—History—21st century | Minority business enterprises—History—21st century | COVID-19 Pandemic, 2020-2023—Economic aspects—United States
Classification: LCC HD2346.U5 F325 2026 (print) | LCC HD2346.U5 (ebook) | DDC 338.6/420973—dc23/eng/20260326
LC record available at https://lccn.loc.gov/2026000055
LC ebook record available at https://lccn.loc.gov/2026000056

10 9 8 7 6 5 4 3 2 1

EU Authorised Representative: Easy Access System Europe, Mustamäe tee 50, 10621 Tallinn, Estonia | Email: gpsr.requests@easproject.com

Contents

Preface

At the beginning of March 2020, no one was ready for what was about to happen. As COVID-19 cases continued to rise, however, one thing became very clear: drastic steps would be needed to slow the spread of the disease. An unprecedented move to "flatten the curve" would entail the widespread shutdown of stores and businesses in the United States and around the world. Small businesses were expected to be hit especially hard by the mandated business closures and because of health concerns on the part of customers, workers, and owners.

When the pandemic began, I started working full-time in the laundry room of my house, which was my new temporary office. My entire family was at home, and the laundry room provided a quiet place for me to work. My older daughter returned home during her sophomore year in college and my younger daughter spent the spring of her senior year in high school on her computer at home instead of in the classroom and on the softball field. Although my family did not appreciate it at the time, we were very fortunate in that our house provided separate spaces for each of us to work or attend school. Stress levels were high. My children, of course, were not happy about the new arrangement and missed hanging out with their friends.

Throughout my career, and well before the pandemic started, I have regularly used the monthly Bureau of Labor Statistics' Current Population Survey (CPS) microdata to study business ownership and unemployment. As early as mid-March of 2020, I used the CPS to analyze business industry patterns by race to predict which groups would be hit the hardest by mandated business closures for a *Washington Post* article. Moving forward in time, it was clear that the April 2020 CPS data would be the first to capture the social distancing restrictions that shut down most businesses in the country. I was prepared for the release of these data, which was scheduled for mid-May. I downloaded the microdata set from the BLS website on the day it became available. Shortly after, I wrote the first paper on the early-stage impacts of COVID-19 on racial inequality in business activity, and Ken Couch, Huanan Xu, and I wrote the first paper on the early-stage impacts of COVID-19 on racial inequality in unemployment.

That first paper, "The Impact of COVID-19 on Small Business Owners: The First Three Months After Social-Distancing Restrictions" (*Journal of Economics & Management Strategy*, 2020), had a large scholarly, societal, and policy impact. It was the first study to document and explore the causes of disproportionate business activity losses by race and gender. One of the key findings was that Black business activity dropped by 41 percent in the first month of the pandemic (compared with 17 percent for white business activity). The findings were reported by hundreds of media outlets, including *The New York Times, The Wall Street Journal,* PBS, NPR and CNN. I was told later that the PBS *NewsHour* story that featured the findings reported in the paper helped PBS win a Peabody Award. The findings on business activity by race and ethnicity were used by the U.S. Congress, the U.S. Vice President's office, the President's office, the California governor's office, and numerous other government agencies. I was also told that the findings were so alarming that they helped justify changing how funds were disbursed in the second round of the $800 billion Paycheck Protection Program (PPP) to help minority-owned businesses.

At the beginning of the pandemic, the National Bureau of Economic Research (NBER) encouraged members to conduct research on the economic impacts of COVID-19 to help inform economic policy during this tumultuous period. Following the NBER's call for research, I devoted a substantial amount of my research time to studying the early impacts of COVID-19. I studied a wide range of topics, including impacts on businesses, unemployment levels, college enrollment, educational technology, health education, and racial and gender inequality. My work on the impacts of COVID-19 was highlighted by the NBER in the *NBER Bulletin,* a Reporter Article, Research Spotlight, Personal Research Summary, and a video.

I received so much interest from policymakers, the media, and researchers that I posted several updates to small business activity on my website through December 2021. My business activity updates were used by the

White House, the Vice President's office, the President-elect's transition team, the U.S. Senate, and U.S. House of Representatives to measure and track small businesses, racial inequality, and the PPP program. I provided similar help to the California state governor's office. I testified two times before the U.S. House of Representatives and two times before the California State Assembly. As a sign of the times, I presented my testimonies from my laundry room except for the one occasion on which I testified in person before the California State Assembly, in July 2021. I also discussed, presented, or wrote reports on the topic for numerous government agencies, including the U.S. Department of Justice, the U.S. Treasury Department, the U.S. Senate Committee on Small Business and Entrepreneurship, the Cleveland, San Francisco, and Boston Federal Reserve Banks, the Minority Business Development Agency, and the National Academy of Sciences.

This book builds on the findings from the early papers, research for my congressional testimonies, and the tracking of business activity posted on my website. The book takes a comprehensive approach to exploring the impacts of the pandemic. I examine trends in COVID-19 cases, GDP growth, and national unemployment rates and provide a detailed discussion of social distancing restrictions and other policies before turning to an analysis of trends in business activity, earnings, sales, closures, PPP receipt, and industry structure using several different data sources. The book extends the analysis of business activity and outcomes through the end of 2024, five years after the arrival of COVID-19. The federal government often revises estimates of economic activity, which are also reported in the book. Additionally, new years of data and new datasets that have only recently become available are used in the book. For example, a new dataset that merges administrative information on employer businesses and PPP loan receipt is examined. I hope that the new findings on the early- and long-term effects of the pandemic on business outcomes and the effects of the PPP prove beneficial for policymakers, business leaders, and small business owners as the country moves forward.

I have many people to thank for providing helpful comments and suggestions over the years spanned by this research project. I benefited from numerous discussions with colleagues and policymakers. Special thanks go to coauthors on earlier papers in the pandemic, among them Ken Couch, Huanan Xu, Frank Fossen, Reid Johnsen, and Gentian Droboniku, who helped with the original ideas, methodology, and analysis. Special thanks also go to coauthors on previous books published with the MIT Press, including Zach Kroff, Javi Miranda, Nick Zolas, and Alicia Robb. I had many useful conversations about the research project with them. I also benefited from discussions with participants at numerous seminars, workshops, conferences, and government presentations. Conversations with Jim Poterba and Karen Mills were inspirational in my continuing to study the impacts on small businesses. I thank Beatriz Rache and Nora Onek for research assistance on the project. Finally, my family members have been incredibly supportive during the writing of this book. I thank Rebecca London, Zoe Fairlie, Jessica Fairlie, and Barbara Fairlie for their patience and support.

1 The Novel Coronavirus and Small Businesses

The world was unprepared for what was about to happen in early 2020. A novel coronavirus, producing a disease that came to be known as COVID-19, emerged on the scene and created one of the largest economic disruptions in history. COVID-19 is an infectious disease caused by the SARS-CoV-2 virus and is spread through coughing, sneezing, and even speaking or breathing. Before vaccines became available, the only ways to prevent the disease, or at least slow its spread, were to keep one's distance from other people, wear masks, and wash or disinfect one's hands frequently. Social distancing early in the pandemic turned out to have the largest impact on commerce, work, and the economy more broadly. Face-to-face interactions in stores, workplaces, and offices are crucial for economic activity, and this importance was perhaps underestimated prior to the pandemic.

The widespread shutdown of stores and businesses in the United States and around the world in an effort to contain the spread of COVID-19 was unprecedented. Stores, factories, and many other businesses shuttered operations early in the pandemic in response to policy mandates, declining consumer demand, health concerns, and other factors. In the months after the start of the pandemic, stores began reopening as social distancing restrictions were relaxed and the number of COVID-19 cases declined, but businesses continued to struggle. Businesses continued to lose revenues from disruptions caused by additional waves of shutdowns, restrictions, and reduced customer demand during the pandemic and after, in the recovery period. Many small businesses closed permanently, but the empty storefronts, the early retirements of some owners, and waves of closures also created new business opportunities.

The effects of social distancing restrictions and health concerns in the pandemic were felt differently across the U.S. population, especially among economically vulnerable groups such as Black and Latinx Americans. Because of limited savings and wealth, these groups were especially vulnerable to negative economic shocks such as layoffs associated with COVID-19. Asian Americans also faced hardships in the pandemic as customers, workers, and fellow employees were nervous about interactions because of the coronavirus's origin in China. Small businesses owned by people of color may have faced disproportionate losses during the pandemic and may have experienced differential recoveries in the following years.

A timeline of the beginning of the pandemic provides a useful starting point. The early timeline sets the stage for better understanding what happened to small businesses overall and small businesses owned by people of color during the pandemic and the recovery phase. For most of us, the early events of the pandemic are a blur because so much was happening so fast. In this chapter I review what happened during the pandemic, focusing on the spread of the disease, and in the next chapter I discuss the emerging government policies to stop or at least slow its spread, before examining the impact of COVID-19 on small businesses.

The Early Timeline of COVID-19

The country, and the world, for that matter, were woefully underprepared for what was about to hit in the beginning of 2020. Although it is well known that COVID-19, which stands for "coronavirus disease 2019," emerged in December 2019 in Wuhan, China, the rapidly developing sequence of events in early 2020 has somewhat faded for most people now. It is insightful to go back to the headlines at the beginning of 2020 to recall how fast information about the disease and the impending crisis was evolving. I focus on the headlines in *The New York Times* to illustrate the timeline of information about the disease.

One of the earliest headlines of 2020 in *The New York Times,* from January 8, 2020, read "China Identifies New Virus Causing Pneumonialike Illness."[1] Interestingly, the article noted "There is no evidence that the new virus is readily spread by humans." Only one week later, however, cases of the new virus were reported in Japan and Thailand, raising concern about the spread of the disease across countries.[2] Only two days later, a few U.S. airports started to screen passengers from Wuhan, China. Cases were starting to spread quickly inside China, and concern was growing around the world.[3]

Those concerns were about to escalate quickly. On January 20, 2020, *The New York Times* reported that a government-appointed expert in China revealed that the new disease could spread from human to human.[4] The disease did not take long to make it to the United States. On January 21, 2020, a *New York Times* headline read "First Patient with Wuhan Coronavirus Is Identified in the U.S."[5] The first case was recorded in Washington state. The person had visited Wuhan and returned to the United States on January 15, before airport screening started at a few airports; he had no symptoms at the time.[6] Additional airports started to screen passengers traveling from Wuhan. On the same day, the coronavirus was reported to have spread to Taiwan and South Korea.[7]

Back in China, drastic measures were being taken to stop the spread of the new disease. On January 22 the Chinese government closed off the city of Wuhan.[8] All means of transport out of the city, including planes and trains, were halted. In a city of 11 million people, public transport such as bus and subway lines was also suspended. A day later the stock market started to drop, and China expanded travel restrictions to twelve cities with a combined population of 35 million people.[9]

The second reported case in the United States occurred on January 24 in Chicago.[10] This person had also traveled to Wuhan and had returned to the United States on January 13 without symptoms. On the same day, COVID-19 cases were reported in France and Australia. On January 26 three more cases were confirmed in the United States, two in California and one in Arizona.[11] All three people had recently visited Wuhan. Just three days later, *The New York Times* reported that there were cases in Thailand, Hong Kong, the United States, Taiwan, Australia, Singapore, South Korea, Malaysia Japan, France, Germany, Canada, Vietnam, Nepal, Cambodia, and the United Arab Emirates.[12] Another major announcement about the new virus came out that same day. Some of the cases involved patients who had not traveled to China, which provided evidence that the disease was spreading through person-to-person contact far from the initial source.

The World Health Organization (WHO) declared a global health emergency on January 30. At the end of January there were roughly 12,000 cases in China and one hundred cases across twenty-one other countries.[13] Governments around the world were starting to take restrictive actions. Nearly two hundred Americans were evacuated from Wuhan and were quarantined for two weeks at a military base in California.[14] Foreign nationals who had recently visited China would be barred entry into the United States. Major U.S. airlines announced that flights between the United States and China would be suspended for several months.

The first extensive business shutdowns prompted by COVID-19 started in China at the end of January. For example, on January 29 the government of Jiangsu Province ordered businesses except those providing necessary items, such as utilities, pharmacies, and supermarkets, to close until February 10.[15] Small to medium-size businesses such as stores and restaurants were expected to get hit the hardest. As reported on February 3, Beijing had mostly shut down, even though it was not under a strict government-ordered lockdown as Wuhan and other nearby cities were.[16] But business was notably affected. Most shops, restaurants, hair salons, and other services were closed. Larger stores and shopping centers imposed restrictions on entry, and customers avoided going out to shop. In less than two months, extensive business shutdowns would come to the United States.

As more and more states reported cases, and as COVID-19 was spreading quickly in most parts of the world, the WHO and the Centers for Disease Control and Prevention (CDC) started to release announcements about the virus. Perhaps the most memorable announcement came on March 11, 2020, when the WHO officially declared COVID-19 a pandemic, ratcheting up concerns over the spread of the disease around the world. The WHO pointed to the more than 118,000 cases of COVID-19 in more than 110 countries and territories around the world. A few days later, on March 15, the CDC recommended that no gatherings of fifty or more people be held for the next eight weeks.[17] To be sure, schools in many states had already started to close, some colleges had moved to online instruction, and several cities had closed restaurants and bars, allowing only takeout and delivery service. But the CDC announcement at the national level underlined the seriousness of the virus and the potential for its rapid spread throughout the country. Perhaps not surprisingly, by March 17 all states in the country had reported COVID-19 cases (National Public Radio 2020).

The Rapidly Growing Number of COVID-19 Cases in the United States

Although the first case of the novel coronavirus infection in the United States was recorded in January 2020, it was not until early March that the CDC began tracking and reporting case numbers. COVID-19 case data start for the week ending March 14. There were 38,878 recorded cases that week. Because much was unknown about the coronavirus at the time, however, there were likely many more cases in the country. Over the following week, the number of new recorded cases in the country more than doubled, to 90,000 new cases that week. Figure 1.1 displays weekly numbers of new COVID-19 cases in March and April 2020. In the last full week in March 2020, new cases of COVID-19 jumped to nearly 120,000. The number of new cases each week continued to climb rapidly in the early days of the pandemic, which was expected because the disease was highly contagious.

The early period of the pandemic was clouded by uncertainty. It is possible that in early to mid-March, customers, workers, and business owners might have started to change their behavior out of fear of catching the disease. The major announcements about the "pandemic" and recommendations on social gatherings by the WHO and CDC might have had at least some chilling effect on business activity in early March. Also, COVID-19 case numbers were rising fast, and there was no hope of a vaccine coming available in the near future. The CDC and health officials were frank about how long it might take to develop a safe and effective vaccine. A vaccine would not be coming in the next few months. In total, small businesses were likely affected by health concerns over COVID-19 in early March, but nothing similar in scale to what was about to happen starting on March 16, when the first social distancing restrictions were implemented in the United States.

COVID-19 and Small Businesses: Why There Could Have Been Impacts

Numbers of reported COVID-19 cases were rising fast in the spring of 2020. Several channels existed by which the emerging pandemic might have affected businesses, and small businesses in particular. The most important channel was likely the mandated social distancing restrictions, which shut down the in-person operations of most businesses starting at the end of March 2020. Chapter 2 provides a detailed discussion of these restrictions, which were undertaken in an attempt to slow the spread of the disease by restricting face-to-face interactions in commercial spaces, the workplace, schools, at social events, and in many other places where people might gather. The social distancing restrictions likely exacted a major toll on business activity, especially among small businesses. Direct-to-consumer and business-to-business sales likely dropped substantially.

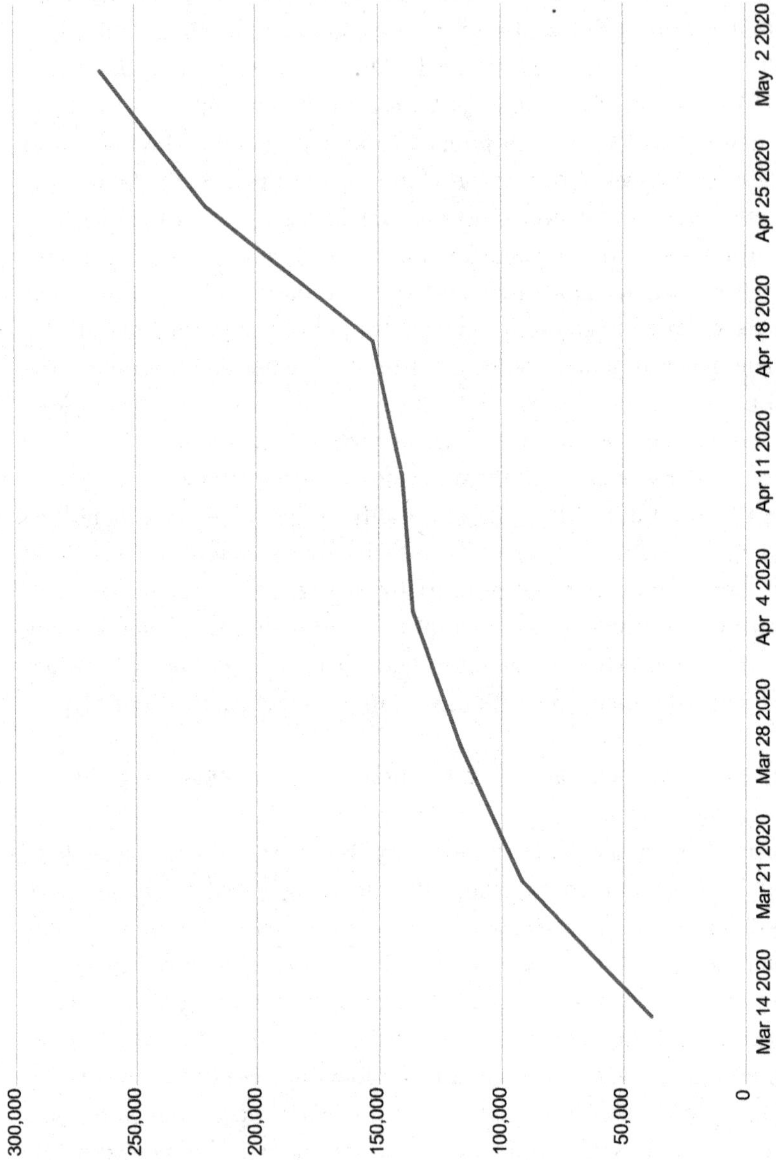

Figure 1.1
New COVID-19 cases in the United States per week for weeks ending March 14, 2020, to May 2, 2020.

Small businesses stood to be particularly hard-hit by COVID-19 because they are often located in sectors where the restrictions on commercial activity were severe, such as tourist spots, retail centers, and transportation hubs and lines. Additionally, many small businesses are in "nonessential" industries rather than "essential" industries—an important distinction for social distancing restrictions at the beginning of the pandemic. To weather the storm of the pandemic, businesses often needed to tap into cash reserves and savings or take out loans from financial institutions. Small businesses often have limited ability to access financing and have only small cash reserves on hand. They are also unlikely to have long-term, established relationships with banks willing to lend money. Large companies, by contrast, receive direct and preferential financing from financial institutions. Perhaps working in their favor, however, small businesses qualified for loans from the Paycheck Protection Program (PPP), which provided nearly a trillion dollars in funding during the pandemic.

Health restrictions were imposed early in the pandemic to slow the spread of the disease. Small businesses were likely affected very quickly by these restrictions. They likely had a difficult time figuring out new regulations regarding operating procedures and legal issues at the very beginning of the pandemic. Small businesses may have had less ability to figure out and implement procedures to align with rapidly changing government regulations regarding healthy operations (e.g., mask wearing, the use of plastic barriers, cleaning, spacing of customers, and so on). Large businesses likely could comply more easily with the measures imposed by government authorities.

COVID-19 disrupted global and national supply chains. Relative to large corporations, small businesses would have been less dependent on global and national supply chains that were disrupted during the crisis. Large companies, however, can choose from among different channels to buy and sell their goods and services. Further, rent on commercial facilities, payment for utilities (electric, gas, and water), salary payments, loan payments to financial institutions, and taxes are expenses with relatively little flexibility. Small businesses would have been hampered in their ability to meet these expenses early in the pandemic.

The consumer side is also important to consider when exploring the impacts of the pandemic on businesses. On the one hand, sales were expected to drop owing to decreased consumer demand during the pandemic. Consumers might have altered their consumption patterns either through either a voluntary decrease in spending or to be in compliance with confinement measures and the restrictions imposed on commercial activities. Consumers might also have reduced their consumption because of the increasing economic uncertainty, income losses, changes in habits (such as spending more time at home than socializing outside the home), or simply because someone living at home caught COVID-19. Under such circumstances, consumers commonly opt for goods and services provided by larger establishments, which find it easier to adapt to and meet health standards and restrictions imposed by the authorities. Consumers might have felt safer shopping at larger retailers. Small businesses are especially susceptible to abrupt drops in demand.

Organization of the Book

Governments around the world responded swiftly and aggressively to curtail the rapid spread of COVID-19. Responses to the disease evolved quickly in mid-March 2020 in the United States, with health authorities making a concerted effort to try to limit interactions between people, especially in crowded settings. One major consequence of these efforts was to limit business commerce, especially at small businesses that provide goods and services directly to customers. Anticipating the economic struggles that would result from these restrictions, the federal government provided the largest aid program to small businesses in history. Nearly 12 million loans totaling a staggering $800 million were provided to small businesses through the PPP. The goal of the program was to help small businesses stay open and retain their employees. In this way, the disruptions caused by mandated shutdowns might be reduced by keeping employees on the payroll of businesses instead of having those employees join the unemployment insurance rolls.

This book examines three overarching questions regarding the impacts of COVID-19 on small businesses resulting from social distancing restrictions; shifts in owner, worker, and customer behavior over health concerns; and federal aid packages. Two additional questions regarding how the economic recovery from COVID-19 affected small businesses are examined.

1. How did COVID-19 affect small business owners? Did it severely reduce their business activity and earnings during the first several months of the pandemic?

2. What types of businesses were hit the hardest? Did the pandemic disproportionately affect and close Black-, Latinx-, and Asian-owned businesses?
3. How did the federal government respond to the crisis to help small businesses? Did the massive, unprecedented levels of government relief for small businesses through the PPP help small businesses survive and retain employees? Did PPP funds get distributed evenly to minority communities?
4. Five years later, have small businesses recovered from the COVID-19–induced recession? Has the recovery been steady or rocky with changes in numbers of reported COVID-19 cases and policies? Has the recovery been uneven by race?
5. What new opportunities for small businesses have appeared in the five years since the start of the pandemic? Which industries have grown and which have contracted since before the pandemic started? What will happen going forward, and how will it be affected by consumer trends, technological changes such as robots and AI, and government policy?

The material covered in each chapter of the book is arranged mostly in chronological order. Chapters 1–4 cover the first few months of the pandemic, when the U.S. economy experienced the largest disruption. Chapters 5 and 6 cover the rest of the first year of the pandemic, 2020. The next three chapters focus on the second year of the pandemic, 2021, which was a pivotal year that saw the arrival of vaccines, a new president, and a rebooted PPP. Chapter 10 crosses from earlier years to later years of the pandemic. Chapters 11–13 cover the economic recovery, and chapter 14 concludes with a summary of findings, areas for further research, and a discussion of future trends.

Overall, the book examines the five-year period from the start of the pandemic in January 2020 to the end of 2024. I weave together evidence from the most up-to-date data on business activity and novel data on PPP receipt and business outcomes recently released by the U.S. Census Bureau. The goal is to reconstruct the story of what happened during one of the most important five-year periods in economic history, from the first cases of COVID-19 reported in the United States, in December 2019, to several years into the recovery, ending in December 2024.

Chapter 2 examines the social distancing restrictions that shut down nonessential businesses, and the distinction made between essential and nonessential businesses. The discussion of the timeline of restrictions placed on nonessential businesses highlights the experience of Santa Clara County, California, the first in the nation to pose these restrictions. The rapidly rising numbers of COVID-19 cases after the initial weeks of the pandemic provide a context for better understanding the potential impacts of social distancing restrictions on small businesses. Chapter 2 also briefly discusses the methodology and measurement issues that are important for estimating the impact of COVID-19 on business activity and earnings in later chapters. Finally, chapter 2 discusses state variation in numbers of COVID-19 cases and two major policies employed to stop the spread of the disease, social distancing restrictions and masking mandates. States had different views on the trade-off between slowing the spread of the disease and minimizing economic activity losses.

Chapter 3 examines the impacts of COVID-19 on business activity in the first few months of the pandemic. The impacts are explored across different types of businesses and between essential versus nonessential businesses. Some industries were hit especially hard during these first few months, while other industries actually experienced growth in business activity. The scramble to find up-to-date data on business activity at the very beginning of the pandemic is also discussed, with suggestions for future work in real-time tracking of business activity, which is not readily available from government sources. Chapter 3 also examines the early impacts of COVID-19 on business owner earnings. Losses to business earnings are estimated across different industries and owner characteristics, such as education, age, and gender. Adjustments are made for prepandemic trends in business earnings. The methodology used to make these adjustments is discussed in an appendix to the chapter.

Additional measures of new business activity and the opportunity versus necessity share of new business activity are presented in chapter 3. Focusing on California, where losses were large, the chapter discusses impacts on business sales, closures, and market concentration. Finally, the broader impacts of COVID-19 on the U.S. economy as measured by the gross domestic product (GDP) and the national unemployment rate are discussed. In sum, the chapter provides a thorough discussion of COVID-19 impacts on small businesses using several measures and data sources, and a comparison with broader impacts on the U.S. economy.

Chapter 4 explores whether there were disproportionate impacts of COVID-19 on business owners by race. The impacts on business activity are examined first, focusing on the first full month, April 2020, after social distancing restrictions were put in place. The second part of chapter 4 examines whether there were disproportionate impacts on business earnings, and, if so, how large those differential impacts were. An important question is whether racial differences in prepandemic owner, business, and geographic characteristics contributed to disproportionate losses in business earnings by race. For example, did industry concentrations place some racial groups at higher risk of business earnings losses in the pandemic? Chapter 4 explores these questions and related questions about whether geographic differences in exposure to COVID-19 and social distancing restrictions contributed to larger earnings losses among business owners of color.

Chapter 5 discusses the Paycheck Protection Program, which represented the largest aid package ever provided to small businesses by the federal government. Nearly $1 billion was provided to small businesses from April 2020 to May 2021 through the PPP with the goal of helping small businesses survive and retain their employees during the pandemic. This chapter focuses on the first two rounds of the program, which ran from April 3, 2020, to August 8, 2020. (The reboot of the program in early 2021 is covered in chapter 9.) The largest providers of loans are discussed for the two rounds and how these changed over time in the first several months of the program. Another important question examined in the chapter is whether PPP funds were evenly disbursed across minority communities in the United States. The chapter also reviews previous research on the Small Business Administration's (SBA's) massive Economic Injury Disaster Loan (EIDL) program and efforts by researchers to address problems of missing race information in the PPP loan data.

Chapter 6 returns to examining the impacts of COVID-19 on business activity by expanding the analysis of chapter 4 to the next two months of the pandemic, May and June 2020. Did business activity drop even further or did it partially rebound in these two months? Did business activity trends over these two months differ by race or industry? The analysis then turns to the impacts on total business activity and racial inequality in business activity through the second half of the year, July to December 2020.

Further losses or rebounds during 2020 are also explored for business sales in California, GDP, and the national unemployment rate. Trends in these measures of the broader economy provide a context for understanding how small business owners fared after the initial disruption caused by COVID-19 and social distancing restrictions.

Vaccines rolled out at the beginning of 2021 to the general public. Chapter 7 examines how numbers of new COVID-19 cases changed in 2021 and whether business activity increased with the resulting optimism and a new presidential administration. Chapter 7 also examines the impacts of COVID-19 on business earnings in 2021. Did businesses rebound strongly during the year? Did businesses rebound differently by industry? The chapter concludes by examining trends in the broader economy over the pivotal year.

Chapter 8 extends the analysis to examine whether there were differential rebounds for Black, Latinx, and Asian business owners through 2021. Differential trends in business activity and earnings are explored. The chapter considers the potential contributions of owner, business, and geographic characteristics to the differential trends observed in 2021.

Chapter 9 examines the reboot of the PPP at the beginning of 2021. The third round of the program differed from the first two rounds in 2020 by placing more emphasis on eligible borrowers in underserved and disadvantaged communities. The chapter first discusses the extensive changes to how the program was marketed, the financial institutions providing loans, and the types of small businesses targeted, including those without employees. During this third round of the PPP, from January to May 2021, a total of $278 billion was provided to small businesses through 6.7 million loans, of which $209 billion and 2.9 million loans were second-draw loans. The chapter then analyzes how the first-draw and second-draw loans were disbursed to minority communities. The analysis builds on the analysis in chapter 5 of the 2020 program.

Chapter 10 examines PPP receipt and small business outcomes. The analysis draws on an exciting new administrative data source providing information on PPP loan receipt, survival, and job destruction among small businesses that recently became available. The new data source, the Business Dynamics Statistics of SBA COVID Response database, links data on the universe of employer businesses to data on the universe of PPP loans. I use the data first to examine the percentage of small businesses receiving

PPP loans. I then analyze whether PPP receipt differed by size of firm and when the first loan was received. The receipt of second-draw loans through the PPP by small businesses is also examined using the data. I next use the new BDS-SBA COVID database to explore the important question of whether the PPP helped small businesses survive and retain employees during the pandemic. The analysis of the association between PPP loan receipt, exits, and job destruction is conducted for firms of different sizes and time of receipt of the first PPP loan. Previous research examining the question is also discussed. Additional aid programs for small businesses, including those targeting small businesses in the struggling food and entertainment industries, are discussed. Finally, the chapter briefly describes the findings from studies examining fraud in the PPP.

Chapter 11 examines the recovery from the COVID-19–induced recession from the beginning of 2022 to the end of 2024. The disease, however, did not disappear. The chapter first examines trends in the number of new COVID-19 cases over the time period before turning to an examination of trends in business activity and earnings. Trends in GDP growth and the national unemployment rate are also presented.

Chapter 12 explores the question of whether there was racial inequality in the recovery for small businesses over the past few years. The chapter first examines how business activity rebounded for each group from the beginning of 2022 to the end of 2024. It then moves on to examine racial patterns in business earnings during the recovery phase. Comparisons are also made with trends in inequality in total earnings and wage and salary worker earnings.

Chapter 13 examines how small businesses in different industries rebounded economically in the recovery. The question of whether businesses that were initially hit the hardest in the pandemic recovered or did not recover by 2024 is explored. I also examine which industries contributed to overall growth in business activity for each racial group. Finally, the chapter presents detailed data on trends in the industry composition of employer business establishments to assess whether there were differential recovery rates.

Chapter 14 concludes by placing the findings in the context of broader issues and lessons learned about long-term inequality, policy impacts, data limitations, and real-time measures of business activity. The chapter provides several suggestions for future research to build on the numerous findings presented in the previous chapters. The last section discusses the implications of trends in consumer behavior, advances in robots and AI, and changes to downtowns for the future of small businesses.

The Context and Big Picture

The detailed and wide-ranging analyses across these chapters of the book provide a better understanding of what happened to small businesses and racial inequality during the pandemic and subsequent economic recovery. Although a flurry of research has examined the impacts of COVID-19 on the economy, workforce, health, and education, much less work has addressed impacts on small businesses and their owners, and even less has focused on the role of racial inequality in those impacts. Furthermore, very few studies have examined the economic recovery or long-term impacts of the COVID-19–related recession.[18] One reason for the lack of research on small businesses is data availability. This book uses the most recent and detailed data possible to examine trends in business ownership activity and earnings during the pandemic and the recovery from the pandemic. The analysis includes novel data only recently released by the U.S. Census Bureau and the SBA.

Some of the analyses contained in the book were prompted by requests by the federal government and the president of the National Bureau of Economic Research (NBER) early in the pandemic. My first research on the impacts of COVID-19 on small business owners at the beginning of the pandemic was released as a working paper in early May of 2020 (Fairlie 2020a). The findings were covered widely in the press and by news outlets (e.g., *The Washington Post, The New York Times, The Wall Street Journal,* PBS, CNBC, BBC) and used in testimony before the U.S. Senate (Busby 2020; Evans 2020), a new Senate bill (U.S. Senate 2020), and the California state governor's office to support small business programs at the very start of the pandemic.[19] The findings helped justify changing how funds were disbursed in the second round of the $800 billion PPP to help minority-owned businesses.

At the beginning of the pandemic, the NBER encouraged members to conduct research on the economic impacts of COVID-19 to help inform economic policy during this unprecedented event. Following the NBER call for research on the economic impacts of COVID, I devoted a substantial amount of research time to studying the impacts of the pandemic on small businesses, unemployment, college enrollment, and racial and gender inequality.[20] As small businesses continued to struggle in the pandemic, I provided updates on whether business owners in total and across different racial groups had recovered or continued to struggle. The findings from continual updates to business owner activity in the pandemic were used by Congress, the U.S. Vice President's office, the President's office, and the California governor's office. I was asked repeatedly for information on how small businesses were doing by Vice President Harris's economic team and President Biden's economic teams (both the transition and the administrative teams). U.S. senators and other government agencies used the findings of my research at the beginning of the pandemic. The U.S. State Department reached out for statistics on how small businesses were doing in the pandemic. For a couple of years, I ran a website that tracked how business owners were doing, and provided the link to the media and policymakers. After studying the PPP, the U.S. Senate was very interested in the PPP and reached out to me to study the third round of providing funds to small businesses.

The research presented here summarizes, revises, and expands on this earlier work at the beginning of the pandemic. The book also delves into the turning point in the pandemic and the continuation of the economic recovery from this turning point through five years after the start of the pandemic. The book picks up where the earlier studies left off and provides a comprehensive analysis of not only business activity but also business earnings, industry structure, PPP receipt and business outcomes, and broader trends in COVID-19 cases, GDP growth, and unemployment rates. When possible, all information is provided from before the pandemic started to the end of 2024.

The findings from the chapters that follow have important implications for improving our understanding of the causes of and shaping policies to address the disproportionate impacts on small businesses. Disproportionate losses to business activity and earnings among business owners of color during the pandemic are additionally concerning because of the potential to widen economic inequality, increase losses in economic efficiency, and hamper job creation and economic stability in low-income and disadvantaged neighborhoods (Boston 1999, 2006; Fairlie and Robb 2008; Stoll, Raphael, and Holzer 2001). Large earnings losses among small businesses in general and those owned by specific groups of the population during the pandemic are worrisome for the longer-term survival of small, local, and diverse businesses throughout the country. Although larger stores and chains with a strong online presence may survive, many small businesses might not have the resources to weather continued reduced demand and longer-term shifts to online shopping. When small business owners were asked just prior to the pandemic what actions they would take if faced with a two-month revenue loss, 17 percent said they would close or sell the business (Mills, Battisto, de Zeeuw, et al. 2020). Very early in the pandemic the U.S. Census Small Business Pulse Survey indicated that only 15–20 percent of businesses had enough cash on hand to cover three months of operations (Bohn, Mejia, and Lafortune 2020; U.S. Census Bureau 2020).

Small business ownership is an extremely important way of making a living. It typically provides local jobs and creates a sense of community. The loss of shops and restaurants and the decline of many downtown areas across the country have created a vacuum in what used to be vibrant areas for commerce and socializing with others in the community. Many downtown areas and neighborhood shopping districts continue to have boarded-up storefronts. Ultimately consumers, robots, and AI might have more impact on the future of small businesses than government policies. The findings from the latest trends in the economic recovery from the pandemic provide insights into what may be next for small businesses.

2 Social Distancing Restrictions

The novel coronavirus arrived in the United States and spread rapidly. The government's response to the disease was also swift and included an effort to try to limit face-to-face interactions, especially in crowded spaces or at mass events, but the response mostly consisted of voluntary or scattered recommendations or restrictions. These early attempts to slow the spread of the new disease were not enough, however, and everything started to change in mid-March. On March 16, 2020, the San Francisco Bay Area imposed the first social distancing restrictions: residents were instructed to stay home and not go to work, school, or stores if possible. By March 17, all states in the United States had reported COVID-19 cases, and most were discussing whether to also implement shelter-in-place or social distancing restrictions. The State of California soon followed the Bay Area by imposing statewide shelter-in-place restrictions on March 19. The shelter-in-place restriction, or more aptly the "social distancing" restriction, noted that the population should "continue sheltering at their place of residence except for essential needs" and urged "essential businesses to implement social distancing protocols" (see appendix 2.A). On March 20, New York state announced an executive order requiring residents to stay indoors except for essential trips and services. Washington state, where the first COVID-19 case was recorded in the United States, imposed social distancing restrictions on March 23. As of April 2, thirty-seven states, along with many cities and counties, had urged residents to stay home as much as possible. By April 5, most, if not all, states had imposed some form of shelter-in-place or social distancing restrictions or recommendations.

The key dates in the early timeline of the pandemic and shelter-in-place or social distancing restrictions are as follows:

- January 20, 2020: First confirmed case of COVID-19 reported, in the State of Washington.
- March 11, 2020: The World Health Organization (WHO) declared COVID-19 a pandemic.
- March 16, 2020: The San Francisco Bay Area imposed social distancing restrictions.
- March 19, 2020: The State of California imposed social distancing restrictions.
- March 20, 2020: New York state imposed social distancing restrictions.
- By early April: Most states had imposed social distancing restrictions.

How did the timing of these announcements and restrictions affect small businesses? The March 11 announcement might have marked the start of negative effects on businesses because of early demand shifts over health concerns predating shelter-in-place or social distancing restriction policies. Or it might have created increased demand because of the uncertainty of what was to come. For example, many of us remember vividly the toilet paper shortages and stockpiling that occurred in the early months of the pandemic. The social distancing restrictions starting on March 16, however, were likely the real kickoff to negative impacts on small businesses. These impacts might have been felt not only in the form of mandated business closures but also in the disruption to consumer behavior. Many customers became nervous about shopping and visiting stores, especially small stores, restaurants, and personal service providers such as hair and nail salons, as COVID-19 was spreading quickly. Furthermore, social distancing restrictions also included shelter-in-place suggestions and restrictions that limited travel outside homes to "essential" trips only. These restrictions certainly resulted in fewer visitors to local businesses. Finally, employees might have become nervous about working in businesses and contracting the disease, placing further pressure on small business owners to shut down operations at least temporarily until new information was provided about the disease or vaccines were developed.

Business Shutdowns in Santa Clara County

Santa Clara County was the first area of the United States to impose any kind of serious social distancing restrictions. Examining these restrictions provides a useful case study for thinking about potential impacts on small businesses. The social distancing restrictions in Santa Clara County officially started on March 16, 2020, but worries about COVID-19 surfaced at least a month earlier. For example, on February 3, 2020, a proclamation by the director of emergency services declared the existence of a local health emergency in the county. On February 10 a resolution by the county's board of supervisors extended the health emergency declaration and ratified it. The State of California followed by proclaiming a state of emergency on March 4. Although these proclamations did not impose the extensive shelter-in-place or social distancing restrictions that were to follow, they likely sparked concern among customers, business owners, and workers about the disease. These earlier concerns might have had at least a small effect of curtailing commerce.

In the original order for social distancing, on March 16, Santa Clara County noted that all businesses with facilities located in the county were required to cease activities except for "essential businesses" and activities that were necessary to keep the business afloat (see appendix 2.A for a complete list). First, the activities that supported basic operations were those needed to maintain the value of the business's inventory, ensure security, process payroll and employee benefits, or perform related functions, including the minimum necessary activities to facilitate employees of the business being able to continue to work remotely from their residences. But the order stated that employees had to comply with social distancing requirements while carrying out such operations. Also, the order made it clear that owners and their employees working from home did not have to cease activities. The extensive movement to working from home began.

Santa Clara County and other local governments defined "essential" businesses in broad terms. The classification of some types of businesses as essential made sense. As expected, health care operations were deemed essential. Anything related to food was deemed essential and thus was not mandated to close. This category included grocery stores, convenience stores, and farm stands on the customer side and farming, fishing, and livestock operations on the production side. Facing a rapidly spreading and mostly unknown disease but a need for people to eat, these food-related stores and production facilities remained open during the early shutdowns. The country was not ready to face the alternative of having the government, possibly through the military, take over all distribution of food in something akin to a scene in an apocalyptic movie.

Related to food sales and production, gas stations, banks, auto supply and repair shops, and hardware stores remained open. Additional exceptions included, for example, media, postal services, plumbing, electricians, and educational institutions (although classes were held remotely). Many of these stores and businesses faced reduced demand as customers avoided them because of disease concerns. Additionally, some of these store types faced less demand because of changes in customers' work and spending behavior. For example, people were not commuting to work or college and so were purchasing much less gasoline at gas stations. The drop in commuting to the office and in business travel had negative effects for a wide range of small businesses. Taxi services, laundry services, and child care centers, for example, were affected by the shift of work from offices to home. Restaurants, coffee shops, and other small stores that catered to downtown or other business districts no longer had a captive audience of workers during the busy lunch hour.

Additional restrictions that affected small businesses focused not on industries but on general business operations. A key factor was the idea of "minimum basic operations." The basic idea was that workers needed to comply with social distancing restrictions to the extent possible to perform the minimum necessary activities to maintain the value of a business's inventory, ensure security, process payroll and employee benefits, or conduct related functions. Furthermore, the minimum necessary activities included those required to facilitate employees of the business being able to work remotely from their residences.

Classification of Essential versus Nonessential Businesses

Early in the pandemic, businesses were categorized into "essential" or "nonessential." Although there were concerns over how contagious and dangerous the disease was at the time, the government decided to allow businesses and stores providing basic services to remain open. Some of the clearest examples of businesses providing essential services that remained open were grocery stores and gas stations. In contrast, movie theaters were considered nonessential and were closed. Schools and colleges were deemed essential but switched to remote classes and operations. It is possible to categorize industries into essential versus nonessential according to state or local government guidelines, although there was a lot of variation across the country in these guidelines in terms of specific industries.

Early in the pandemic, the State of Delaware provided probably the most detailed and comprehensive list of essential businesses at the 4-digit industry level, using the same 4-digit industry codes as the widely used North American Industry Classification System (NAICS). This made the list easier to implement for research and policymaking at the beginning of the pandemic.[1] Delaware also made its list of essential businesses available to policymakers, businesses, the public, and researchers.

Table 2.1 reports these industries for 2-digit NAICS code approximations to simplify. The classification is likely to be imperfect, however, because definitions, enforcement, business owner compliance, and health- and economic-related consumer reactions varied across the country. The classification is useful for showing generally which groups of industries were included and which were excluded from social distance restriction shutdowns.

COVID-19 Cases After April 2020

The number of new cases of COVID-19 increased by 137 percent from the first to the second week of March 2020, which is the first time period on record by the CDC (figure 2.1). After the implementation of social distancing restrictions the weekly rise in the number of new cases slowed. The increase in the number of COVID-19 cases from the week ending April 4 to the week ending April 11 was much lower, 3 percent.

The question of whether shelter-in-place or social distancing restrictions slowed the spread of COVID-19 has been studied extensively. The findings range from large reductions in the spread of the disease due to lockdowns to small reductions to relatively no effects of government mandates (see, e.g., Berry et al. 2021; Dave et al. 2021; Fowler et al. 2020; Hsiang et al. 2020; Lewis 2022; Wagner et al. 2020). Social distancing restrictions likely slowed the spread in the early months but it is unlikely that there will ever be an

Table 2.1
Essential and Nonessential Industries in the Early Stages of COVID-19

Essential industries
Agriculture
Forestry, Logging, Fishing and Hunting
Mining, Quarrying, and Oil and Gas Extraction
Construction
Nonmetallic Mineral Product Manufacturing
Primary Metals and Fabricated Metal Products
Machinery Manufacturing
Computer and Electronic Product Manufacturing
Electrical Equipment, Appliance Manufacturing
Transportation Equipment Manufacturing
Wood Products
Furniture and Fixtures Manufacturing
Miscellaneous and Not Specified Manufacturing
Food Manufacturing
Beverage and Tobacco Products
Textile, Apparel, and Leather Manufacturing
Paper and Printing
Petroleum and Coal Products Manufacturing
Chemical Manufacturing
Plastics and Rubber Products
Wholesale Trade
Transportation and Warehousing
Utilities
Internet Publishing and Broadcasting
Telecommunications
Internet Service Providers and Data Processing Services
Finance
Insurance
Rental and Leasing Services
Professional, Scientific, and Technical Services
Management of Companies and Enterprises
Waste Management and Remediation Services
Educational Services
Hospitals
Health Care Services, Except Hospitals
Social Assistance Services
Repair and Maintenance
Private Households
Public Administration
Armed Forces

Nonessential industries
Retail Trade
Publishing Industries (Except Internet)
Motion Picture and Sound Recording Industries
Broadcasting (Except Internet)
Other Information Services
Real Estate
Administrative and Support Services
Arts, Entertainment, and Recreation
Accommodation
Food Services and Drinking Places
Personal and Laundry Services
Membership Associations and Organizations

Notes: Essential versus nonessential industry designations are reported here as 2-digit code approximations based on actual codes at the 4-digit level from the Delaware state list.

agreed-upon estimate of the reduction in COVID-19 cases resulting from these restrictions.

After the initial waves in March and April, for most weeks during the spring and early summer of 2020 new case numbers increased at a slower rate, though still increasing overall. Figure 2.1 expands the time period to display weekly COVID-19 case numbers through the end of 2020. For the week ending July 18, 2020, slightly more than three quarters of a million new cases of COVID-19 were reported in the United States. The number of new cases finally reversed course: the week ending July 25 had 701,985 new cases. New case numbers mostly declined over the summer but ticked up again in September: for the week ending September 19, the number of new cases increased by more than 100,000 from the previous week, and new cases were nearly at the three-quarter-million mark again.

Numbers of new cases were rising into unchartered territory. On November 14, 2020, the nation witnessed more than one million new COVID-19 cases over the previous week. The following week, ending November 21, a peak number of 1,094,536 new cases of COVID-19 were reported. The number of new cases per week remained high mostly through the end of 2020.

These trends in the number of new COVID-19 cases are important for understanding how social distancing restrictions might have shut down small businesses and affected their activity, earnings, and other outcomes. Also, concerns over health likely led customers, workers, and owners to

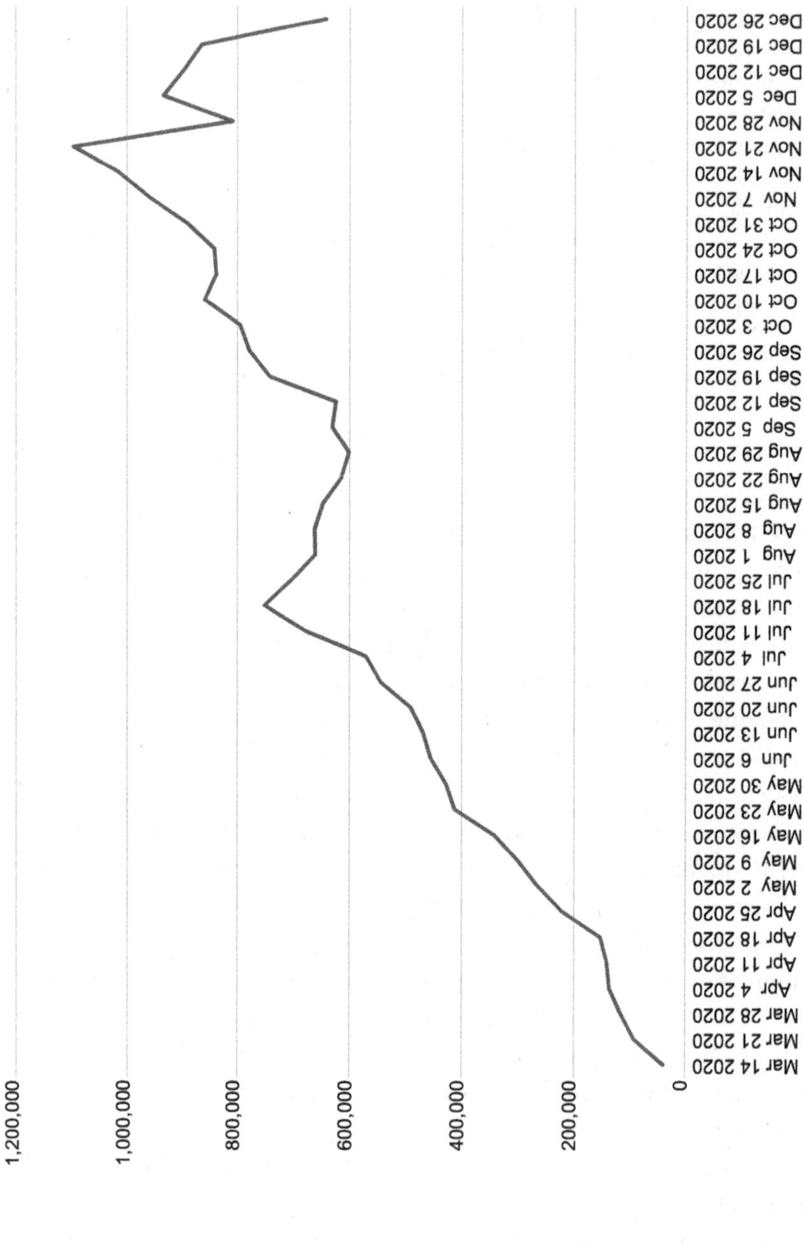

Figure 2.1
New COVID-19 cases in the United States per week for weeks ending March 14, 2020, to December 26, 2020.

alter their shopping behavior during this time period when COVID-19 was spreading so rapidly.

Measuring the Impacts of COVID-19: Timing

The timing of events is important for analyzing the impacts of COVID-19 on small business owners and the broader economy. The number of COVID-19 cases was not recorded until the second week of March 2020 but rose quickly after that, and social distancing restrictions were rolled out at the end of March and early April. The standard methodological approach would be to compare business activity in a time period prior to COVID-19 ("pre-period") with business activity in a time period after the arrival of COVID-19 ("post-period"). There are two key decisions for the analysis of impacts. First, when did COVID-19 first have an effect? Was it after social distancing restrictions were imposed? Or was it before restrictions were imposed, when customers, business owners, and employees started to worry about catching the contagious disease and changed their behavior?

Second, most data on business activity are collected monthly, quarterly, or annually. Even for higher-frequency data such as monthly data (which are used extensively in subsequent chapters), the decisions over which months are included in the pre-period and which months are included in the post-period are not always straightforward. With COVID-19 in particular, March 2020 might be included in either category. Most of the month did not include mandated business shutdowns through social distancing restrictions across the country, but in at least part of March, restrictions were in place for some locations. Additionally, consumer, owner, and employee behavior might have started to change in March, resulting in closures or at least reduced business activity during that month. To address this issue, most of the analyses in subsequent chapters exclude March 2020, so that the pre-period is considered to be the months through February 2020 and the post-period the months starting in April 2020. This approach is sometimes characterized as a "donut hole" comparison because one time period is left out of the analysis. In this case, March 2020 is the hole in the donut.

Using quarterly data such as gross domestic product (GDP), the first quarter of 2020 includes January, February, and March. The second quarter includes April, May, and June. Quarterly data do not include as clean a break around the timing of COVID-19 restrictions because they do not permit leaving out the ambiguous month of March 2020. By chance, however, they do line up fairly closely with COVID-19 because of the April 1 cutoff for the start of the second quarter. Most analyses of the impacts of COVID-19 using quarterly data define the pre-period as ending with the first quarter of 2020 and the post-period as starting with the second quarter of 2020. It was unlikely that COVID-19 had a major effect on most of the month of March 2020, suggesting that the first quarter of 2020 is "clean" and that this approach is reasonable. Trends in GDP growth defining the pre-period as including 2020Q1 and the post-period as starting with 2020Q2 are presented in later chapters.

Annual data create more difficulty in clearly defining the pre- and post-periods but also provide a reasonable approximation. The calendar year 2020 includes January and February, which were before COVID-19. Thus, only two months, or at worst two to three months, of calendar year 2020 were unaffected by COVID-19. Taking this approach, it is possible to define the pre-period as ending with the end of 2019 and the post-period as starting with 2020. As discussed in more detail in later chapters, information on business earnings by race is collected only by calendar year. The effects of COVID-19 on inequality in business earnings are explored using 2019 as the last pre-period year and 2020 as the first post-period year in subsequent chapters.

Additional Analysis Issues

In most research examining the effects of policy interventions, often referred to as "natural experiments," a control group is needed. The control group by definition cannot be affected by the policy intervention. The use of a natural experiment is akin to a randomized controlled trial (RCT), in which researchers randomly assign study subjects to a treatment group or a control group. For example, the largest evaluation of the effectiveness of entrepreneurship training in the United States randomly assigned individuals signing up for training to a treatment group that received training program classes and services or a control group that did not receive training program classes and services (see, e.g., Fairlie, Karlan, and Zinman 2015).

A natural experiment differs from an RCT in that individuals are not randomly assigned to a policy or program and instead are assigned based on a purported exogenous circumstance, such as living in a different state or having low versus high income. The general approach for a natural experiment is that there are two groups (e.g., states): a treatment group that is hypothesized to be affected by the policy or other intervention and a control group that is not affected by the intervention. By comparing the change from the pre-period to the post-period for the treatment group with the change from the pre-period to the post-period for the control group, the true "effect" of the intervention can be estimated. One might be tempted to use "nonessential" versus "essential" businesses. But this does not work well because the definition of a control group is that it is not affected by the intervention. The problem is that even in some industries, such as agriculture, or types of stores, such as grocery stores, that were considered essential businesses and were not closed, customers, business owners, and employees nevertheless likely changed their behavior in respect to these businesses because of COVID-19. It is likely that the entire population and every business in the country was affected by COVID-19 at least in some way. In this sense, there is no true control group of businesses or jobs that were entirely unaffected by COVID-19. More broadly, COVID-19 led to massive changes in almost every aspect of society, such as education, health care, and other social activities, in March and April of 2020, creating additional complications for the natural experiment methodology.

The impact of COVID-19 was so severe and broad that most analyses refer to the comparison between the post-period and the pre-period as the "effect" or "impact" of COVID-19. The worldwide reaction in the early stages of the pandemic affected people in so many different ways that it would be difficult to argue that there was no effect or that something else was happening at the same time. The effects of the government's reaction to the pandemic are also extremely difficult to disentangle from the broader impacts of COVID-19.

What was happening before the novel coronavirus arrived? Many analyses, including those reported in subsequent chapters, also attempt to control for previous trends in economic outcomes before the start of the pandemic to examine how COVID-19 bumped these economic outcomes off their trajectory. For example, economic growth was strong in the years leading up to COVID-19. The unemployment rate was declining nearly every month before COVID-19 arrived.

As an illustration of this trend, figure 2.2 displays the national unemployment rate in the decade prior to the start of the pandemic. The unemployment rate was steadily declining over the decade prior to the start

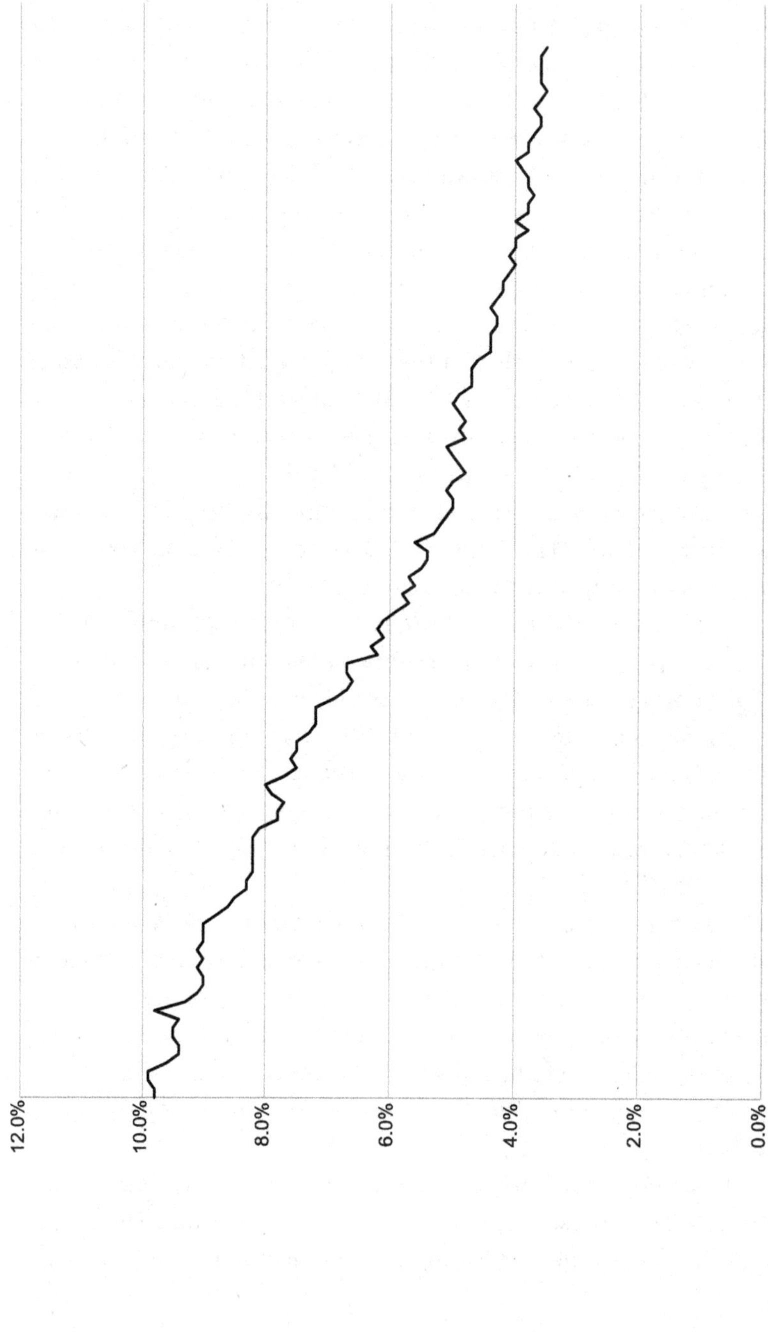

Figure 2.2
Unemployment rate, January 2010–February 2020.

of the pandemic. It is reasonable to expect that the unemployment rate would have continued a downward trend had the pandemic not occurred (although not indefinitely). Thus the expected unemployment rate in April 2020 would not be at the February 2020 level but at a slightly lower level. The difference in months alters the estimated effect of COVID-19. The downward trend can be adjusted by using regression analysis, as discussed in the next chapter. The same issue arises when quarterly data are used. If there is a downward trend prior to COVID-19, then an adjustment is needed to accurately estimate the effects of the pandemic.

Some measures of the economy do not show as clear a downward trend. One example is the GDP growth rate. Because it captures growth from quarter to quarter, it typically does not show longer-term upward or downward trends similar to trends in the unemployment rate (which is not a growth rate). Quarterly GDP growth rates tend to fluctuate between 1 and 3 percent, with 2.5 percent representing a long-term average. There is no positive or negative trend in growth rates over the decade leading up to the start of the COVID-19 pandemic.

Theoretical Perspective

Theoretical models of the choice to become self-employed are generally based on a comparison of potential earnings from business ownership and wage and salary work. In the classic economic model by Evans and Jovanovic (1989), individuals can obtain an income, Y^W, from the wage and salary sector: $Y^W = w + rA$, where w is the wage earned in the market, r is the interest rate, and A represents the consumer's assets. Earnings in the self-employed business ownership sector, Y^{SE}, are defined as $Y^{SE} = \theta f(k)\varepsilon + r(A\text{-}k)$, where θ is entrepreneurial ability, $f(.)$ is a production function whose only input is capital, ε is a random component of the production process, and k is the amount of capital purchased by the worker. Individuals choose to become business owners if the potential income from business ownership and investing remaining personal wealth after using it for startup capital is higher than the potential income from wage and salary work and investing personal wealth.

This simple theoretical model is useful for illustrating the main avenues through which business cycles might affect entrepreneurship (Fairlie 2013). One of the main effects is that recessions reduce consumer and firm demand for products and services provided by startups, thus decreasing potential entrepreneurial earnings, Y^{SE}. Recessions may also reduce total wealth, A, which in turn would lower the likelihood of entrepreneurship. In the presence of liquidity constraints, lower levels of wealth may make it more difficult for entrepreneurs to find the required startup capital to launch new ventures. Personal wealth may have declined substantially through declining home values and home ownership rates. Recessions also make it more difficult to acquire financing from banks, other financial institutions, angel investors, and venture capitalists.

On the other hand, the costs of production are lower in a recession, especially rent and labor, increasing Y^{SE}. The opportunity cost of capital, r, is also likely to be lower in recessions, placing upward pressure on entrepreneurship. Perhaps the largest factor having a positive effect on the entrepreneurial decision is that compensation in the wage and salary sector decreases in economic contractions. The positive effect of lower wages on entrepreneurship may be tempered somewhat in recessions, however, because some workers may be reluctant to leave their jobs in a recession because of concerns about finding another one if the business fails. The net effect of these opposing forces in recessions on entrepreneurship is ambiguous.

The COVID-19–induced recession, however, was very different from the Great Recession or previous recessions. The mandated shutdowns of nonessential businesses, shifts in consumer demand, health concerns, an increase in working from home, the move to remote education, and numerous other social and economic changes during the pandemic suggest that the standard theoretical model is too simple to capture all potential forces working in each direction on the choice. It is also not clear that an expanded theoretical model could capture everything that happened during the pandemic.

State Variation in Policies

Early in the pandemic, states opted for different strategies to slow the spread of COVID-19. One of the main reasons for the adoption of different policies was that states had different views on the trade-off between slowing the spread of the disease and encouraging economic activity. Another reason was that states were having different experiences with the spread of COVID-19. Figure 2.3 displays a map of state variation in

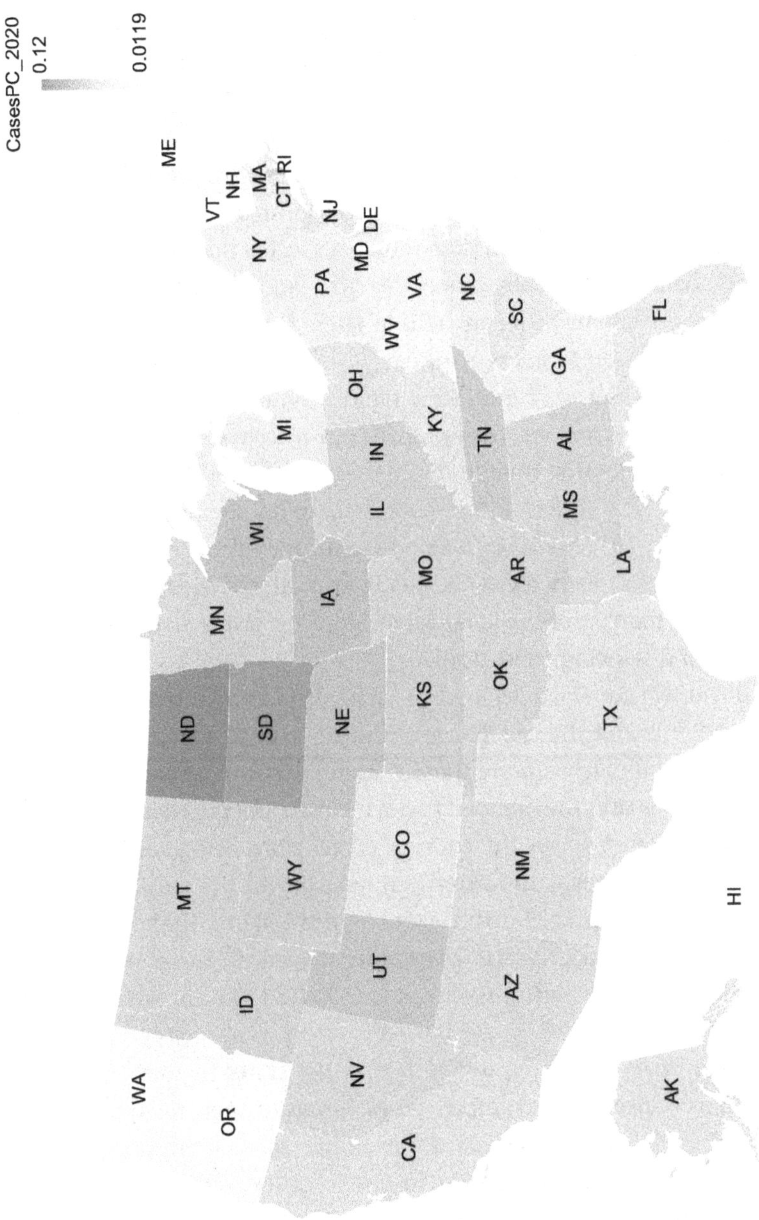

Figure 2.3
COVID-19 cases per capita in 2020 by state.

COVID-19 cases per capita over the year 2020. Large states did not vary much in the degree of COVID-19 spread throughout their populations. For example, California, Florida, New York, and Texas had similar COVID-19 per capita levels.

Several studies use state variation in the manner or timing (or both) of the implementation of pandemic-related policies to assess health and other outcomes. These policies include but are not limited to social distancing restrictions, mask mandates, vaccine rollouts, vaccine mandates for certain occupations and enrollments, school closures, and remote learning.[2] For brevity, I present the two that are used in later chapters for the analysis of COVID-19's effects on business earnings.

As COVID-19 cases were increasing rapidly, states began implementing social distancing restrictions, such as shelter-in-place restrictions. The State of California was the first state to impose restrictions, on March 19, 2020, and the State of New York was the second state to impose restrictions. Early in the pandemic *The New York Times* posted a list of states with social distancing restrictions.[3] Early social distancing restrictions were those imposed in the first few months of the pandemic. Figure 2.4 displays state variation in early social distancing restrictions.

The norm was for states to impose social distancing restrictions early in the pandemic and the exception was to impose no mandated restrictions. The commonality among states that did not impose social distancing restrictions is that they tended to have more rural populations. These states were scattered across the country rather than being confined to a few regions. The states without restrictions early in the pandemic were Arkansas, Iowa, Nebraska, North Dakota, South Dakota, Utah, and Wyoming. Having populations that were more dispersed, these states were possibly less concerned with the spread of COVID-19 in the early months of the pandemic.

Some less easily measured differences across states in social distancing policies occurred. For example, states varied in their restrictions on large social gatherings. California, for example, set strict restrictions on social gatherings, whereas Florida had few to no restrictions on gatherings. States also differed in the social distancing restrictions they placed on businesses and workplaces related to essential businesses, and in how early in the pandemic they lifted those and other social distancing restrictions.

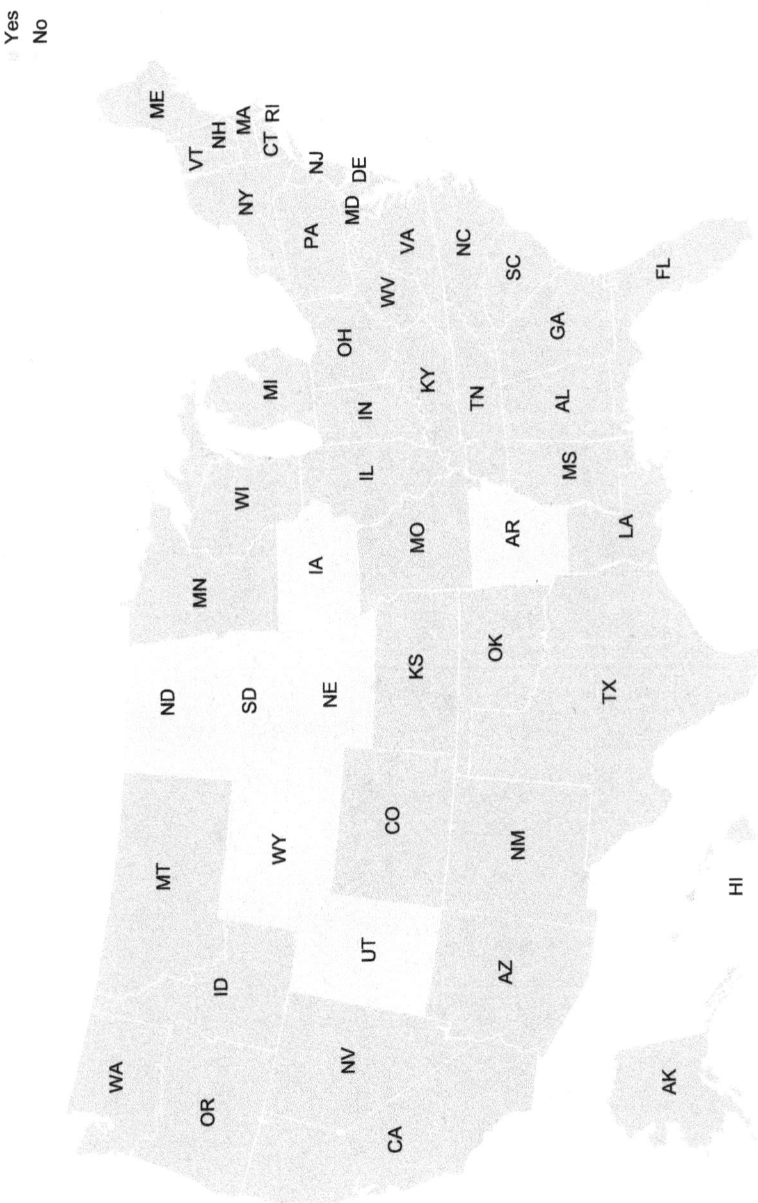

Figure 2.4
Early social distancing restrictions in 2020 by state.

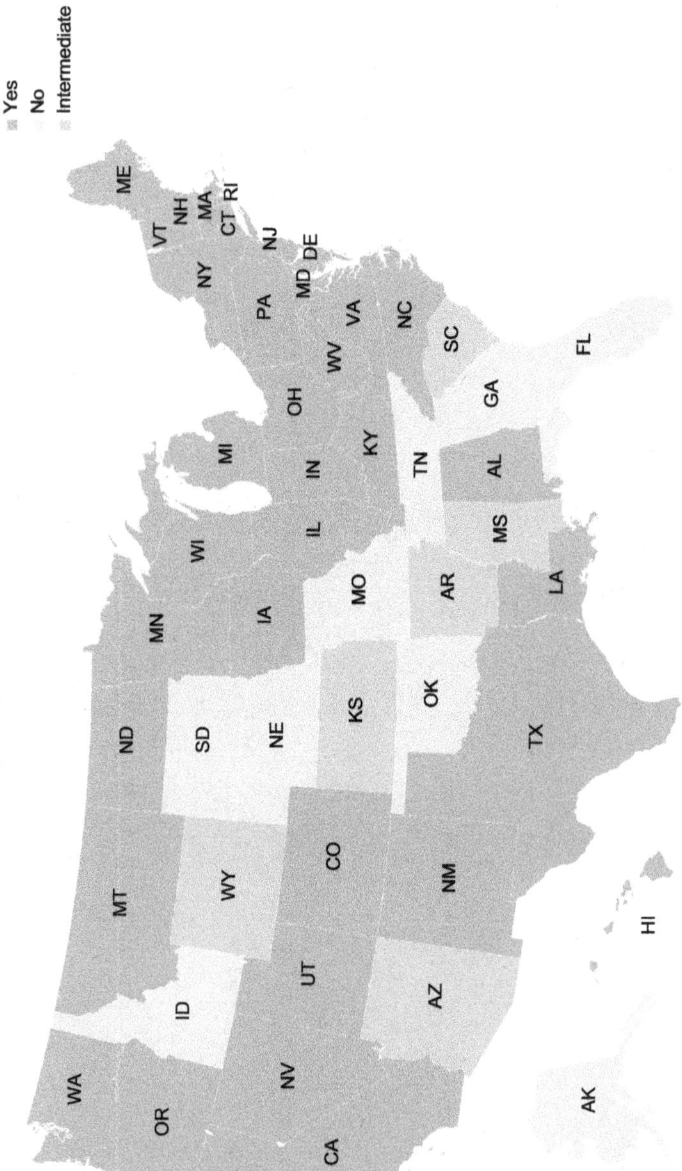

Figure 2.5
Mask mandates in 2020 by state.

Mask Mandates

As COVID-19 continued to spread and social distancing restrictions were relaxed across the country, a common approach was to impose mask mandates instead of returning to the strict social distancing policies that limited social interactions and gatherings. States differed in terms of imposing mask mandates in various locations. Figure 2.5 displays mask mandates at the end of 2020 for every state as reported by *The New York Times*.[4]

Most states imposed mask mandates around the end of 2020. A few of the same states that did not impose early social distancing restrictions did not impose mask mandates, but the overlap is not perfect. The states that did not impose mask mandates tended to be in the middle of the country and less urban than other states. A handful of states imposed intermediate policies around mask mandates that were not full mandates but represented a policy more restrictive than no mask mandate at all. These states are also noted in figure 2.5.

Later, in 2021, when vaccines started to become available, states also differed in vaccine requirements. For example, California and New York had very strict vaccine mandates for health care workers, and most businesses required their employees to be vaccinated. New York implemented a program called "Key to NYC" that required proof of vaccination for entry into many restaurants, gyms, performance venues, and other businesses. In contrast, states such as Texas and Florida enacted laws that restricted businesses from requiring their employees to be vaccinated. These states also made it much easier for residents to be granted exemptions from vaccination when vaccines were required.

Appendix 2.A

Original Santa Clara County Novel Coronavirus Health Order: March 16, 2020

> All businesses with a facility in the County, except Essential Businesses as defined below in Section 10, are required to cease all activities at facilities located within the County except Minimum Basic Operations, as defined in Section 10.[5] For clarity, businesses may also continue operations consisting exclusively of employees or contractors performing activities at their own residences (i.e., working from home). All Essential Businesses are strongly encouraged to remain open. To the

greatest extent feasible, Essential Businesses shall comply with Social Distancing Requirements as defined in Section 10 below, including, but not limited to, when any customers are standing in line.

a. For the purposes of this Order, "Essential Businesses" means:
   i. Healthcare Operations and Essential Infrastructure;
   ii. Grocery stores, certified farmers' markets, farm and produce stands, supermarkets, food banks, convenience stores, and other establishments engaged in the retail sale of canned food, dry goods, fresh fruits and vegetables, pet supply, fresh meats, fish, and poultry, and any other household consumer products (such as cleaning and personal care products). This includes stores that sell groceries and also sell other non-grocery products, and products necessary to maintaining the safety, sanitation, and essential operation of residences;
   iii. Food cultivation, including farming, livestock, and fishing;
   iv. Businesses that provide food, shelter, and social services, and other necessities of life for economically disadvantaged or otherwise needy individuals;
   v. Newspapers, television, radio, and other media services;
   vi. Gas stations and auto-supply, auto-repair, and related facilities;
   vii. Banks and related financial institutions;
   viii. Hardware stores;
   ix. Plumbers, electricians, exterminators, and other service providers who provide services that are necessary to maintaining the safety, sanitation, and essential operation of residences, Essential Activities, and Essential Businesses;
   x. Businesses providing mailing and shipping services, including post office boxes;
   xi. Educational institutions—including public and private K–12 schools, colleges, and universities—for purposes of facilitating distance learning or performing essential functions, provided that social distancing of six-feet per person is maintained to the greatest extent possible;
   xii. Laundromats, drycleaners, and laundry service providers;
   xiii. Restaurants and other facilities that prepare and serve food, but only for delivery or carry out. Schools and other entities that typically

provide free food services to students or members of the public may continue to do so under this Order on the condition that the food is provided to students or members of the public on a pick-up and take-away basis only. Schools and other entities that provide food services under this exemption shall not permit the food to be eaten at the site where it is provided, or at any other gathering site;

xiv. Businesses that supply products needed for people to work from home;

xv. Businesses that supply other essential businesses with the support or supplies necessary to operate;

xvi. Businesses that ship or deliver groceries, food, goods or services directly to residences;

xvii. Airlines, taxis, and other private transportation providers providing transportation services necessary for Essential Activities and other purposes expressly authorized in this Order;

xviii. Home-based care for seniors, adults, or children;

xix. Residential facilities and shelters for seniors, adults, and children;

xx. Professional services, such as legal or accounting services, when necessary to assist in compliance with legally mandated activities;

xxi. Childcare facilities providing services that enable employees exempted in this Order to work as permitted. To the extent possible, childcare facilities must operate under the following mandatory conditions:

A. Childcare must be carried out in stable groups of 12 or fewer ("stable" means that the same 12 or fewer children are in the same group each day).

B. Children shall not change from one group to another.

C. If more than one group of children is cared for at one facility, each group shall be in a separate Groups shall not mix with each other.

D. Childcare providers shall remain solely with one group of children.

b. For the purposes of this Order, "Minimum Basic Operations" include the following, provided that employees comply with Social Distancing

Requirements as defined this Section, to the extent possible, while carrying out such operations:

i. The minimum necessary activities to maintain the value of the business's inventory, ensure security, process payroll and employee benefits, or for related functions.

ii. The minimum necessary activities to facilitate employees of the business being able to continue to work remotely from their residences.

Appendix 2.B

Updated on March 31, 2020: Order of the Health Officer of the County of Santa Clara

ORDER OF THE HEALTH OFFICER OF THE COUNTY OF SANTA CLARA DIRECTING ALL INDIVIDUALS LIVING IN THE COUNTY TO CONTINUE SHELTERING AT THEIR PLACE OF RESIDENCE EXCEPT FOR ESSENTIAL NEEDS; REQUIRING ESSENTIAL BUSINESSES TO IMPLEMENT SOCIAL DISTANCING PROTOCOLS; CLARIFYING AND FURTHER LIMITING ESSENTIAL BUSINESS ACTIVITIES, INCLUDING CONSTRUCTION; AND DIRECTING ALL BUSINESSES AND GOVERNMENTAL OPERATIONS TO FURTHER CEASE NON-ESSENTIAL OPERATIONS[6]

DATE OF ORDER: MARCH 31, 2020

- For the purposes of this Order, a "business" includes any for-profit, non-profit, or educational entity, whether a corporate entity, organization, partnership or sole proprietorship, and regardless of the nature of the service, the function it performs, or its corporate or entity structure.
- For the purposes of this Order, "Essential Businesses" are:

1. Healthcare Operations and businesses that operate, maintain, or repair Essential Infrastructure;
2. Grocery stores, certified farmers' markets, farm and produce stands, supermarkets, food banks, convenience stores, and other establishments engaged in the retail sale of unprepared food, canned food, dry goods, non-alcoholic beverages, fresh fruits and vegetables, pet supply, fresh meats, fish, and poultry, as well as hygienic products and household consumer products necessary for personal hygiene or the habitability, sanitation, or operation of residences. The businesses

included in this subparagraph (ii) include establishments that sell multiple categories of products provided that they sell a significant amount of essential products identified in this subparagraph, such as liquor stores that also sell a significant amount of food.

3. Food cultivation, including farming, livestock, and fishing;
4. Businesses that provide food, shelter, and social services, and other necessities of life for economically disadvantaged or otherwise needy individuals;
5. Construction, but only of the types listed in this subparagraph below:
    1. Projects immediately necessary to the maintenance, operation, or repair of Essential Infrastructure;
    2. Projects associated with Healthcare Operations, including creating or expanding Healthcare Operations, provided that such construction is directly related to the COVID-19 response;
    3. Affordable housing that is or will be income-restricted, including multi-unit or mixed-use developments containing at least 10% income-restricted units;
    4. Public works projects if specifically designated as an Essential Governmental Function by the lead governmental agency;
    5. Shelters and temporary housing, but not including hotels or motels;
    6. Projects immediately necessary to provide critical non-commercial services to individuals experiencing homelessness, elderly persons, persons who are economically disadvantaged, and persons with special needs;
    7. Construction necessary to ensure that existing construction sites that must be shut down under this Order are left in a safe and secure manner, but only to the extent necessary to do so; and
    8. Construction or repair necessary to ensure that residences and buildings containing Essential Businesses are safe, sanitary, or habitable to the extent such construction or repair cannot reasonably be delayed;
6. Newspapers, television, radio, and other media services;

7. Gas stations and auto-supply, auto-repair (including, but not limited to, for cars, trucks, motorcycles and motorized scooters), and automotive dealerships, but only for the purpose of providing auto-supply and auto-repair services (and not, by way of example, car sales or car washes). This subparagraph (vii) does not restrict the on-line purchase of automobiles if they are delivered to a residence or Essential Business;
8. Bicycle repair and supply shops;
9. Banks and related financial institutions;
10. Service providers that enable residential transactions (including rentals, leases, and home sales), including, but not limited to, real estate agents, escrow agents, notaries, and title companies, provided that appointments and other residential viewings must only occur virtually or, if a virtual viewing is not feasible, by appointment with no more than two visitors at a time residing within the same household or living unit and one individual showing the unit (except that in person visits are not allowed when the occupant is still residing in the residence);
11. Hardware stores;
12. Plumbers, electricians, exterminators, and other service providers who provide services that are necessary to maintaining the habitability, sanitation, and operation of residences and Essential Businesses, but not for cosmetic or other purposes;
13. Arborists, landscapers, gardeners, and similar service professionals, but only to the limited extent necessary to maintain the habitability, sanitation, operation of businesses or residences, or the safety of residents, employees, or the public (such as fire safety or tree trimming to prevent a dangerous condition), and not for cosmetic or other purposes (such as upkeep);
14. Businesses providing mailing and shipping services, including post office boxes;
15. Educational institutions—including public and private K–12 schools, colleges, and universities—for purposes of facilitating distance learning or performing essential functions, provided that social distancing of six-feet per person is maintained to the greatest extent possible;

16. Laundromats, drycleaners, and laundry service providers;
17. Restaurants and other facilities that prepare and serve food, but only for delivery or carry out. Schools and other entities that typically provide free food services to students or members of the public may continue to do so under this Order on the condition that the food is provided to students or members of the public on a pick-up and take-away basis only. Schools and other entities that provide food services under this exemption shall not permit the food to be eaten at the site where it is provided, or at any other gathering site;
18. Funeral home providers, mortuaries, cemeteries, and crematoriums, to the extent necessary for the transport, preparation, or processing of bodies or remains;
19. Businesses that supply other Essential Businesses with the support or supplies necessary to operate, but only to the extent that they support or supply these Essential Businesses. This exemption shall not be used as a basis for engaging in sales to the general public from retail storefronts;
20. Businesses that have the primary function of shipping or delivering groceries, food, or other goods directly to residences or businesses. This exemption shall not be used to allow for manufacturing or assembly of non-essential products or for other functions besides those necessary to the delivery operation;
21. Airlines, taxis, rental car companies, ride-sharing services (including shared bicycles and scooters), and other private transportation providers providing transportation services necessary for Essential Activities and other purposes expressly authorized in this Order;
22. Home-based care for seniors, adults, children, and pets;
23. Residential facilities and shelters for seniors, adults, and children;
24. Professional services, such as legal, notary, or accounting services, when necessary to assist in compliance with non-elective, legally required activities;
25. Services to assist individuals in finding employment with Essential Businesses;
26. Moving services that facilitate residential or commercial moves that are allowed under this Order;

27. Childcare facilities providing services that enable owners, employees, volunteers, and contractors for Essential Businesses, Essential Governmental Functions, or Minimum Basic Operations to work as allowed under this Order. Children of owners, employees, volunteers, and contractors who are not exempt under this Order may not attend childcare facilities. To the extent possible, childcare facilities must operate under the following conditions:
    1. Childcare must be carried out in stable groups of 12 or fewer ("stable" means that the same 12 or fewer children are in the same group each day).
    2. Children shall not change from one group to another.
    3. If more than one group of children is cared for at one facility, each group shall be in a separate room. Groups shall not mix with each other.
    4. Childcare providers shall remain solely with one group of children.

- For the purposes of this Order, "Minimum Basic Operations" means the following activities for businesses, provided that owners, employees, and contractors comply with Social Distancing Requirements as defined this Section, to the extent possible, while carrying out such operations:
    1. The minimum necessary activities to maintain and protect the value of the business's inventory and facilities; ensure security, safety, and sanitation; process payroll and employee benefits; provide for the delivery of existing inventory directly to residences or businesses; and related functions.
    2. The minimum necessary activities to facilitate owners, employees, and contractors of the business being able to continue to work remotely from their residences, and to ensure that the business can deliver its service remotely.

- For the purposes of this Order, all Essential Businesses must prepare and post by no later than 11:59 p.m. on April 2, 2020 a "Social Distancing Protocol" for each of their facilities in the County frequented by the public or employees. The Social Distancing Protocol must be substantially in the form attached to this Order as Appendix A. The Social Distancing Protocol must be posted at or near the entrance of the relevant facility, and shall be easily viewable by the public and employees. A copy of the Social Distancing Protocol must also be provided to each employee performing work at the facility. All Essential Businesses shall implement the Social Distancing Protocol and provide evidence of its implementation to any authority enforcing this Order upon demand. The Social Distancing Protocol must explain how the business is achieving the following, as applicable:

1. Limiting the number of people who can enter into the facility at any one time to ensure that people in the facility can easily maintain a minimum six-foot distance from one another at all times, except as required to complete the Essential Business activity;
2. Where lines may form at a facility, marking six-foot increments at a minimum, establishing where individuals should stand to maintain adequate social distancing;
3. Providing hand sanitizer, soap and water, or effective disinfectant at or near the entrance of the facility and in other appropriate areas for use by the public and employees, and in locations where there is high-frequency employee interaction with members of the public (e.g. cashiers);
4. Providing for contactless payment systems or, if not feasible to do so, the providing for disinfecting all payment portals, pens, and styluses after each use;
5. Regularly disinfecting other high-touch surfaces; and
6. Posting a sign at the entrance of the facility informing all employees and customers that they should: avoid entering the facility if they have a cough or fever; maintain a minimum six-foot distance from one another; sneeze and cough into one's elbow; not shake hands or engage in any unnecessary physical contact.
7. Any additional social distancing measures being implemented (see the Centers for Disease Control and Prevention's guidance at: https://www.cdc.gov/coronavirus/2019-ncov/community/guidance-business-response.html).

3 Early Impacts of COVID-19 on Business Activity and Earnings

At the beginning of the pandemic, there was a scramble to understand the early effects of COVID-19 on small businesses and entrepreneurs. There was much concern over the effects on small businesses of the mandated social distancing restrictions and changes in customer behavior resulting from health concerns. A major problem in tracking the fate of small businesses early in the pandemic, however, is that virtually no up-to-date or real-time business-level data were released by the government or any other source.

Early in the pandemic, I provided the first analysis of the impacts of COVID-19 in the first month of social distancing restrictions on business activity (Fairlie 2020a, 2020b). To address real-time data limitations, I tracked the number of active business owners using monthly data released by the U.S. Bureau of Labor Statistics (BLS). The BLS uses the data to provide up-to-date information on the unemployment rate in its monthly Employment Situation Summary (aka the monthly jobs report). The much-anticipated report is released at 8:30 a.m. Eastern time on the first Friday of every month for the prior month. By compiling and analyzing information on business ownership in the underlying data used for the jobs report, I provided the first estimates of the impacts of COVID-19 on business owner activity in April 2020 and released these findings in May 2020.

In this chapter, I present business activity patterns over time using microdata from the BLS's Current Population Survey (CPS) to determine the impacts of COVID-19. The focus is on how the trend leading up to the pandemic was disrupted in the first months of the pandemic. The social distancing restrictions and mandated shutdowns of nonessential businesses were implemented at the end of March 2020. Not all types of businesses might have been affected in the same way, however. I explore the impacts on business activity across different industries, including differences between businesses deemed nonessential and those deemed essential.

The Devastating First Month of the Pandemic Shutdowns

Business activity was affected strongly and immediately after social distancing restrictions were imposed. Figure 3.1 displays trends in the number of active business owners from January 2005 to April 2020. Business activity includes business owners who are actively working during the survey week but not business owners who are not actively working during the survey week. All active business owners, including those who owned incorporated or unincorporated businesses and those who are employers or nonemployers, are captured. Although some business owners own large businesses, by far the most common type are small businesses, and thus the data can be interpreted as predominantly capturing the number of active small business owners.[1]

In the fifteen years from January 2005 to March 2020, the number of active business owners in the United States exhibited a relatively smooth pattern over time, with a slight upward trend. Notable, however, is the dramatic drop in the number of active business owners in April 2020. The number of working business owners dropped from 15.0 million in February 2020 to 11.7 million in April 2020 because of COVID-19. March 2020 shows only a small drop in the number of active business owners, likely because of the limited effect from social distancing restrictions in the middle of that month, when the survey was taken. If the survey had been taken at the end of March, then the findings likely would have been different. Throughout this book, I focus on April 2020 as the first month in which business activity was fully affected by COVID-19. By the middle of April, when the survey was conducted, the social distancing restrictions were in place.

The loss of 3.3 million active business owners (or 22 percent) from February to April 2020 is the largest drop on record. In contrast, the Great Recession, which lasted eighteen months, resulted in a drop of only 5 percent in business activity. The National Bureau of Economic Research (NBER) officially dates the Great Recession as occurring from December 2007 to June 2009. December 2007 was the peak of the long economic growth period leading up to the recession, and June 2009 was when the economy started to grow again. The NBER officially dates the start of the COVID-19–related

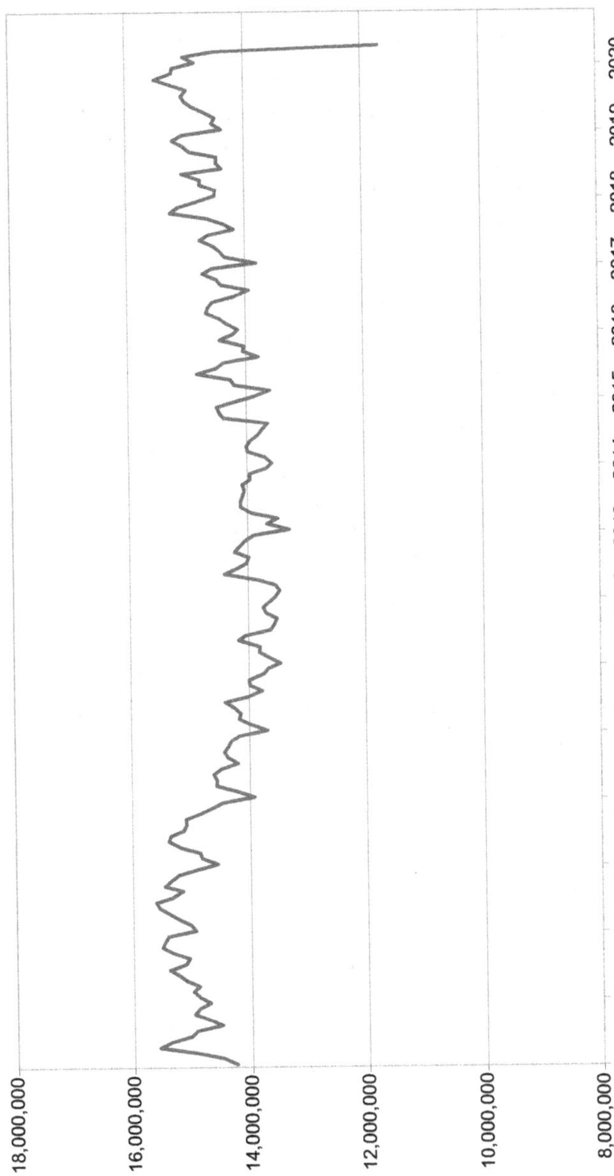

Figure 3.1
Number of active business owners in the United States, January 2005–April 2020.

recession as February 2020, indicating that March 2020 was the first full month of the recession and February was the peak of the preceding growth period.

As with any measures of economic activity, numbers of business owners can be sensitive to business cycle fluctuations, especially recessions. Do the conclusions change when one alters the definitions of business activity? The main definition here focuses on any work by business owners during the survey week. Another approach is to condition on more hours of work in the business during the survey week. One possible choice is to condition on working at least two days per week. In this case, I use fifteen hours per week of work effort by the business owner to approximate two days a week and accommodate lumpy hours reporting. For example, survey respondents often report fifteen, twenty, or forty hours instead of fourteen, twenty-one, or forty-two hours. When conditioning on business owners working at least fifteen hours in the survey week, the losses were even larger. Table 3.1 reports business activity numbers based on different definitions. There were 13.6 million business owners working fifteen or more hours in February 2020 and only 9.8 million in April 2020. The drop of 3.8 million business owners, or 28 percent, was unprecedented.

Table 3.1 also reports business activity based on working thirty or more hours per week. Conditioning on an even higher number of hours worked per week results in losses of 3.4 million active business owners, or 31 percent. Finally, table 3.1 reports the total number of hours worked during the

Table 3.1
Number of Active Business Owners Before and After COVID-19 Social Distancing Restrictions Were Mandated

Month	No. of business owners who worked during the survey week	Percent change from February 2020	No. of business owners who worked 15+ hours	No. of business owners who worked 30+ hours	Total hours worked in the business (000s)
April 2020	11,710,360	−22	9,821,255	7,684,501	394,678
March 2020	14,475,704	−4	12,803,107	10,392,909	523,558
February 2020	15,012,692	0	13,582,876	11,086,054	558,440
January 2020	14,832,717	−1	13,293,991	11,093,877	551,153

Notes: Author's calculations from compiled monthly Current Population Survey microdata.

Table 3.2
Number of Active Business Owners by Incorporation

Month	No. of active business owners	No. of active unincorporated business owners	No. of active incorporated business owners
April 2020	11,710,360	6,392,480	5,317,880
March 2020	14,475,704	8,545,156	5,930,548
February 2020	15,012,692	8,828,513	6,184,179
January 2020	14,832,717	8,649,659	6,183,059

Notes: Author's calculations from compiled Current Population Survey microdata. Active business owners are those who worked during the survey week.

survey week among all business owners by month. (Figures are reported in 1,000s.) From February to April there was a 29 percent drop in total hours worked in businesses by owners.

These reductions in business hours worked have important ramifications for the take-home earnings of business owners. Without working in their businesses at the start of the pandemic, owners were unlikely to have earned much or anything at all. Business owners are likely to have experienced large reductions in earnings from prepandemic levels. Unfortunately, the monthly CPS data do not provide information on these losses to business earnings (as it would be hard to gather this information through a monthly survey). I focus on impacts on business earnings using an annual survey in the next section of this chapter.

Separating the number of business owners into unincorporated and incorporated status shows large drops in activity for both groups. Table 3.2 reports business activity numbers for unincorporated and incorporated businesses. Incorporated businesses are viewed as more growth-oriented, committed, pro-cyclical, and entrepreneurial (e.g., Fairlie et al. 2023; Levine and Rubinstein 2017). The number of active unincorporated business owners dropped 28 percent from February to April. Incorporated business owners realized a drop in active business owners of 14 percent from February to April 2020.

Industry Patterns

Did the social distancing restrictions and other impacts of COVID-19 have differential effects on businesses in different industries? Store closures were rampant, but some business owners were able to switch to working remotely and others owned essential businesses. Using the same data source, I examine how the number of active business owners changed in the first full month of the pandemic by major industry. Table 3.3 reports the number of active business owners by major industry groups for February 2020 and the change to April 2020. The number of active business owners for March 2020 is not reported.

Almost every industry experienced sizable drops in the number of active business owners from February to April. The only exception was Agriculture, for which the number of active business owners increased slightly.[2]

Table 3.3
Number of Active Business Owners by Industry and Percent Change, February to April 2020

Industry	February 2020		Percent change, February to April 2020
	No. of active business owners	Percent of total	
Agriculture	869,661	6	7
Construction	2,436,057	16	–27
Manufacturing	566,192	4	–11
Wholesale Trade	260,151	2	–14
Retail Trade	1,068,484	7	–10
Transportation	798,325	5	–22
Information	235,847	2	–10
Financial Activities	1,301,769	9	–12
Professional and Business Services	3,295,875	22	–18
Educational Services	329,544	2	–39
Health Services	1,238,335	8	–16
Arts, Leisure, and Accommodations	685,009	5	–35
Restaurants	409,605	3	–22
Repair and Maintenance	512,403	3	–25
Personal and Laundry Services	926,409	6	–79

Notes: Author's calculations from compiled monthly Current Population Survey microdata.

Construction, one of the largest industries for U.S. business ownership, experienced a major decline of nearly 670,000 (27 percent) active business owners in the United States from February to April. Although construction businesses typically experience swings in demand, the 27 percent drop was extremely large.

Storefronts across the country were closed because of COVID-19–mandated restrictions, especially in April. Retail Trade showed a decline of 108,000 business owners in April, representing 10 percent of February 2020 levels. Restaurants experienced a decline of 22 percent in April, even though many of those remaining open turned to take-out or delivery services. The broad sector of Arts, Leisure, and Accommodations was hit especially hard, losing 35 percent of active business owners in April.

Both high-skill and lesser-skill services were hit hard by COVID-19–related restrictions. The sector Personal and Laundry Services was especially hard-hit, with losses of 79 percent of business owner activity in April. Transportation services, a category that includes taxi and some ride-sharing (e.g., Uber and Lyft) drivers, dropped by 22 percent in April.[3] Higher-skill services such as found in the Financial Activities sector and Professional and Business Services lost 12 percent and 18 percent, respectively. Even Health Services experienced a drop of 16 percent.

Essential versus Nonessential Businesses

Industries were categorized as "essential" or "nonessential" according to state or local government guidelines, although there was a lot of variation across these guidelines with respect to specific industries. At the beginning of the pandemic, Delaware state provided the most detailed and comprehensive list of essential businesses at the 4-digit industry level and following the same 4-digit industry codes as the CPS, the North American Industry Classification System (NAICS).[4] The classification was imperfect, however, because definitions, enforcement, business owner compliance, and health- and economic-related consumer reactions varied across the country. Under this categorization, 76 percent of business owners worked in essential industries. Table 3.4 reports business activity number by essential business status. Losses in the number of active business owners are lower for essential industries, 17 percent in April, compared with 38 percent among nonessential industries (as expected).

Table 3.4
Number of Active Business Owners by Essential versus Nonessential Business and Percent Change, February to April 2020

	February 2020		Percent change, February to April 2020
Industry	No. of active business owners	Percent of total	
Nonessential industry	3,675,939	24	–38
Essential industry	11,336,752	76	–17

Notes: Author's calculations from compiled monthly Current Population Survey microdata. Essential industries are defined using the classification provided by Delaware state for essential and nonessential businesses (see appendix 2.A in chapter 2).

What Would Have Happened Without COVID-19?

What would have happened to business activity had the pandemic never happened? Of course, we cannot answer that question, but we can examine what was *likely* to have happened without the pandemic by examining trends just prior to the start of the pandemic. Was business activity rising quickly or was it declining leading up to the mandated shutdowns to stop the spread of the disease at the beginning of the pandemic?

To estimate the disruption to business activity caused by COVID-19, it is potentially important to control for what was happening prior to the start of the pandemic and the implementation of early social distancing restrictions. The goal is to compare the predicted or forecasted level of business activity to the realized level of business activity after the implementation of COVID-19–related restrictions. The answer comes down to whether there were preexisting trends in business activity. Business activity over the five or so years before spring 2020 appears to have been trending slowly upward, as displayed in figure 3.1. Furthermore, there appear to be some month-to-month fluctuations that are likely attributable to seasonality. For example, small business activity typically is higher in the summer and during the year-end holiday period because consumer demand is higher.

Before we turn to regression-adjusted estimates, a simpler approach is to compare April 2020 levels with February 2020 levels and April 2020 levels with April 2019 levels. April 2020 and February 2020 are only two

Table 3.5
Change in Number of Active Business Owners Calculated over Different Comparison Time Periods

		Percent change relative to:		
Month	No. of active business owners	February 2020	Same month in previous year	Regression-adjusted estimates
March 2019	14,488,307		0.0	
April 2019	14,662,821		0.0	
February 2020	15,012,692	0.0		0.0
March 2020	14,475,704	−3.6	−0.1	−3.6
April 2020	11,710,360	−22.0	−20.1	−22.7

Notes: Author's calculations from compiled monthly Current Population Survey microdata. Regression-adjusted estimates are based on regression analysis accounting for trends and seasonality (monthly).

months apart, and thus any forecasted trend over that short time period would be minimal. On the other hand, April 2020 and April 2019 are a year apart but the same month of the year, which controls for seasonality, and a comparison of business activity should capture an upward or downward trend. Table 3.5 reports estimates of COVID-19–related impacts on business activity using these two reference months. Business activity in April 2020 dropped by 22.0 percent compared with its level in February 2020, whereas it dropped slightly less, 20.1 percent, compared with its level in April 2019. The two comparison time periods do not show a major difference in the estimated impact of COVID-19 on business activity.

Table 3.5 also reports estimated changes in business activity in March 2020, which might have been partly affected, even though business activity was measured in mid-March. Relative to February 2020, business activity dropped by 3.6 percent, but this figure might reflect monthly seasonality in business activity because business activity was essentially the same in March 2020 as it was in March 2019. In any case, using monthly data, the focus should be on impacts showing up in April 2020, not March 2020.

A convenient method for adjusting simultaneously for a longer time trend and monthly seasonality is to use regression analysis. The regression model can "adjust" for business activity fluctuations attributable to both preexisting trends and monthly seasonality by using a longer time period than just one month prior to COVID-19. Table 3.5 also reports estimates of COVID-19–related impacts in April 2020 that adjust for a time trend and monthly seasonality using regressions and monthly data back to January 2015. By using data back to January 2015, it is possible to capture longer-term trends in the regression adjustment. The regression-adjusted estimate of the COVID-19–related effect is a 22.7 percent drop in business activity, which is similar to the 22.0 percent drop estimated based on the comparison of April 2020 with February 2020.

The simple comparison of business activity in February 2020, which was right before the pandemic kicked into gear, with business activity in April 2020, which was the first full month of social distancing restrictions, provides an accurate assessment of the impact of COVID-19. Business activity dropped by more than 20 percent at the start of the pandemic. Comparing April 2020 business activity with April 2019 activity or using regression adjustments does not change this conclusion.

Real-Time Measures of Business Activity

At the beginning of the pandemic, the scramble to track the early effects in April and May 2020 led to several innovative ways of measuring business activity. The goal was to find measures that were continually updated through various sources, including surveys that were fielded quickly or administrative data generated from nongovernmental sources. The monthly CPS data used as the primary measure of business activity in this book have existed since the 1940s. Because of the BLS's need for a timely measure of the national and state unemployment rates in its monthly jobs report, the underlying microdata are made available quickly. Unfortunately, other governmental sources of data on businesses have a longer lag time.

Early in the pandemic the intense search for additional data sources on how businesses were doing led to the development of several innovative measures. Starting with government innovations, one approach taken early in the pandemic was to examine the intent to start a business and how this changed at the start of the pandemic. Employer business applications as measured by the U.S. Census weekly Business Formation Statistics (BFS) fell in the five weeks from mid-March to mid-April by over 27 percent relative to the previous year (Wilmoth 2020). The BFS data show a bounce back from this initial drop, but the numbers vary quite a bit from month to month, making it difficult to discern a clear trend (U.S. Census Bureau 2020). One problematic observation is that the number of applications increased to a record high of 550,000 in July 2020. The number was considerably higher than the number one year or a few months earlier. There were 280,000 applications in July 2019 and 300,000 applications in February 2020. The BFS was intended to predict future employer business creation but is limited in that it measures only the intent to start a business, and not the survival or employment of businesses during the pandemic. However, over the long run, and without the major disruption of the early months of the pandemic, it provides a useful forecast of future employer business creation (e.g., Asturias et al. 2021; Bayard et al. 2018). Furthermore, in thinking about a timeline for measuring startup activity, Fairlie et al. (2023) note that the BFS captures a stage in the process closer to the formation of a business idea than do measures based on first revenues or employment. Indeed, Decker and Haltiwanger (2023) find that the increase in employer business applications early in the pandemic was accompanied by an increase in actual new employer businesses and job creation.

The U.S. Census Bureau scrambled early in the pandemic to address the limitation and quickly put together a weekly survey to track what was happening to business owners during the pandemic. Estimates from the weekly U.S. Census Small Business Pulse Survey indicated that roughly 50 percent of businesses were experiencing a large negative effect from the COVID-19 pandemic and that only 15–20 percent of businesses had enough cash on hand to cover three months of operations (Bohn, Mejia and Lafortune 2020; U.S. Census Bureau 2020). The surveys provided more insight into what was happening early in the pandemic. For example, findings from one weekly survey indicated that decreased demand was more problematic for small businesses early in the pandemic than supply factors such as accessing materials and goods (Desai and Looze 2020).

Nongovernmental sources were also used to examine how small businesses were doing early in the pandemic. These sources included surveys of members of private business networks, cell phone data (to examine where customers stopped going to stores compared with activity in previous months), payroll information from payroll processing companies such as Automatic Data Processing (ADP), or reviews of businesses on Yelp. For example, Bartik, Bertrand, Cullen, et al. (2020) conducted a survey in late March of nearly six thousand small businesses that were members of the Alignable business network. They found that 43 percent of businesses were temporarily closed, large reductions in staffing had occurred, and the majority of businesses had less than one month of cash on hand. Alekseev et al. (2023) used two waves of a survey conducted on Facebook in April and December 2020 and found that larger and older firms were more likely to remain open, roughly one-fourth of firms reduced prices, and one-fourth of firms had access to formal sources of financing, which in turn affected how they responded early in the pandemic. Using their own network of businesses, the Stanford Latino Entrepreneurship Initiative (2020) surveyed 224 high-revenue Latinx-owned businesses and found that 86 percent of respondents reported immediate negative effects such as delayed projects and closure from the pandemic.

Additional studies used "real-time" data collected by private companies for their business purposes. Bartik, Bertrand, Feng, et al. (2020) used data from Homebase, a provider of clock-in, clock-out tracking software, and measured business shutdowns by firms that had stopped reporting clock events. Kurmann, Lale, and Ta (2021) also used the Homebase data but additionally checked whether business owners had updated their status in Google Places (the database behind Google Maps) or stopped posting on Facebook. Rigobon et al. (2022) used data from Google Places in the retail and food service sectors in downtown Ottawa and measured business exits when a business was removed from the data. De Vaan et al. (2021) relied on foot traffic data from mobile applications provided by SafeGraph, focusing on service-oriented businesses, and used changes in the number of visitors to identify closures. Yelp (2020) used its online platform of business reviews to track business closures when owners updated their Yelp pages. Chetty et al. (2020) relied on Womply, which aggregates transaction and revenue data from several credit card processors. Firms that reported zero credit card revenue for three days in a row were counted as closures.

The Impacts of COVID-19 on Business Earnings

COVID-19's disruption of business activity in April 2020 is clear. Small business owners were severely affected, which often led to shutting down operations. An important question is how the disruptions in operations from the pandemic affected business earnings. Did owners lose substantial amounts of income in the early stages of the pandemic? Large losses could have implications for broader economic inequality.

The vast majority of data collected on earnings either by business owners or by wage and salary workers are collected on an annual basis instead of monthly. For surveys, an annual measure makes the most sense because people tend to have a better sense of how much they earn per year than how much they earn per month. Salaries for different jobs are advertised at annual levels and taxes are filed annually, not monthly. Even administrative datasets typically include annual measures of household or business income over the calendar year. The CPS data collected by the BLS and the Census Bureau are no different. All earnings measures are included in an annual survey in March that refers to the previous calendar year. The timing is convenient because it lines up closely with when individuals complete and file their tax forms for the previous calendar year.

To explore the impacts of COVID-19 on business earnings, I examine CPS data for the calendar year 2020. These annual data are used to examine the effects of COVID-19 on business earnings in the first year of the pandemic. It is important to keep in mind that calendar year 2020 includes both months prior to the start of the pandemic and the recovery from the first month of social distancing restrictions. In chapter 6, when we return to monthly data on business activity, we will see that business activity started to recover from the shutdowns in 2020, although not fully.

Figure 3.2 displays trends in business earnings by calendar year from 2015 to 2020. Mean and mean log business earnings are shown. All estimates are adjusted for inflation and are measured in 2019 dollars. Mean business earnings dropped from $62,675 in calendar year 2019 to $59,715 in calendar year 2020, for a loss of 5 percent. Prior to the start of the pandemic, the trend in mean business earnings was relatively flat from 2015 to 2017, then rose from 2017 to 2018 (8 percent), dropping from 2018 to 2019 (–8 percent).

Trends in mean log business earnings are also displayed in figure 3.2. The standard approach in analyzing earnings is to take logs to remove the influence of outliers and because the transformation often fits the data better when estimating regressions.[5] Mean log business earnings dropped by 17 log points from 2019 to 2020, which represents approximately a 17 percent drop in business earnings. The COVID-19–induced loss in business earnings is the largest when measured in logs, which reduces the influence of large

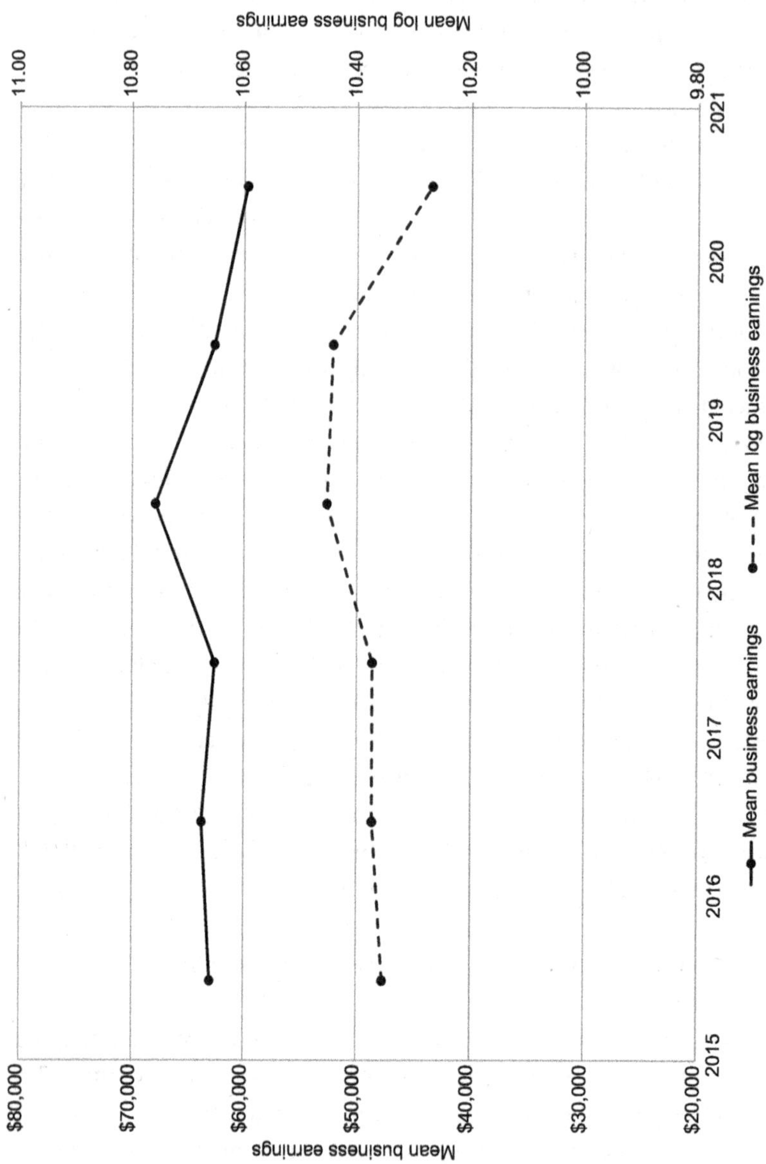

Figure 3.2
Business earnings trends, 2015–2020.

outliers represented by very successful business owners and instead focuses more on losses in all other parts of the earnings distribution. See Fairlie (2024) for additional analyses.

Business Earnings Losses by Business and Owner Characteristics

Which types of businesses and owners experienced the largest losses in business earnings in the pandemic? The question is of broad interest. First, such information should help us better understand which industries experienced the largest business earnings losses in the pandemic. Second, looking ahead to the next chapter, it could also shed light on the causes of differential impacts of COVID-19 by race and ethnicity because it reveals the types of businesses and owners that experienced the largest losses in business earnings, which might the same ones in which minority-owned businesses are concentrated.

Table 3.6 reports mean business earnings by industry of the business. There is wide variation in mean business earnings across major industry groups. In 2019, mean business earnings range from $40,000 in Other Services to $98,000 in Financial Activities. In the pandemic, some sectors experienced large losses: Wholesale and Retail Trade and Other Services each suffered losses over 20 percent, and Leisure and Hospitality lost a startling 43 percent in average earnings. Agriculture and Information (which include technology) both experienced large positive gains in business earnings in the pandemic.

What about other characteristics of the business or owner? How did these types of businesses and owners fare in the first year of the pandemic? Do they differ by the education/skill level of the owner or by major industry, region, central city status, or other characteristics of the business? Table 3.7 reports mean business earnings for 2019 and 2020 and the percent change between the two years. There is a clear positive relationship between education level and mean business earnings. For example, in 2019, college graduate business owners had average earnings of $86,000, compared with $46,000 for high school graduate owners (who did not obtain any higher level of education). Interestingly, however, there is not a strong negative relationship between business earnings losses from 2019 to 2020 and education level. The largest business earnings losses occurred for owners with some college, which is defined as those who have some

Table 3.6
Business Earnings by Industry and Percent Change, 2019 to 2020

	Mean business earnings			
Industry	2019	2020	Percent change, 2019 to 2020	Average *N*
Agriculture	$42,262	$64,556	53	376
Construction	$50,512	$54,384	8	1136
Manufacturing	$70,465	$57,092	–19	215
Wholesale and Retail Trade	$66,539	$49,211	–26	590
Transportation	$51,185	$42,537	–17	340
Information	$49,958	$70,624	41	99
Financial Activities	$98,315	$87,787	–11	478
Professional and Business Services	$73,437	$76,025	4	1,285
Educational and Health Services	$71,215	$72,453	2	679
Leisure and Hospitality	$60,032	$33,934	–43	435
Other Services	$40,154	$31,476	–22	605

Notes: Author's calculations from Current Population Survey microdata, 2019–2020. All estimates use CPS-provided sample weights. The sample includes only individuals with longest-job-held work activity as self-employed business owner in calendar year.

college credits but did not graduate with a bachelor's degree. This group most notably includes owners with two-year associate's degrees and vocational degrees.

Across regions, the South and West experienced business earnings losses, whereas the Northeast experienced essentially no change and the Midwest experienced gains. Within metropolitan status, businesses located in central cities experienced the largest losses in average business earnings. Those in suburban areas also experienced losses during the pandemic, while businesses in rural areas experienced some gains in average business earnings from 2019 to 2020. By gender, male and female business owners experienced similar mean earnings losses during the pandemic. Older business owners experienced larger mean earnings losses than younger ones.

Table 3.7
Business Earnings by Owner and Business Characteristics and Percent Change, 2019 to 2020

Owner and business characteristic	Mean business earnings 2019	2020	Percent change, 2019 to 2020	Average *N*
High school dropout	$36,671	$35,788	−2	525
High school graduate	$45,992	$43,587	−5	1,606
Some college	$51,776	$45,108	−13	1,691
College graduate	$85,824	$84,670	−1	2,413
Northeast	$61,529	$63,003	2	929
Midwest	$60,806	$64,972	7	1,180
South	$63,181	$57,274	−9	2,109
West	$64,112	$57,533	−10	2,018
Central city	$61,788	$56,276	−9	1,544
Suburbs	$70,098	$65,889	−6	2,468
Rural	$46,891	$50,303	7	1,213
Not identified local geography	$55,510	$55,062	−1	1,011
Female	$45,750	$43,245	−5	2,369
Male	$72,480	$70,084	−3	3,866
Below median age	$57,708	$56,449	−2	3,506
Above median age	$68,738	$63,579	−8	2,729

Notes: Author's calculations from Current Population Survey microdata, 2019–2020. All estimates use CPS-provided sample weights. The sample includes only individuals with longest-job-held work activity as self-employed business owner in calendar year.

Adjusting for Prepandemic Trends in Business Earnings

To probe further whether COVID-19 negatively affected business earnings, it is helpful to examine and control for trends that existed prior to the start of the pandemic, as discussed in chapter 2. The question becomes whether and how much COVID-19 knocked any preexisting trends in business earnings off of their predicted course to 2020. To accomplish this goal and thus more formally test whether COVID-19 had an impact on business earnings, I estimate regressions. The regressions build on the underlying patterns displayed in the figures by controlling for pre-COVID-19 trends and owner, business, and geographic characteristics. For example, if there was an upward trend in business earnings, the regression equation can simulate where these trends would likely have led in 2020 had COVID-19 not happened.

When COVID-19 disrupts these patterns, there are two possible comparisons. One comparison is with what existed in 2019 (static) and the other comparison is with what likely would have happened in 2020 (trend-adjusted). The regressions thus estimate the impacts of COVID-19 on relative patterns in business earnings using both comparisons. Table 3.8 reports estimates from equations (3.1) and (3.2) in appendix 3.B. Specification 1 starts with a stripped-down model that includes no additional variables except the race indicators. The loss in business earnings in 2020 is reported as the "Post-COVID 2020" coefficient. The coefficient estimate indicates that business earnings losses from COVID-19 were roughly 17 percent.

Specification 2 reports estimates from equation (3.1). The regression equation includes a time trend, and controls for owner, business, and geographic

Table 3.8

Regressions for Log Business Earnings, Current Population Survey, 2015–2020

Explanatory variables	(1)	(2)	(3)	(4)
Black	−0.309	−0.209	−0.209	−0.208
	(0.041)	(0.022)	(0.022)	(0.022)
Latinx	−0.332	−0.138	−0.138	−0.138
	(0.031)	(0.018)	(0.018)	(0.018)
Asian	0.124	0.054	0.054	0.054
	(0.046)	(0.025)	(0.025)	(0.025)
Post-COVID-19 2020	−0.168	−0.190	−0.190	−0.163
	(0.023)	(0.021)	(0.021)	(0.020)
Main controls	No	Yes	Yes	Yes
Industry controls	No	Yes	Yes	Yes
Time trend	No	Yes	Yes	Yes
Pre-2019 indicator	No	No	Yes	No
Full 2015–2019 indicators	No	No	No	Yes
Sample years	2019–2020	2015–2020	2015–2020	2015–2020
Sample size	12,470	40,611	40,611	40,611

Notes: Author's calculations from compiled monthly Current Population Survey microdata. The sample consists of business owners (ages 20–64) who worked in their business in the calendar year. Coefficient estimates and their standard errors (in parentheses) are reported. Main controls include female, age, education, region, and central city status indicator variables.

characteristics. The inclusion of the time trend and controls results in business earnings dropping by approximately 19 percent in the first calendar year of the pandemic. The losses are estimated from the prediction of where business earnings should in 2020 based on prior trends absent the pandemic.

Specification 3 reports estimates from the slight variation of equation (3.1) noted above. In this model, I add an indicator variable that captures years 2015 to 2018 as "Pre-2019 indicator" in table 3.8. The addition of this indicator variable focuses the estimation of COVID-19 effects on using 2019 as the comparison year instead of the average, de-trended level in previous years. The coefficients from this specification are similar to the previous specification. The estimate is similar to the previous specification showing an estimated effect of COVID-19 of roughly a 19 percent loss in business earnings. Specification 4 reports estimates of equation (3.2) which is an event-study regression. In this specification, a full set of year indicators for each pre-COVID-19 year (2015 to 2019) are included. The effect of COVID-19 on business earnings is also similar at roughly –16 percent.

Overall, the robustness of estimates is impressive and reassuring that prior-trends, choice of comparison pre-COVID-19 time period, or inclusion of baseline controls for individual and business characteristics do not affect the results. Business earnings losses were 16–19 percent in 2020.

The Rate of New Business Formation During the Pandemic

The pandemic likely affected individuals starting business activities. On the one hand, social distancing restrictions and customer health concerns limited opportunities to start small businesses, but on the other hand, the labor market was also struggling, and individuals might have turned to engaging in some kind of business activity out of necessity. Indeed, previous research on prior business cycles indicates that recessions can decrease potential business income and access to capital, but also restrict opportunities in the wage and salary sector, leaving the net effect on business activity starts slightly positive (Fairlie 2013).[6] Furthermore, the discussion of the standard theoretical model of entrepreneurship in the previous chapter indicates that there are potentially opposing factors working on business activity in recessions.

To explore the question of how the flow into business activity changed in the pandemic I examine a measure of new business activity. The rate of new business activity reflects how many adults start a business activity, on average each month, in a year.[7] Figure 3.3 presents the rate of new business activity from 2005 to 2020. In 2020, an average of 0.38 percent of the adult population, or 380 out of 100,000 adults, created a new business activity each month.[8] The rate of new business owners increased sharply from 2019 to 2020. During tumultuous times such as the pandemic, the rate of new business activity can increase substantially as businesses close and reopen and as workers are laid off and turn to part-time business activities. The measure captures "churning" among business owners, potentially including frequent starts and stops that are not always optimal for the long-run success of the business.

How much of the increase in new business activity in the first year of COVID-19 was due to necessity and how much to opportunity? Previous research has examined how new business formation can arise out of opportunity or necessity, and how this differs over time and for different groups of the labor force (e.g., Fairlie 2014; Fairlie and Fossen 2019). I turn to exploring whether the increase in new business activity was primarily due to necessity veersus opportunity creation. The necessity share of new business activity provides a barometer of the effects of economic conditions on business creation among new business owners. It distinguishes between new business owners who come out of work, school, or another labor market status, or "opportunity entrepreneurs," and new business owners who come out of unemployment, or "necessity entrepreneurs" (Fairlie and Fossen 2019). Although the motivations for starting businesses and the background economic and labor market conditions can differ, businesses started out of necessity could eventually become very successful. Interestingly, Stangler (2009) found that the majority of Fortune 500 companies were started during recessions or bear markets.

Trends in the necessity share of new business activity from 2005 to 2020 are displayed in figure 3.4. The necessity share of new business activity jumped in 2020. It increased from 13.1 percent in 2019 to 30.3 percent in 2020, representing the largest increase over the past fifteen years and perhaps much longer. The sharp increase in the necessity share in 2020 reflects the massive economic losses during the pandemic. As nonessential businesses closed to stop the rapid spread of COVID-19 and consumers cut back on in-person consumption, the share of new business activity originating in opportunity fell precipitously. The increase in the necessity share

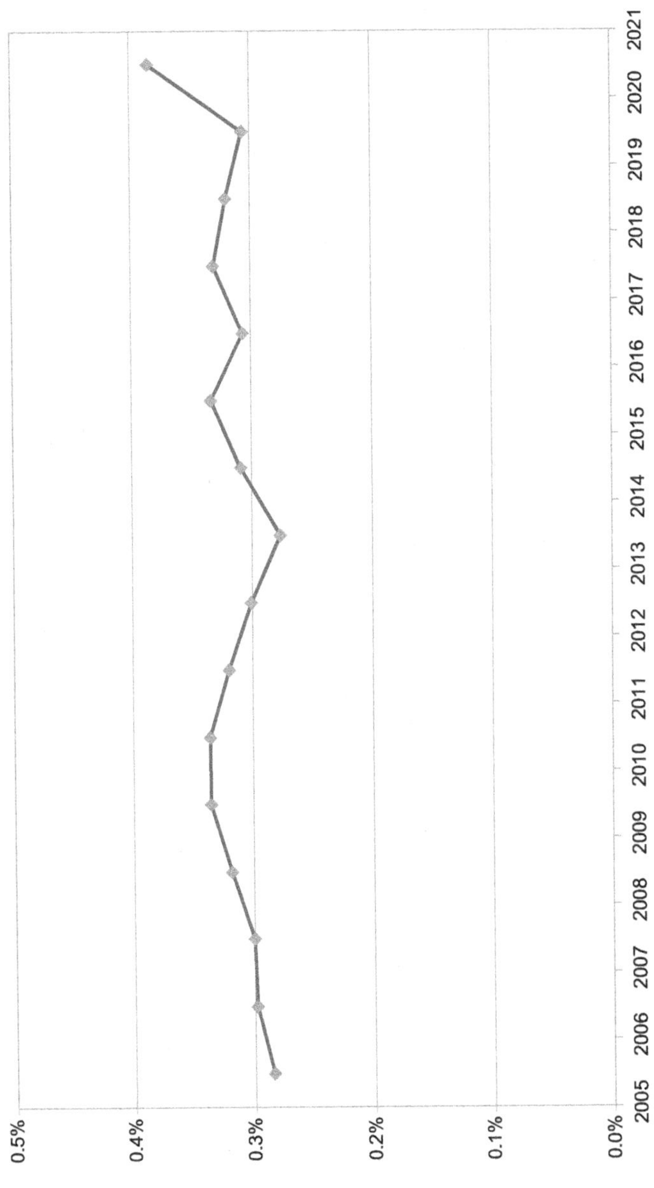

Figure 3.3
Rate of new business activity, 2005–2020.

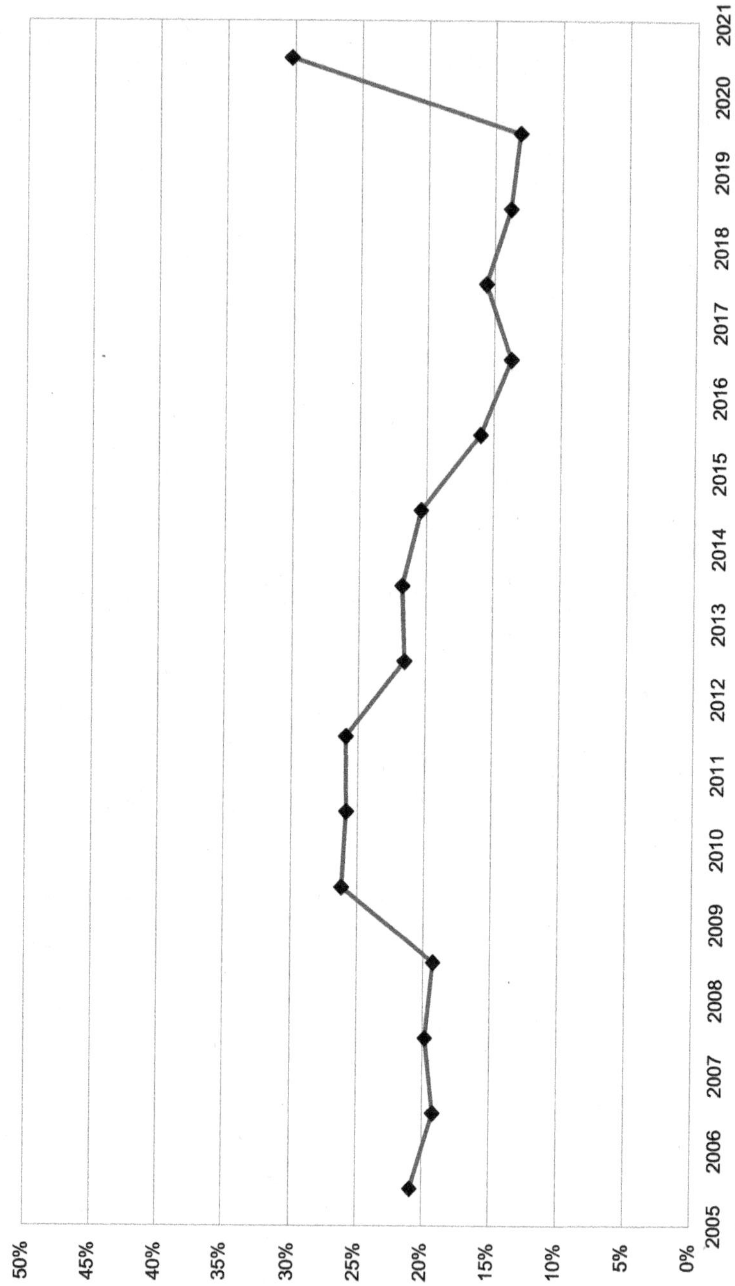

Figure 3.4
Necessity share of new business activity, 2005–2020.

of new business activity from 2019 to 2020 was 17.1 percentage points. The increase in the necessity share from 2008 to 2009 during the Great Recession was much lower, at 6.9 percentage points.

The increased rate of new business activity shown in figure 3.3 appears to be driven by workers who were laid off in the first year of the pandemic. Because many firms were reluctant to hire workers early in the pandemic some of these unemployed workers started self-employed business activities to make ends meet. Consistent with what has been seen in prior recessions, necessity entrepreneurship increased substantially as a result of layoffs, a weakened labor market, and worsening economic conditions.

Business Sales Losses Were Large at the Beginning of the Pandemic

Did businesses experience sizable sales and revenue losses in the first stages of the pandemic? To examine this question, I use administrative data from California on business sales losses at the beginning of the pandemic. Information on taxable sales by businesses is available for all sectors reporting taxable sales in the State of California. The data come from the California Department of Tax and Fee Administration (CDTFA).[9] The data are reported quarterly and thus capture the effects on business sales in the first complete quarter of the pandemic, which was 2020Q2. The second quarter of each year includes April, May, and June. One limitation of these data is that they include all businesses and are not limited to small businesses.

The information was first presented as testimony before the U.S. House of Representatives Committee on Small Business on February 4, 2021, and the California State Assembly Committee on Jobs, Economic Development and the Economy on February 23, 2021 (Fairlie 2021a, 2021b). Further analyses were reported in Fairlie and Fossen (2021 and 2022b). Since that time the numbers have been revised slightly by the CDTFA. Most important, the loss in total taxable sales from 2019Q2 to 2020Q2 has been revised slightly downward from the previously reported number.

Figure 3.5 displays year-over-year changes in taxable sales by businesses reporting taxable sales in California. Taxable sales decreased substantially in the second quarter of 2020, which directly followed the strict social distancing restrictions imposed by the state. Total taxable sales in California were $152 billion in 2020Q2, which represents a drop of 15.4 percent from 2019Q2. Typically, year-over-year growth for the same quarter is an

Figure 3.5
Year-over-year change in taxable sales in California.

increase of 3–4 percent. The sharp decline in sales was not due to a loss in the number of sales permits, which actually grew slightly from 2019Q2 to 2020Q2. This finding implies that average sales losses per firm increased with COVID-19.

To slow the spread of COVID-19, governments enforced social distancing restrictions that shut down businesses in jobs and industries deemed nonessential. Less drastic restrictions were also imposed on essential businesses, such as capacity limitations for grocery stores. Health concerns also dissuaded customers from visiting stores that had person-to-person contact. Finally, the ability to telecommute in jobs allowed certain businesses, or at least certain jobs in those businesses, to continue to operate.

Taxable sales losses across business types can be examined. Table 3.9 reports the percentage change in sales from 2019Q2 to 2020Q2 and sales levels in 2020Q2 for business types for California. Starting with stores that were mostly considered nonessential and had person-to-person contact, we find major losses. Clothing and Clothing Accessories Stores lost 53.7 percent in taxable sales from the second quarter of 2019 to the second quarter of 2020.

Food services and drinking places were not shut down but faced restrictions in terms of switching to takeout and delivery service only and then later adding outside dining service. These restrictions and consumers' concerns over health led to a major drop in demand. Sales at restaurants, bars, and other eating establishments dropped by 45.8 percent in taxable sales from 2019Q2 to 2020Q2. In contrast, this business type category was experiencing year-over-year growth of 3–6 percent prior to the pandemic. Gasoline was deemed essential, but as workers stayed home and business travel was mostly shut down, gasoline stations lost substantial revenue. From 2019Q2 to 2020Q2, sales dropped by 46.0 percent. Larger purchases and ones with more flexibility in timing experienced large but lesser drops in taxable sales. The category of Furniture and Home Furnishings Stores dropped 16.4 percent over the year. Similarly, Motor Vehicle and Parts Dealers dropped by 13.2 percent.

Not all businesses experienced large losses. Businesses that were deemed essential were not forced to close and remained open during the first three months of the pandemic (i.e., 2020Q2). The category of Food and Beverage Stores experienced an increase of 3.8 percent, but the growth rate was lower than average year-over-year growth in sales. Building Material and Garden

Table 3.9
California Taxable Sales Losses by Business Types

Business type	Percent change, 2019Q2 to 2020Q2	Taxable transactions, amount	Percent of total tax
Total all outlets	–15.4	$156,172,000,000	100.0
Total Retail and Food Services	–15.3	$107,147,000,000	68.6
Motor Vehicle and Parts Dealers	–13.2	$19,644,600,910	12.6
Furniture and Home Furnishings Stores	–16.4	$2,668,985,145	1.7
Electronics and Appliance Stores	–13.0	$3,695,857,833	2.4
Building Material and Garden Equipment and Supplies	12.7	$12,312,127,035	7.9
Food and Beverage Stores	3.8	$7,740,217,184	5.0
Health and Personal Care Stores	–7.9	$3,524,764,595	2.3
Gasoline Stations	–46.0	$7,882,536,415	5.1
Clothing and Clothing Accessories Stores	–53.7	$4,822,146,701	3.1
Sporting Goods, Hobby, Musical Instruments, Book Stores	–17.3	$2,066,810,169	1.3
General Merchandise Stores	–9.6	$12,529,894,237	8.0
Miscellaneous Store Retailers	–14.5	$4,572,483,652	2.9
Food Services and Drinking Places	–45.8	$12,348,097,303	7.9
Total all other outlets	–15.6	$49,025,258,867	31.4

Source: Administrative data from the California Department of Tax and Fee Administration.

Equipment and Supplies grew by 12.7 percent, which might reflect home and garden repair and improvement projects started by homeowners with more time on their hands during the pandemic.

The category of General Merchandise Stores captures both essential and nonessential goods, and so these stores were often open during the pandemic. They experienced a drop of 9.6 percent from 2019Q2 to 2020Q2 in taxable sales. All other outlets experienced a drop of 15.6 percent in taxable sales. When all business types are combined, as shown in table 3.9, total taxable sales dropped by 15.4 percent. Total Retail and Food Services dropped by a similar amount, 15.3 percent.

Sales losses were extremely large for even more detailed industries as reported in Fairlie and Fossen (2022b). For example, sales losses were more than 90 percent for Accommodations, a category that includes hotels and motels. Almost as large were the sales losses at drinking places, a category that includes bars, and sales losses in Arts, Entertainment and Recreation. Full-service restaurants lost roughly 60 percent in year-over-year sales. The largest losses were for business types severely affected by mandatory lockdowns because they typically had many people in interior spaces. In contrast to the losses experienced by most business types, several business types actually experienced gains in taxable sales. The biggest gains were for online sales, which grew by 181 percent as consumers substituted online for in-store purchases. Taxable sales in Agriculture businesses grew by 40 percent in 2020Q2, and notably, taxable sales in Beer, Wine, and Liquor Stores grew by 10 percent.

The pandemic-induced recession created large losses for many types of businesses. The large losses in sales in the second quarter of 2020 for so many different types of business but especially those shut down through mandatory restrictions are worrisome for the longer-term survival of small, local businesses throughout the country. Although larger stores and chains with a strong online presence may survive, many small businesses will not have the resources to weather prolonged closures, continued reduced demand from consumers' health concerns, and a more comprehensive recession.

The findings are generally consistent with the findings from a few other early studies of the impacts of COVID-19 on business sales that used different data sources. Timely information on business sales is not easy to find. Data from the transactions of financial accounts at JPMorgan Chase indicate that small business revenues dropped 30–50 percent at the end of March and early April and 40 percent into May (Farrell, Wheat, and Mac 2020; Kim, Parker, and Schoar 2020). In surveys conducted by the Kauffman Foundation, Desai and Looze (2020) found that 60 percent of business owners reported lower sales in April 2020 and 50 percent of owners reported lower sales in May. The Opportunity Insights Economic Tracker. which reports small business revenue data from Womply, and found a drop of 50 percent in April from January and losses of roughly 20 percent by the end of May from January levels.[10] Bloom, Fletcher, and Yeh (2021) partnered with a large payments technology company to collect survey data from 2,500 small businesses and found an average loss of 29 percent in sales in 2020Q2.

Business Closures due to COVID-19

Business activity, earnings, and sales dropped substantially at the beginning of the pandemic. The analysis of CPS data presented earlier in the chapter clearly indicates that COVID-19 led to a large drop in the number of businesses active and operating early in the pandemic, but did these shutdowns turn into permanent closures or were they only temporary? The CPS data do not allow for an analysis of longer-term business closures. To measure closures, panel data are needed but are difficult to find. Each business in the data needs to be followed over time and for a long enough period of time (at least a year or two) to measure a permanent closure.

The CDTFA data that were used to examine taxable sales losses for California businesses can be used to measure business closures. As part of a research project with the CDTFA that started in 2021, we examined permanent business closures in the pandemic using administrative firm-level panel data covering the universe of businesses filing sales taxes (Fairlie et al. 2022). These are the underlying microdata that created the sales losses numbers presented above. The goal of the project was to provide some of the first estimates of permanent business closures in the pandemic. There was very limited information at the time. By using panel data we could track whether a business that ceased operations came back later to reopen or not. We followed taxable sales for four consecutive quarters to determine whether a business was not active for a long enough period of time before defining a closure.[11] Findings from this research project are reported for the first quarter of the pandemic to gauge how much of the losses to business owner activity and earnings in the very beginning of the pandemic were from permanent closures.[12]

A large percentage of businesses with taxable sales closed in the first quarter of the COVID-19 pandemic. Figure 3.6 displays the business closure rate in California by quarter from 2015Q2 to 2020Q2. The business closure rate increased substantially in 2020Q1 and remained high in 2020Q2,

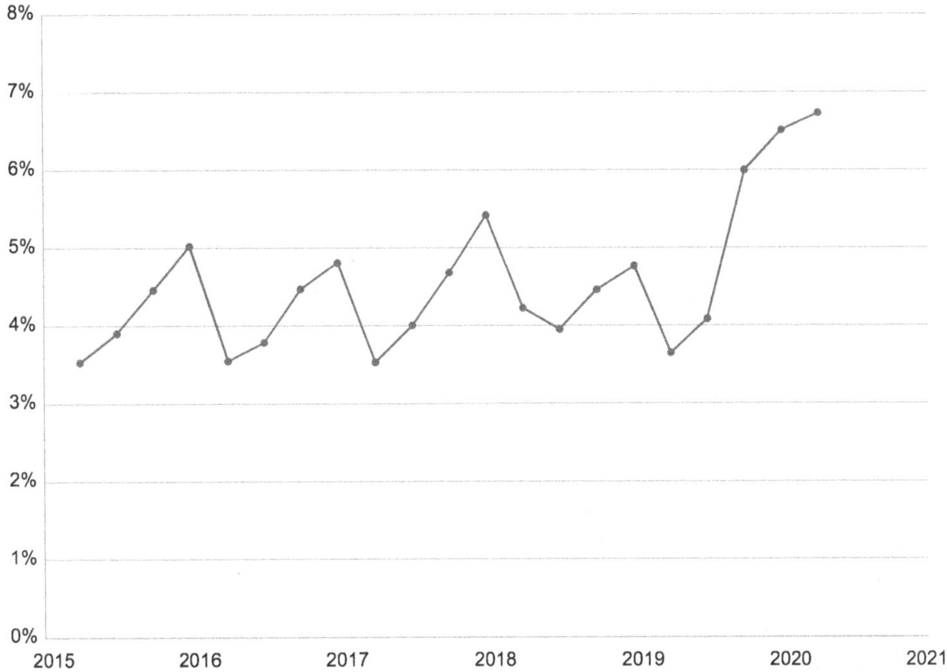

Figure 3.6
Quarterly closure rates for all businesses in California, 2015Q2 to 2020Q2.

capturing the early effects of COVID-19. A focus on the year-over-year change shows the closure rate was 3.7 percent in 2019Q2 and jumped to 6.7 percent in 2020Q2. From 2019Q1 to 2020Q1 the closure rate increased from 4.8 percent to 6.5 percent. Closure rates display strong seasonality patterns but do not show a strong downward or upward trend prior to the pandemic. Insofar as the second quarter of the year typically has relatively low business closure rates, the jump in 2020Q2 is especially large and notable relative to prepandemic levels.

Did small businesses close at a higher rate than larger businesses? Surprisingly, this question also was very difficult to answer because of a lack of available timely data. The CDTFA panel data allow one to examine whether business closure rates differed by initial size of the business. Indeed, the large increase in the closure rate of California businesses from 2019Q2 to 2020Q2 was felt very differently by size of the business. Figure 3.7 displays

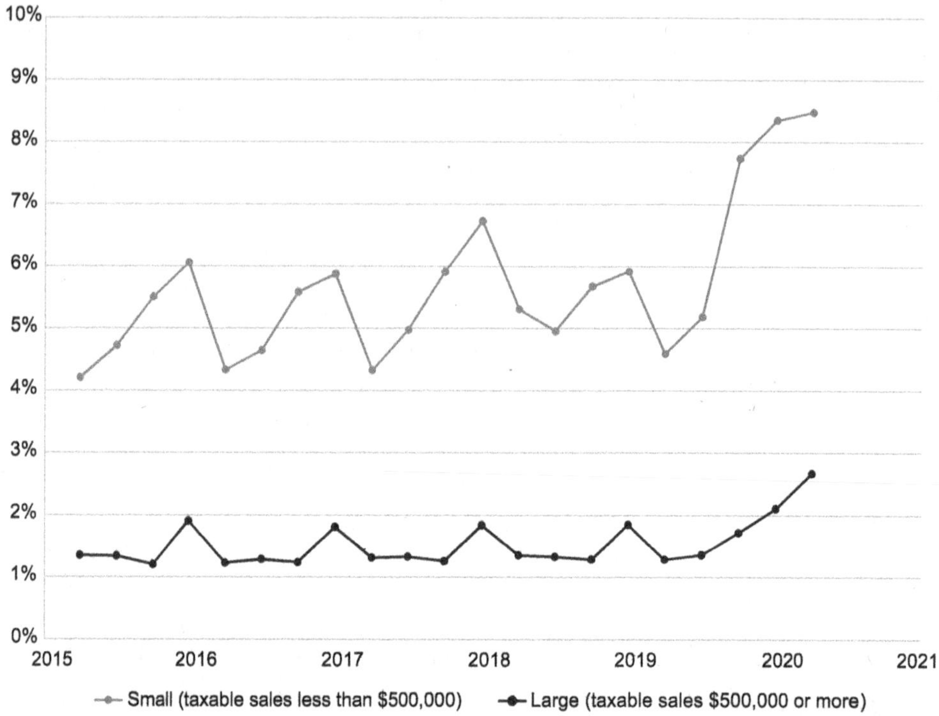

Figure 3.7
Quarterly closure rates for small and large businesses in California, 2015Q2 to 2020Q2.

closure rates for small businesses and large businesses from 2015Q2 to 2020Q2. Small businesses are defined as those with average quarterly taxable sales annualized to less than $500,000. Large businesses are defined as those with $500,000 or more in annualized taxable sales over the previous four quarters. There is a clear pattern of lower closure rates with larger initial size of the business. Closure rates are much higher for small businesses than for large businesses, and this differential holds both prior the pandemic and at the start of the pandemic. On average, 5.4 percent of small businesses closed each quarter from 2015Q1 to 2019Q4. In comparison, an average of 1.4 percent of large businesses closed each quarter during the same time period.

Another clear pattern is that all business sizes experienced an increase in closure rates in the pandemic. The increases in closure rates for for businesses of both size classes were large enough to disrupt seasonality patterns.

Another finding is that there does not appear to be a strong upward or downward trend prior to the pandemic in closure rates for either large or small businesses.

Market Share Concentration

Did the disproportionate closing of small businesses during the pandemic lead to an increase in the concentration of taxable sales at large businesses in California? In other words, was there a large increase in market share concentration caused by the pandemic? Fairlie et al. (2022) also report findings for changes over time in market concentration using the commonly used Herfindahl-Hirschman Index (HHI). The HHI captures the thought experiment of how consumer dollars are spent at different retailers. The HHI divided by 100 is the probability (in percentage terms) that two dollars chosen at random among all dollars spent in California in a given quarter are spent at the same retailer. An increase in the HHI indicates an increasingly concentrated market. For example, if there is only one retailer for a certain business type that all customers purchase from, the HHI will be 100 percent. If instead every dollar is spent at a different retailer, then the HHI will be very small.

Fairlie et al. (2022) found that the HHI increased only slowly and mostly steadily from 19.8 in 2015Q1 to 21.4 in 2019Q3 before the pandemic. In the early months of the pandemic, however, the HHI increased to 38.0 in 2020Q2. There was a clear increase in market concentration at the start of the pandemic. This increased concentration is consistent with higher closure rates among small businesses during the pandemic. Sales shifted from small businesses to large businesses as small businesses closed at a disproportionate rate.

What Happened to the Broader Economy?

Did the pandemic result in major losses to the U.S. economy? One of the main indicators used to measure the pulse of the economy is the growth rate of the national gross domestic product (GDP). Another widely used barometer of the health of the economy, especially in the labor market, is the national unemployment rate. Both measures are often used to provide information on current economic conditions.

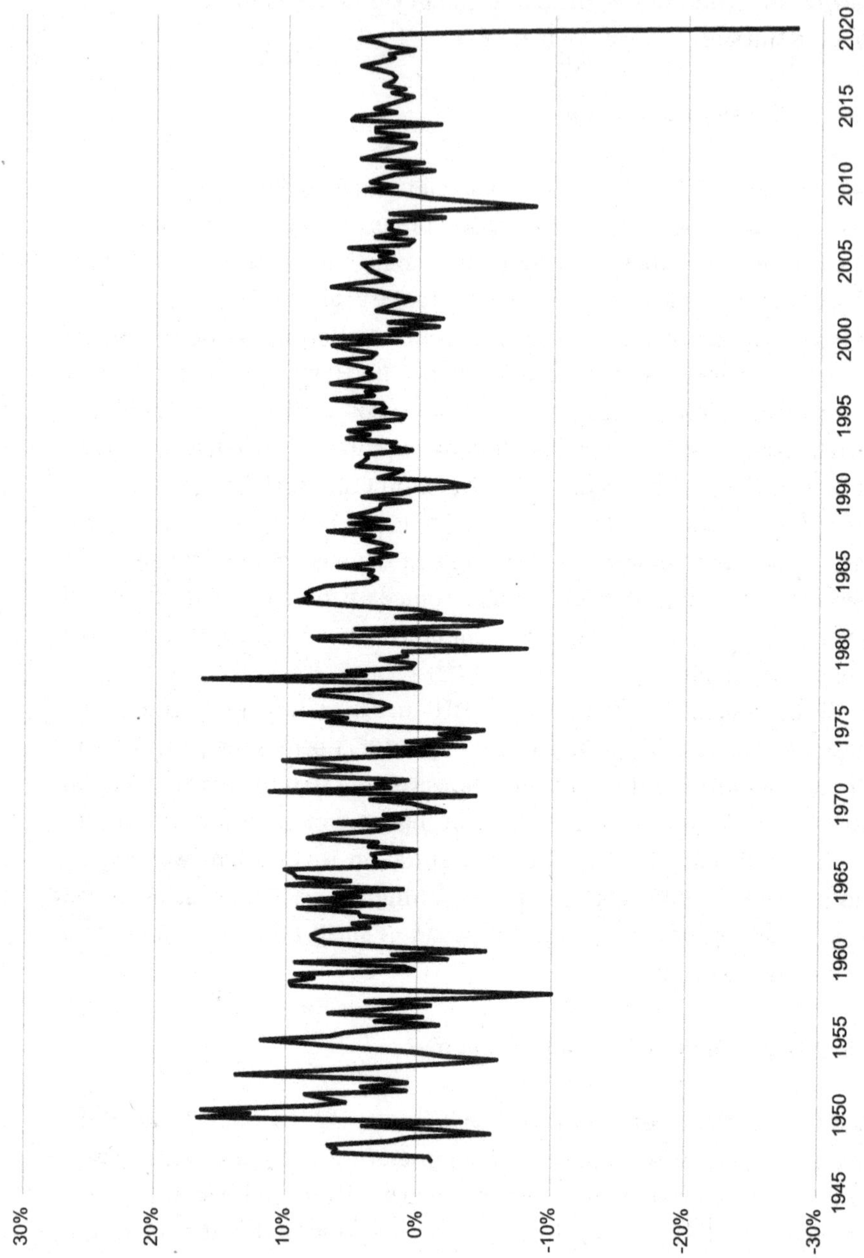

Figure 3.8
Quarterly GDP growth rate, 1947Q2–2020Q2. *Source:* GDP quarterly growth data from U.S. Bureau of Economic Analysis.

Perhaps the broadest measure used to track U.S. economic conditions is the growth rate in the GDP. Figure 3.8 displays trends in quarterly GDP growth rates from the first year it was tracked quarterly, 1947, to the second quarter of 2020. The second quarter of 2020 includes April, May, and June. The pandemic led to an unprecedented disruption of the U.S. economy. GDP growth plummeted in early 2020. Over the numerous recessions in the second half of the twentieth century and the first two decades of the twenty-first century there has never been such a large quarter-to-quarter change in GDP as in the first full quarter of the pandemic, 2020Q2. GDP fell by 28.1 percent in 2020Q2.[13]

If we focus on the past fifteen years, the disruption caused by the pandemic is even clearer (figure 3.9). GDP growth plummeted in early 2020. In contrast, during the Great Recession GDP dropped by much less, 8.5 percent, in 2008Q3. The pandemic created an extremely severe but short recession. GDP reversed course quickly and grew substantially the next quarter. The NBER officially dates the pandemic-induced recession as occurring from February 2020 (peak) to April 2020 (trough).

The disruption to the national unemployment rate, which is measured monthly, is examined next. Figure 3.10 displays the national unemployment rate from January 2000 to April 2020. The unemployment rate rose to recessionary peaks in 2003 and 2009 before starting the long, steady decline to extremely low levels just prior to the start of the pandemic. The unemployment rate reached a long-term low of 3.5 percent in February 2020. Two months later, unemployment skyrocketed to an all-time high of 14.8 percent in April 2020. For several reasons related to measurement issues, the true unemployment rate in April 2020 was likely much higher (Couch, Fairlie, and Xu 2020a, 2020b).

There was much concern over the devastating number of job losses during the Great Recession. Unemployment rates tend to keep rising even after the official end of the recession. The national unemployment rate hit a peak of 10.0 percent in October 2009. The official trough during the Great Recession occurred in June 2009. In contrast, the COVID-19 recession had an immediate effect on unemployment rates, mostly because it was an economic shutdown by design. The goal was to "flatten the curve," or slow the increase in the spread of COVID-19 by shutting down business activity and other forms of social interaction. The COVID-19 shutdown also resulted in a much larger increase in unemployment rates than did the lengthy Great Recession.

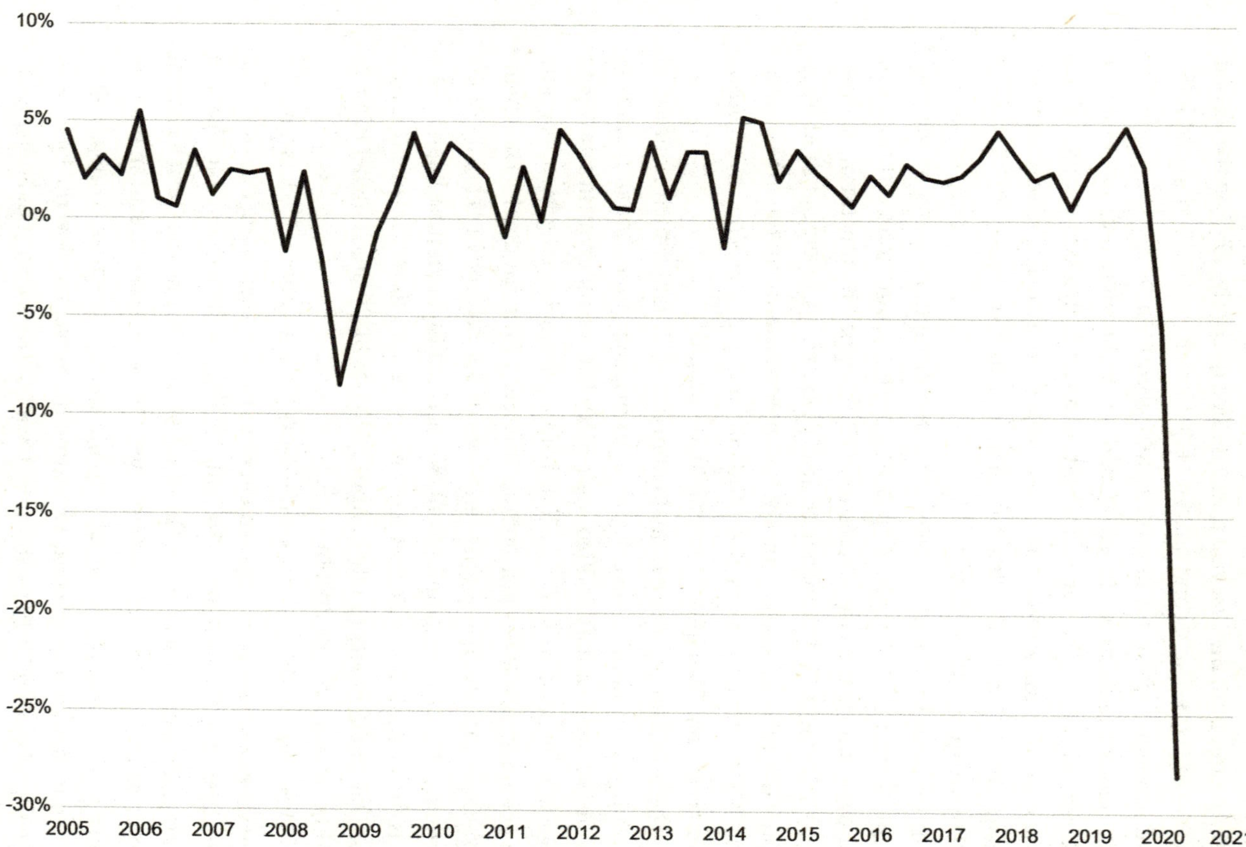

Figure 3.9
Quarterly GDP growth rate, 2005Q1–2020Q2. *Source*: GDP quarterly growth data from U.S. Bureau of Economic Analysis.

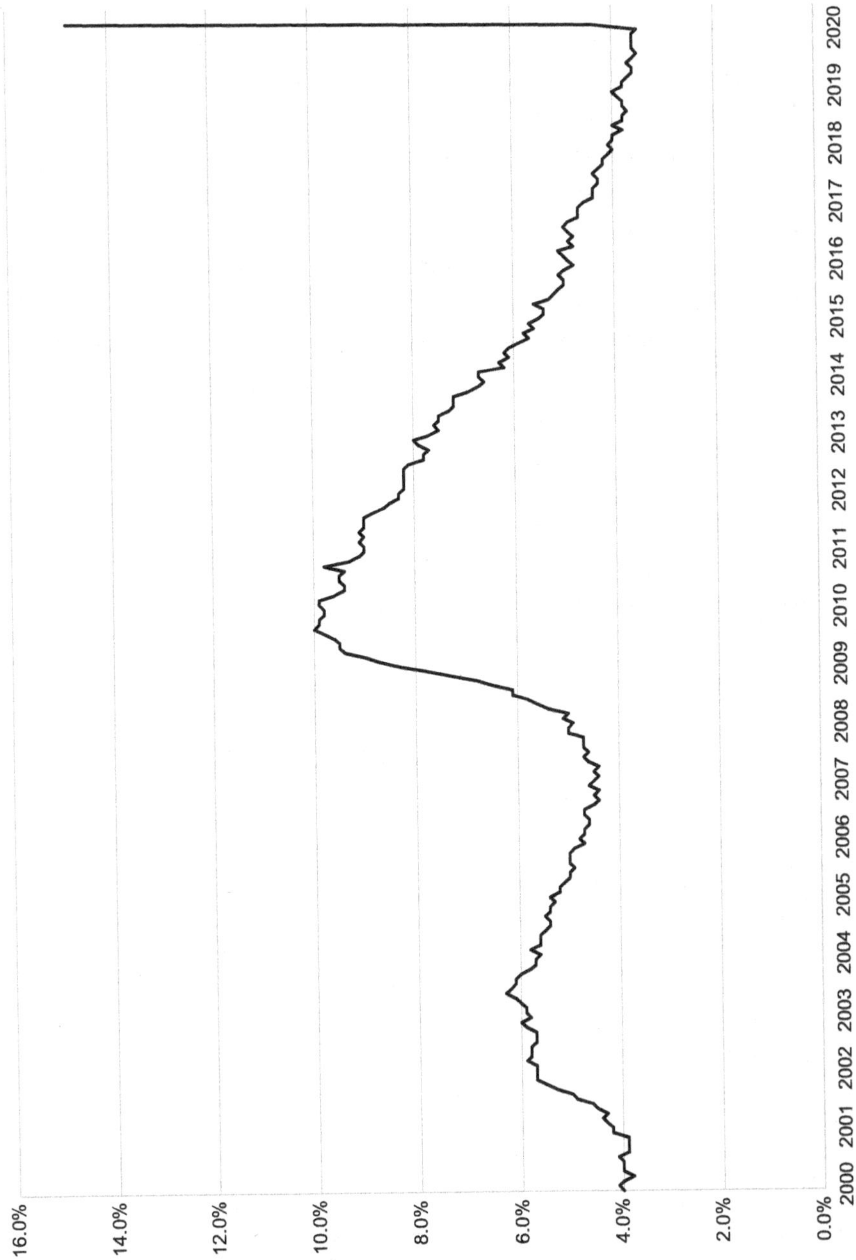

Figure 3.10
Unemployment rate, January 2000–April 2020.

The COVID-19 Recession: The Official Dating

The COVID-19 recession as defined by the NBER started in March 2020 and ended in May 2020. Table 3.10 reports the official business cycle dates from the NBER. It was very unusual recession not only in that it was self-enforced through social distancing restrictions but also because it was extremely short, lasting only two months. It is the shortest contraction period on record. The NBER business cycle dating goes back to the 1850s. Also, as seen above in the data, March only partially captures the impacts of the social distancing restrictions.

The Great Recession was much longer. The U.S. economy peaked in December 2007 and slipped into a deep recession that lasted until June 2009. The Great Recession lasted eighteen months, compared with two months for the pandemic recession. The early 2000 and early 1990 recessions both lasted longer, at eight months. The two recessions in the 1980s also lasted longer.

Another notable characteristic of the pandemic recession was the lengthy economic expansion period leading up to the contraction. The expansion period was the longest on record. It lasted 128 months (more than ten years). The economic growth period leading up to the recession starting in April 2001 lasted nearly the same length of time, at 120 months. Other recessions, however, were preceded by much shorter expansion periods.

Table 3.10
NBER-Dated Business Cycles

Peak month	Trough month	Economic contraction (mos.)	Preceding economic expansion (mos.)
January 1980	July 1980	6	58
July 1981	November 1982	16	12
July 1990	March 1991	8	92
March 2001	November 2001	8	120
December 2007	June 2009	18	73
February 2020	April 2020	2	128

Source: National Bureau of Economic Research: US Business Cycle Expansions and Contractions, https://www.nber.org/research/data/us-business-cycle-expansions-and-contractions.

Appendix 3.A: The Current Population Survey

The CPS is the only nationally representative dataset that provides (1) a measure of business ownership, (2) information on the demographic characteristics of owners, and (3) a timely measure of business activity. Using microdata from the basic monthly files of the CPS, I measured self-employed business ownership at the individual owner level. These surveys, conducted monthly by the U.S. Bureau of the Census and the U.S. Bureau of Labor Statistics, are representative of the entire U.S. population and contain observations for more than 130,000 people. The CPS is usually released within a month of when the data are collected.

The CPS has been conducted monthly since 1940 and is the underlying source of official government statistics on employment and unemployment. Data are collected by personal interview. The data cover all persons in the civilian noninstitutionalized population of the United States living in households. The CPS is the only source of monthly estimates of employment, self-employed persons, wage and salary employees, and unemployment. Although the main purpose of the CPS is to collect information on the employment situation, a secondary purpose is to collect information on the demographics of the population.

Measures of business ownership are available from only a handful of other large, nationally representative government datasets, such as the Survey of Business Owners (SBO) and the American Community Survey (ACS). Measures of business ownership based on these cross-sectional data, however, cannot capture recent patterns because there is often a one- to two-year delay in release of the data. The CPS microdata are released very quickly after the surveys are collected.

To estimate business ownership from the CPS data, I identified all individuals who owned a business as their main job in the survey month (based on the class-of-worker question and monthly labor force recode). The main job is defined as the one with the most hours worked during the survey week. Thus individuals who start side businesses are not counted if they work more hours in a wage and salary job. The CPS captures the current work activity of the business owner and whether that business owner is currently operating the business. Thus the number of *active* business owners can be captured in the data, but there is no way of telling whether these are temporary or permanent business closures. But inactive business owners, regardless of whether the business is temporarily or permanently closed, suffer losses in business income during months of nonoperation.

The measure of business ownership in the CPS captures all business owners, including those who own incorporated or unincorporated businesses and those who are employers or nonemployers. Although some business owners own large businesses, small businesses predominate. I interpret the data as predominantly covering small business owners. In addition to providing information on business ownership and current activity, the CPS data include detailed demographic information, such as gender, race, and immigrant status of the owner. The data also include information on the industry and incorporation status of the business. The CPS data have been used in previous research to study self-employment, business ownership and entrepreneurship (see, e.g., Chatterji, Chay, and Fairlie 2014; Fairlie and Chatterji 2013; Fairlie and Fossen 2019; Hipple and Hammond 2016; Levine and Rubenstein 2017; Wang 2019; and Wilmoth 2021).

Survey Timing and Social Distancing Restrictions

The CPS survey reference period is generally the calendar week that contains the twelfth day of the month. For April, the week was Sunday, April 12, through Saturday, April 18. The March survey reference week was March 8 through March 14. For May, the week was Sunday, May 10, through Saturday, May 16, and for June, the week was Sunday, June 14, to Saturday, June 20. Insofar as shelter-in-place restrictions started after this reference week, the April 2020 release is the first CPS survey fully covering the early-stage impacts of COVID-19. On March 16, 2020, the San Francisco Bay Area imposed shelter-in-place restrictions, followed by the State of California on March 19. New York state followed the next day. By early April most states had imposed social distancing restrictions. The analysis below mostly relies on comparisons between February 2020 (prior to social distancing policy mandates) and April, May, or June 2020 (the first three months after policy mandates). March 2020 is not included in most analyses because there were only partial effects in this month.

CPS Data on Business Earnings

Only a few national datasets provide information on business ownership, the demographic characteristics of business owners, and business owner earnings. I use microdata from the Annual Social and Economic (ASEC) supplement to the CPS to measure self-employed business owner earnings at the individual owner level and explore patterns by race and ethnicity. To estimate business earnings in the ASEC CPS data, I identified all individuals who reported owning a business as their main job over the previous calendar year (based on the class-of-worker question). The main job is defined in the ASEC as the one with the most hours worked during the year. Thus individuals who start side businesses are not counted if they work more hours in a wage or salary job. Although some business owners own large businesses, most own small businesses. I calculated business earnings from a survey question that asks for net earnings from the business (or farm) after expenses during the calendar year. For incorporated business owners, the question asks for earnings from the business before deductions in the calendar year. The ASEC file includes a measure of earnings from the longest job held during the calendar year. The question refers to annual earnings and captures the previous calendar year. Thus, for example, the 2021 ASEC file asks about earnings in the 2020 calendar year.

In addition to providing information on business ownership and earnings, the CPS data include detailed demographic information, such as gender, race, and ethnicity of the owner. The education level and geographic location of the owner are also captured, as is the industry of the business.

Measures of business ownership and outcomes are available from only a handful of other large, nationally representative government datasets such as the Annual Survey of Entrepreneurs (ASE), the SBO, and the ACS. Measures of business ownership based on these data, however, cannot capture recent patterns because there is typically a one- to two-year delay in release of the data. Another complication is that the 2020 ACS microdata, which also have annual business earnings, are only being released through "experimental" estimates, with a limited number of data tables and geographies covered because of the impact of the COVID-19 pandemic on data collection (U.S. Census Bureau 2021). In contrast, the BLS went to great lengths to make sure that CPS response rates were high even in the early months of the pandemic, and 2020 calendar year earnings are measured from the 2021 March survey, when most social restrictions were lifted.

Survey and Pandemic Timing with Annual Data

The ASEC provides information on the previous calendar year. For example, the 2021 ASEC covers calendar year 2020. The months of January and

February 2020 were likely unaffected by the pandemic. March 2020 is less clear. GDP growth in 2020Q1, which captures March 2020, shows a large drop. Even if only January and February 2020 are unaffected, in calendar year 2020 the estimated impacts will be smaller than if measured over the entire calendar year. It is not possible to remove earnings in these two months from a person's reported earnings for the calendar year. Using this approach, 2019 is the last prepandemic year. Thus my estimates of COVID-19's effects focus on comparisons of 2020 with 2019. For the early-stage economic recovery period the analysis focuses on comparisons of 2021 with 2019.

Appendix 3.B: Regression Equations for Adjusting for Prepandemic Trends

To more formally test whether COVID-19 had disproportionate impacts on minority business owner earnings, I estimated regressions in which log business earnings was the dependent variable. The regressions control for trends prior to COVID-19 and prepandemic differences in business, owner, and geographic characteristics. Controlling for prior trends in business earnings might be important for identifying the disruption created by COVID-19. To start, I estimated the following base equation:

$$Y_{it} = \alpha + \delta COVID20_t + \beta' X_{it} + \lambda_t + \varepsilon_{it}, \quad (3.1)$$

where Y_{it} is annual log business earnings for owner i in calendar year t, $COVID20_t$ is a dummy variable for the post-COVID-19 year 2020, X_{it} includes owner, business, and geographic characteristics, λ_t is a linear time trend, and ε_{it} is the error term. The analysis sample covers seven years, with five pre-COVID-19 years (2015–2019) and one post-COVID-19 year (2020). As noted above, 2020 includes the months of January and February, prior to social distancing restrictions being imposed, and March only partially captures the effects of those restrictions. Estimates of *annual* losses in the pandemic will be downward biased because of this limitation.

The parameter of interest is δ, which captures the estimate of COVID-19 effects on business earnings. The regressions control for business (industry), owner (education/skill level, age, gender, race), and geographic (region, central city status) characteristics. The main specification includes a linear time trend. All specifications are estimated with OLS using CPS sample weights.

Equation (3.1) could be expanded to create a "difference-in-difference" estimator of the impact of COVID-19 but, owing to the widespread impact of restrictions and the disease, no group was unaffected. However, I am not evaluating the impact of a specific policy but am estimating whether there are impacts of COVID-19 relative to prepandemic levels and trends. There is no control group because all groups were affected by the pandemic.

Equation (3.1) implicitly calculates the second or post-pre difference from a comparison of 2020 business earnings with mean business earnings from 2015 to 2019 (detrended). Although this approach provides more precise estimates because of a longer pre-COVID-19 time period, it has the disadvantage of including years that are further away from the beginning of the pandemic in the calculation of COVID-19 effects. One way to address this issue is to narrow the prepandemic period comparison to 2019 only. The simplest way to do this is to include a dummy variable that equals one for the entire 2015–2018 time period and include its interactions with the race dummies. Pre2019 is a dummy variable equal to one if the year is in 2015–2018 and zero otherwise.

Another approach is to include a full set of year dummies instead of combining all pre-COVID-19 years prior to the base year, 2019. This "event-study" style regression is specified as follows:

$$Y_{it} = a + \sum_{s=-5}^{1} \delta_s Year_{it} + \beta' X_{it} + \varepsilon_{it}, \tag{3.2}$$

where the reference year is $s = 0$ (2019) and $Year_t$ are dummy variables for each year. This event-study regression estimates log business earnings in pre-COVID-19 years. Insofar as the economy was steadily growing during this time period, examining years prior to 2019 should not reveal big jumps in earnings, at least not at the level created by COVID-19 in 2020.

4 Early Impacts of COVID-19 on Racial Inequality in Business Activity and Earnings

The mandated closings of nonessential businesses to slow the spread of COVID-19 and disruptions of consumer demand from health concerns had widespread effects on small businesses starting in the spring of 2020. As noted in the previous chapter, business activity dropped by 22 percent from February 2020 to April 2020, and business earnings losses were on the order of 16–19 percent. Business activity and earnings losses were much larger for some types of businesses, such restaurants, hotels, and personal services. Additional measures such as the opportunity versus necessity share of new businesses and taxable sales by businesses also showed large losses at the beginning of the pandemic.

Although the losses to small businesses were unprecedented, a pressing concern for economic inequality is whether they were felt disproportionately by people of color. The impact on minority-owned businesses is of special concern. Roughly one-tenth of the workforce owns a business instead of working for someone else as their primary job, and these business owners hold a disproportionate amount of total wealth and often create jobs for others (Fairlie et al. 2023; Headd 2021; Hipple and Hammond 2016; U.S. Bureau of Labor Statistics 2020; U.S. Census Bureau 2016). Minority-owned businesses are important for local job creation, economic advancement, and longer-term wealth equality (Boston 1999, 2006; Bradford 2003, 2014; Fairlie and Robb 2008; Stoll, Raphael, and Holzer 2001).

Large and persistent racial disparities in business ownership and outcomes have also existed for some time in the United States, but their causes are not entirely understood.[1] The lack of research attention is surprising given the magnitude of the racial disparities and the importance of business ownership as a way to make a living for many Americans. Only 5 percent of Black workers and 8 percent of Latinx workers own businesses, compared with more than 11 percent of non-Latinx white workers (Hipple and Hammond 2016). Similarly troubling is that Black- and Latinx-owned businesses have substantially lower average sales and hire fewer employees than white-owned businesses (Davila and Mora 2013; Fairlie and Robb 2008; U.S. Census Bureau 2016). The pandemic may have widened these preexisting inequalities. To date, however, there exists much less evidence on whether small businesses owned by minority groups were more (or less) negatively affected by COVID-19, and if so, why. This chapter explores whether there were disproportionate impacts of COVID-19 on small businesses by race.

Impacts on Business Owners of Color

Business activity by race in the first month of the pandemic is first examined. Building on the analysis presented in the previous chapter, figure 4.1 displays losses in the number of active business owners by major racial groups. I provided the first report of these numbers on the impact of COVID-19 on business activity by race in May 2020 (Fairlie 2020a, 2020b).

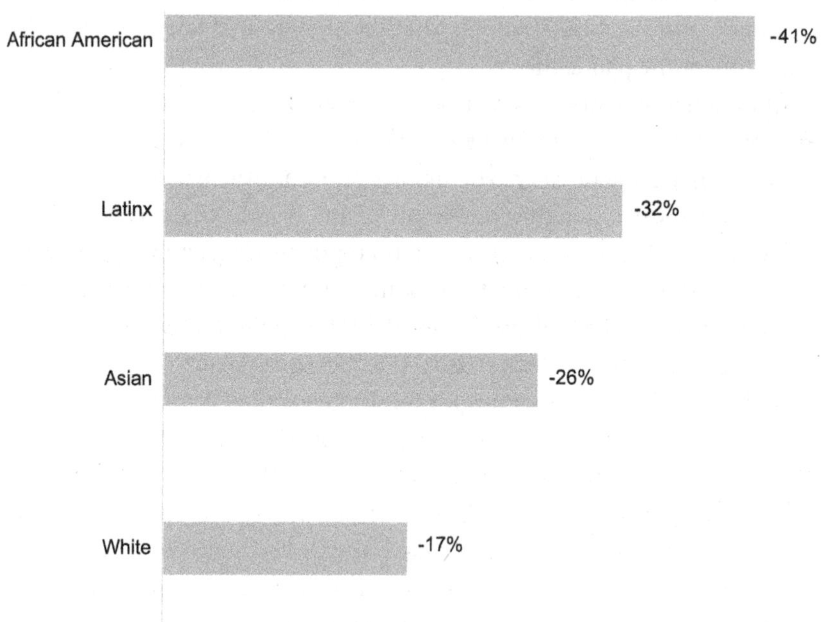

Figure 4.1
Losses in the number of active business owners by race from before to after COVID-19 restrictions, February to April 2020.

The levels of losses in business activity among owners of color are alarming. The number of African American or Black business owners plummeted by 41 percent in the first full month of the pandemic-mandated shutdowns. The percentage loss was the largest for any major racial or ethnic group.

The 41 percent drop in Black business activity reflects the loss of nearly half a million Black business owners actively working in their businesses. The number of active Black business owners dropped from 1.1 million in February 2020 to 640,000 in April (table 4.1). The implications for lost

Table 4.1

Change in Number of Active Business Owners by Race or Ethnicity in the United States, February to April 2020

Racial/ethnic group and month, 2020	No. of active business owners	Percent change relative to February 2020
Total		
February 2020	15,012,692	0
March 2020	14,475,704	–4
April 2020	11,710,360	–22
Black		
February 2020	1,079,116	0
March 2020	1,074,478	0
April 2020	637,769	–41
Latinx		
February 2020	2,070,896	0
March 2020	1,936,739	–6
April 2020	1,412,925	–32
Asian		
February 2020	888,528	0
March 2020	936,072	5
April. 2020	657,896	–26
White		
February 2020	10,553,415	0
March 2020	10,155,913	–4
April 2020	8,761,531	–17

Notes: Author's calculations from compiled monthly Current Population Survey microdata.

income from having 41 percent of business owners not working in April likely caused major economic difficulties for owners.

Latinx business owners also suffered major losses in business activity. The number of active Latinx business owners dropped from 2.1 million to 1.4 million (32 percent) from February to April 2020. These losses were large and likely created financial hardship for owners.

Asian business owners suffered losses in business activity of 230,000 in April 2020, representing 26 percent of February levels. Consumer discrimination against Asian-owned businesses was a concern because of the coronavirus's first appearance in China. The drop in business activity from February to April for whites was also large, at 1.8 million business owners, but smaller as a percentage of starting levels (17 percent).

When the comparison is changed to April 2019 (i.e., to detect year-over-year change) instead of February 2020, the conclusions about the early impacts of COVID-19 on business activity levels by race do not differ. For all the racial groups, the number of business owners dropped precipitously from April 2019 to April 2020. In general, the number of self-employed business owners for each group does not change substantially over time, especially during stable economic conditions, and thus February 2020 accurately captures prepandemic levels. April 2020 clearly posed an unprecedented shock to business owners that hit all groups hard, throwing active business totals off their relatively stable longer-term levels.

These findings for April 2020 were covered widely in the early press and news outlets (e.g., *The Washington Post, The New York Times, The Wall Street Journal,* PBS, CNBC, BBC) covering the pandemic. The findings also were used in government policy discussions at the beginning of the pandemic to address concerns over disproportionate losses. The findings were used in testimony before the U.S. Senate (Busby 2020; Evans 2020), a new Senate bill (U.S. Senate 2020), arguments for the Shop at Black-Owned Businesses movement, and other policies.

Losses in April 2020 Were Much Larger Than Losses During the Great Recession

The losses for each racial group were the largest over time. Figure 4.2 displays trends for the number of active Black, Latinx, and Asian business owners back to January 2005. Although there is some fluctuation from month

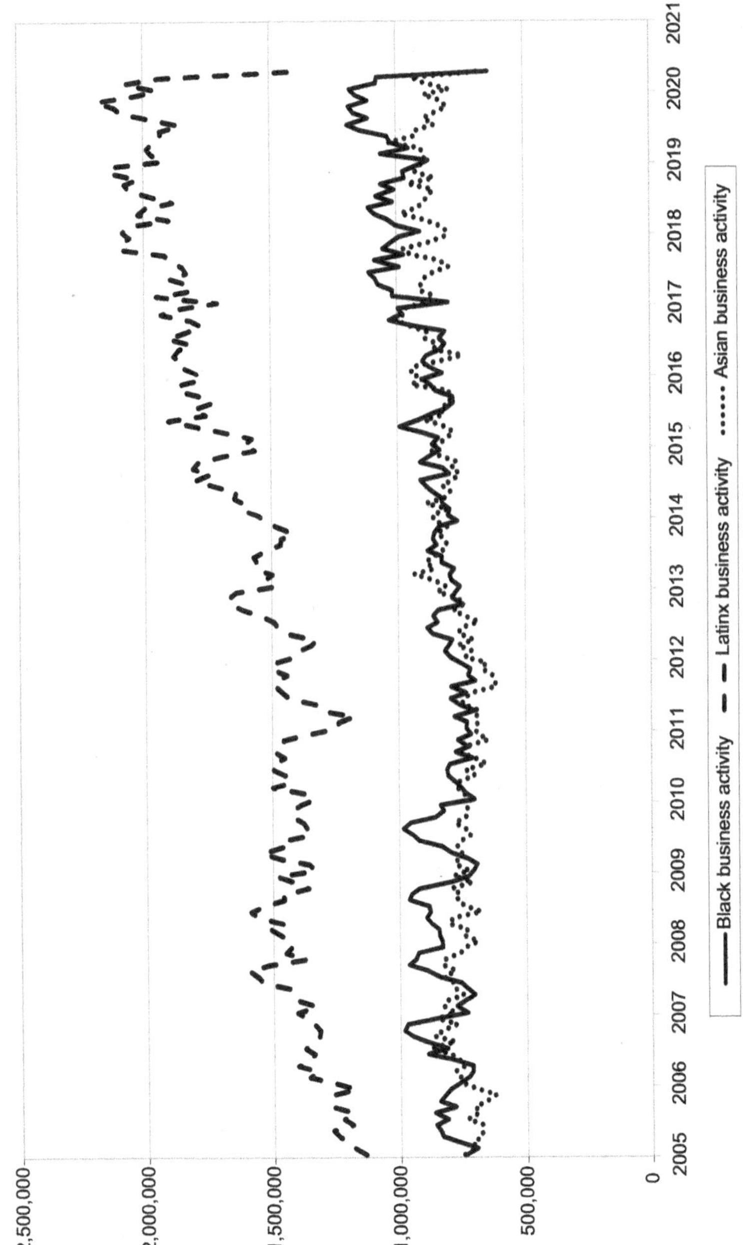

Figure 4.2
Number of active business owners by race, January 2005–April 2020.

to month because of sampling variation, the drop in April 2020 in business activity is clear and much larger than any other fluctuations over time. During the Great Recession, business owner activity dropped at a much lower rate of 6 percent for Latinx owners and 3 percent for Asian owners, and did not decrease for Black owners. The disruption from COVID-19 was unprecedented for business owners of color.

Causes of Disproportionate Losses: The Importance of Industry Distributions

Did the industry distribution of businesses owned by different racial groups place them at a higher or lower risk of negative impacts from COVID-19–related shutdowns? As shown in table 3.3 in the previous chapter, business activity fell by differing rates by industry. For example, Personal and Laundry Services lost 79 percent of business owner activity in April, and Arts, Leisure, and Accommodations lost 35 percent of business activity in April. If a minority group was overrepresented in these two industries compared with others, then it might have experienced larger losses in business activity at the start of the pandemic.

To explore this question, I simulated the total number of business owners for each racial group by switching their industry distribution for the U.S. national industry distribution. The industry distributions are both from February 2020. The simulation essentially uses the national industry shares and multiplies them by the group-specific changes in the number of active business owners between February and April 2020.[2]

Table 4.2 reports estimates from the simulations. The number of Black business owners declined by 41 percent from February to April 2020. The industry distribution of Black business owners was partly responsible for relatively large business activity losses from February to April. When switching to the U.S. national industry distribution, the decline in active business owners is less, at 35 percent. Thus the Black business industry distribution was "unfavorable" in terms of placing these owners at a higher risk of business activity losses in April 2020 due to COVID-19.

A similar pattern is found for Latinx business owners. When switching from the Latinx industry distribution to the U.S. national industry distribution, the drop in the predicted number of active Latinx business

Table 4.2
Business Losses by Racial/Ethnic Group and Simulations of Losses from Switching Industry Distributions, February to April 2020

	Actual losses, February to April 2020		Predicted using national industry distribution	
Group	No.	Percent change	No.	Percent change
Total	−3,302,331	−22	−3,302,331	−22
Black	−441,347	−41	−379,452	−35
Latinx	−657,971	−32	−583,009	−28
Asian	−230,632	−26	−195,041	−22
White	−1,791,884	−17	−1,928,907	−18

Notes: Author's calculations from compiled monthly Current Population Survey microdata.

owners improves slightly, from 32 percent (actual losses) to 28 percent (predicted national), for April. Latinx business owners thus had an "unfavorable" industry distribution, placing them at higher risk of business activity losses.

Asian business owners show a similar pattern in April 2020. For April, I also found that Asian business owners were more concentrated in industries placing them at a higher risk of losses in business activity. Business activity losses were larger in industries with a higher Asian business owner concentration.

Another way to estimate industry impacts is to examine the percentage of each racial group that is in essential industries. As noted earlier, the classification is not perfect, and other factors, such as differences in customer demand, enforcement of tactics to limit the spread of COVID-19, and compliance by businesses, also influenced whether these businesses were open at the beginning of the pandemic. The percentage of Black business owners in essential industries was 66 percent, lower than the national percentage of 76 percent and consistent with the less favorable industry distribution placing them at higher risk of losses from COVID-19. On the other hand, Latinx business owners were slightly more likely to be concentrated in essential industries, at 80 percent. Asian business owners had the same concentration in essential industries as the national average. The patterns are interesting, but it is important to note that the classification is not perfect and does not completely align with patterns of group-specific losses.

Racial Disparities in Business Earnings Trends

As noted in the previous chapter, monthly information on business earnings does not exist. Instead, Bureau of Labor Statistics (BLS) data include an *annual* measure of business owner earnings. The annual survey is conducted each March and collects information on the previous calendar year's earnings. I switch to using these data to examine the effects of COVID-19 on business earnings in the first year of the pandemic by necessity.

All racial and ethnic groups experienced business earnings losses from 2019 to 2020. Figure 4.3 displays trends in mean business earnings from 2015 to 2020 by race and ethnicity. Mean business earnings dropped by 11 percent for Black business owners. Asian business owners lost 15 percent in 2020, and Latinx business owners lost 7 percent in the pandemic.[3] In comparison, white business owners experienced smaller business earnings losses of 2 percent.

Business earnings trends by group show much more year-to-year variation, likely owing to smaller sample sizes. Table 4.3 reports annual business earnings estimates and average sample sizes underlying figure 4.3. Although there is more year-to-year fluctuation, mean business earnings show large losses from 2019 to 2020. Business earnings losses appear to be the largest for Black business owners and Asian business owners. Business earnings losses early in the pandemic appear to be the smallest for white business owners. Prior to the pandemic there appears to be either a flat or slightly increasing upward trend in business earnings for all groups. The fluctuations from year to year make it difficult, however, to see a clear pattern.

Estimated business earnings losses are larger when measured in logs. Figure 4.4 displays trends in mean log business earnings by race and ethnicity. Using logs, business earnings dropped by 28 percent for Black business owners. which was considerably larger than the loss of 15 percent for white business owners. Asian business owners lost 21 percent and Latinx business owners lost 19 percent in the pandemic.

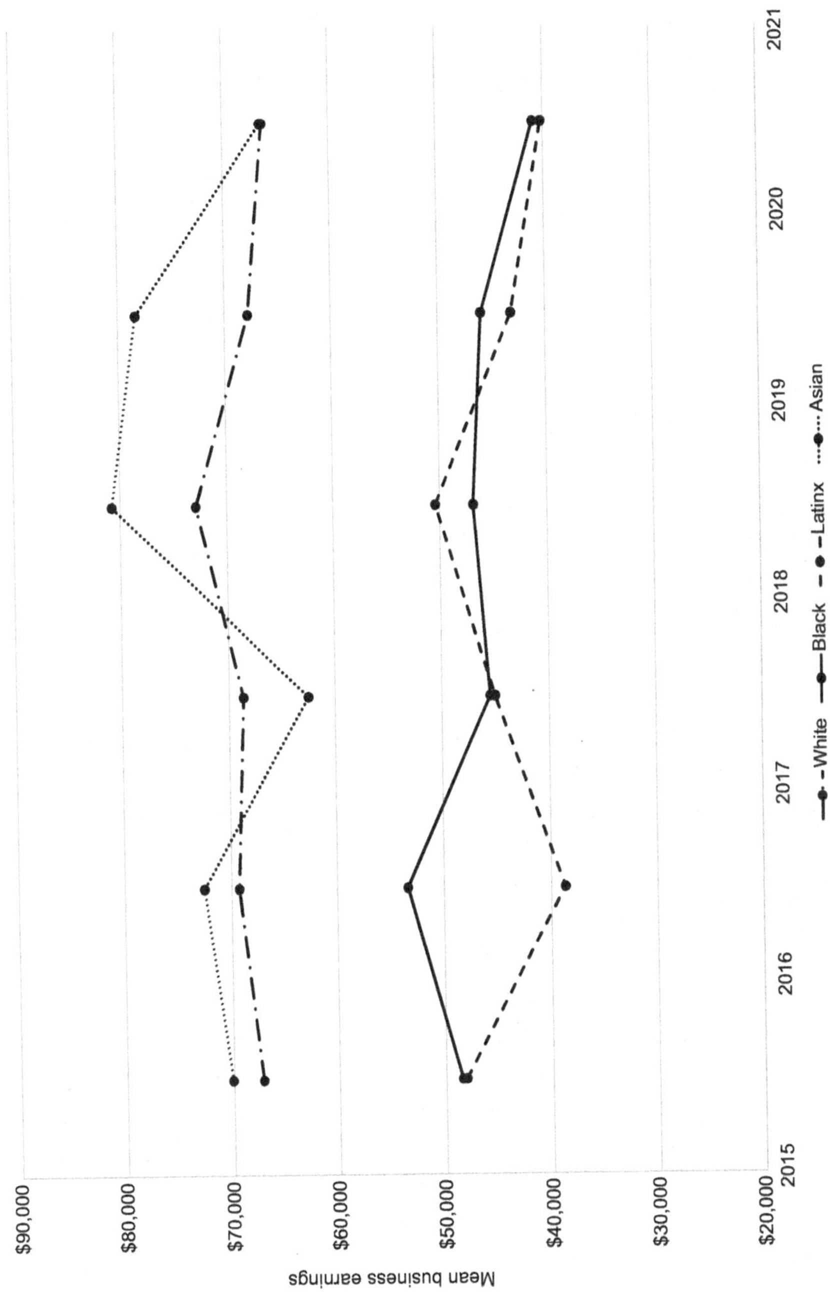

Figure 4.3
Mean business earnings trends by race, 2015–2020.

Table 4.3
Mean Annual Business Earnings Trends by Race and Ethnicity, 2015–2020

Business earnings and growth rates	Total	Black	Latinx	Asian	White
Mean business earnings ($)					
2015	63,029	48,461	48,076	70,093	67,131
2016	63,797	53,393	38,679	72,565	69,267
2017	62,636	45,494	45,022	62,482	68,627
2018	67,934	46,845	50,419	80,763	72,932
2019	62,675	45,961	43,152	78,350	67,777
2020	59,715	40,947	40,209	66,434	66,235
Growth rates (%)					
2015–2016	1	10	−20	4	3
2016–2017	−2	−15	16	−14	−1
2017–2018	8	3	12	29	6
2018–2019	−8	−2	−14	−3	−7
2019–2020	−5	−11	−7	−15	−2
Avg. annual *N*	6,769	473	1,169	462	4,673

Notes: Author's calculations from compiled annual Current Population Survey microdata.

Table 4.4 reports annual mean log business earnings estimates and average sample sizes. Similar to the estimates reported in table 4.3, there is a lot of year-to-year variation by group. Mean log business earnings show large losses from 2019 to 2020, with the largest losses for Black and Asian business owners and the smallest losses for white business owners.

Another important finding from the analysis of business earnings is that consistent across the two measures of business earnings, there is an unambiguous, time-invariant pattern of relative business earnings across groups.[4] Asian business owners and white business owners have higher business earnings in all years than Black business owners and Latinx business owners. Mean annual business earnings for the five years prior to the pandemic were roughly $73,000 for Asian business owners, $69,000 for white business owners, $48,000 for Black business owners, and $45,000 for Latinx business owners. Mean log business earnings were 9 log points higher for Asian business owners, 28 log points lower for Black business owners, and 32 log points lower for Latinx business owners than for white business owners. These long-term disparities in business performance across racial and

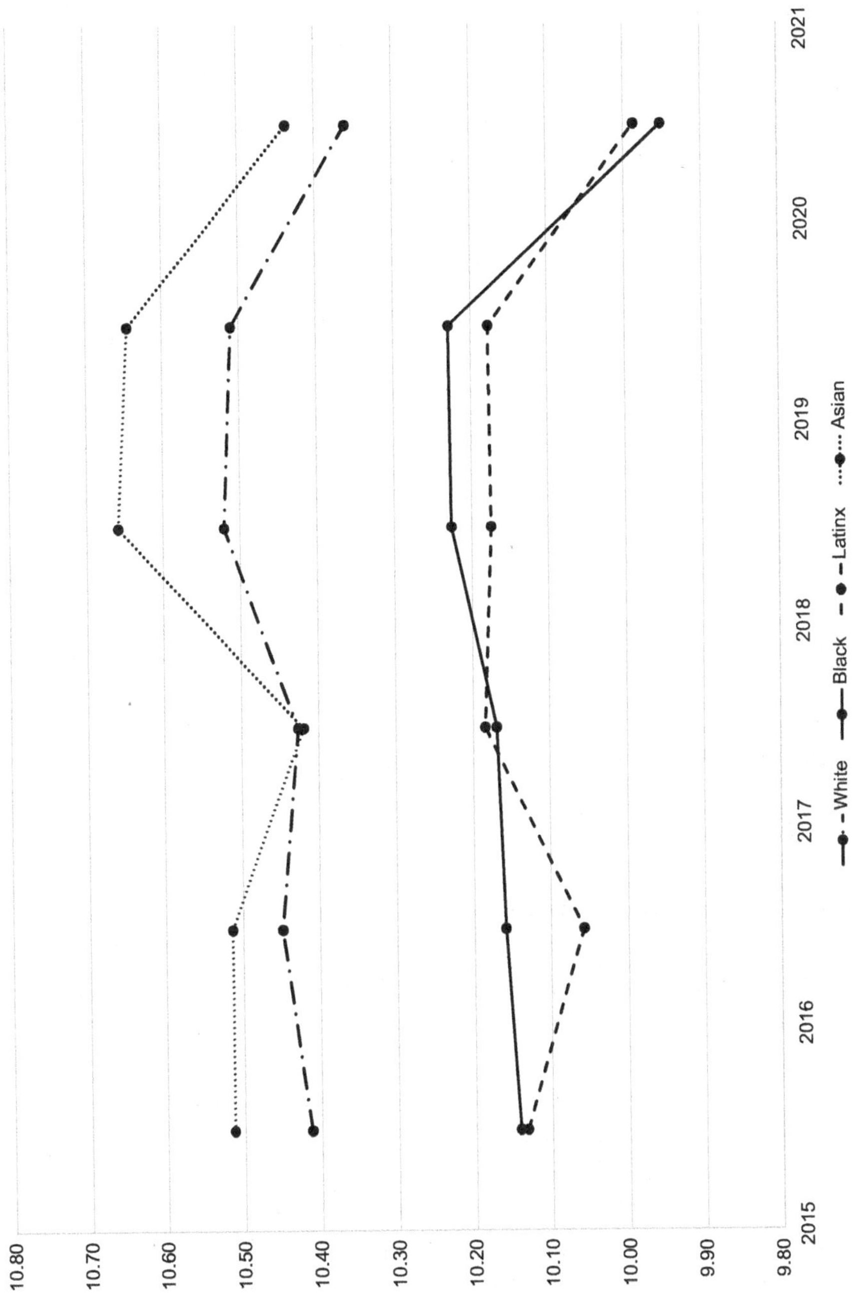

Figure 4.4
Mean log business earnings trends by race, 2015–2020.

Table 4.4
Mean Annual Log Business Earnings Trends by Race and Ethnicity, 2015–2020

Log business earnings and growth rates	Total	Black	Latinx	Asian	White
Mean log business earnings					
2015	10.35	10.14	10.13	10.51	10.41
2016	10.37	10.16	10.06	10.51	10.45
2017	10.37	10.17	10.18	10.42	10.43
2018	10.45	10.23	10.18	10.66	10.52
2019	10.44	10.23	10.18	10.65	10.51
2020	10.27	9.95	9.99	10.44	10.36
Growth rates (%)					
2015–2016	2	2	–8	0	4
2016–2017	0	1	13	–10	–2
2017–2018	8	6	–1	24	9
2018–2019	–1	0	0	–1	–1
2019–2020	–17	–28	–19	–21	–15
Avg. annual *N*	6,769	473	1,169	462	4,673

Notes: Author's calculations from compiled annual Current Population Survey microdata.

ethnic groups have been documented using a wide range of data sources and time periods (for reviews, see Bates 1997; Davila and Mora 2013; Fairlie and Robb 2008; Parker 2018).

Disproportionate Impacts of COVID-19 by Race and Ethnicity

To more formally test whether COVID-19 had disproportionate impacts among business owners of color, I estimate equation 4.1 in appendix 4.A for log business earnings. The regressions build on the underlying patterns displayed in the figures by controlling for pre-COVID-19 trends and owner, business, and geographic characteristics. For example, if there were converging trends in business earnings between two racial groups, the regression equation can simulate where these trends would likely have led in 2020 had COVID-19 not happened. When COVID-19 disrupts these patterns, there are two possible comparisons. One comparison is with what existed in 2019 (static) and the other comparison is with what likely would have happened in 2020 (trend-adjusted). The regressions thus estimate the impacts of COVID-19 on relative patterns in business earnings using both comparisons.

Table 4.5 reports estimates from equations (4.1) and (4.2) in appendix 4.A. Specification 1 starts with a stripped-down model that includes no additional variables except the race indicators and their interactions with 2020 (i.e., the "post-COVID-19" by race interactions).[5] The loss in business earnings for all groups in 2020 is captured by the "post-COVID-19" coefficient, which was roughly –15 percent. Focusing on whether there were differential impacts by race/ethnicity, the estimates indicate that Black business owners disproportionately experienced losses in earnings in 2020 relative to just prior to the

Table 4.5

Regressions for Log Business Earnings, Current Population Survey, 2015–2020

Explanatory variables	(1)	(2)	(3)	(4)
Black	–0.249	–0.182	–0.169	–0.169
	(0.058)	(0.041)	(0.052)	(0.052)
Latinx	–0.313	–0.143	–0.154	–0.155
	(0.044)	(0.032)	(0.040)	(0.040)
Asian	0.149	0.072	0.098	0.098
	(0.064)	(0.045)	(0.058)	(0.058)
Post-COVID-19 2020	–0.147	–0.168	–0.165	–0.138
	(0.027)	(0.025)	(0.026)	(0.025)
Post-COVID-19 2020 × Black	–0.120 (0.081)	–0.132 (0.075)	–0.139 (0.076)	–0.144 (0.072)
Post-COVID-19 2020 × Latinx	–0.035 (0.062)	–0.032 (0.057)	–0.024 (0.058)	–0.027 (0.055)
Post-COVID-19 2020 × Asian	–0.052 (0.093)	–0.070 (0.085)	–0.084 (0.087)	–0.094 (0.083)
Main controls	No	Yes	Yes	Yes
Industry controls	No	Yes	Yes	Yes
Time trend	No	Yes	Yes	Yes
Pre-2019 interactions	No	No	Yes	No
Full 2015–2019 interactions	No	No	No	Yes
Sample years	2019–2020	2015–2020	2015–2020	2015–2020
Sample size	12,470	40,611	40,611	40,611

Notes: Author's calculations from compiled annual Current Population Survey microdata. Main controls include female, age, education, region, and central city status indicator variables. Standard errors in parentheses.

pandemic, 2019. The Black coefficient estimate of –0.12 implies that Black business owner earnings dropped by 12 log points, or approximately 12 percent more than white (only) business owner earnings.[6] The point estimates for the relative COVID-19 effect on Latinx business earnings and Asian business earnings in 2020 are not statistically significant.

Specification 2 reports estimates from equation (4.1) in appendix 4.A. The regression equation includes a time trend and controls for owner, business, and geographic characteristics. The inclusion of the time trend and controls results in Black business earnings dropping by 13 percent more than white business earnings early in the pandemic. The coefficient on the COVID-19 effect on Latinx business earning remains roughly similar in magnitude and not statistically significant. The COVID-19 Asian business earnings loss increases in magnitude to 7 log points but remains statistically insignificant. The overall "post-COVID-19" coefficient indicates that all groups experienced losses of roughly 17 percent from prediction of where business earnings should in 2020 based on prior trends absent the pandemic.

Specification 3 reports estimates from the slight variation of equation (4.1) in appendix 4.A noted above. In this model, I added an indicator variable that captures years 2015–2018 as "-pre-2019 interactions" in table 4.5. The addition of this set of indicator variables focuses the estimation of COVID-19 effects on using 2019 as the comparison year instead of the average, detrended level over 2015–2018. The coefficients from this specification are similar to those of the previous specification. They indicate, for example, a similarly large relative drop for Black business earnings of roughly 14 percent in 2020. The point estimates for the Latinx versus white business earnings effect and Asian versus white business earnings effects are similar to the ones in the previous specification but remain statistically insignificant. Altering the comparison year also results in a similar estimate of the COVID-19 effect for all groups of a 17 percent loss in business earnings in 2020.

Specification 4 of table 4.5 reports estimates of equation (4.2), which is an event-study regression. In this specification, a full set of race indicator interactions with each pre-COVID-19 year (2015–2019) are included.[7] The coefficient estimate for the COVID-19 Black versus white effect is 14 percent. The point estimates for the Latinx and Asian relative COVID-19 effects are similar but remain statistically insignificant. The overall COVID-19 effect on all groups is estimated at 14 percent in 2020.

Overall, the robustness of estimates is impressive and reassuring that prior trends, choice of comparison pre-COVID-19 time period, or inclusion of baseline controls for individual and business characteristics do not affect the results.[8] Black business earnings dropped disproportionately as a result of COVID-19. Latinx and Asian business earnings might have also disproportionately dropped owing to COVID-19, but the imprecision of coefficient estimates rules out making strong conclusions regarding these findings.

It is important to note that the emphasis here is on testing for disproportionate effects of COVID-19 on business earnings among owners of color but that all groups, including white business owners, experienced earnings losses. The total pandemic-induced earnings losses for whites are estimated by the regressions to be from 14 to 17 percent, depending on the specification. As noted above, Black business owners lost an additional amount in business earnings, which, added to these base effects, totaled to a loss of 27–30 percent. Latinx business owners lost a total of 17–20 percent in business earnings, and Asian business owners lost a total of 20–25 percent in business earnings. When the COVID-19 interactions with race and ethnicity are removed and the regressions are reestimated, the estimated total effect of COVID-19 on business earnings is between 16 and 19 percent, as shown in table 3.8 in the previous chapter.

What Caused the Disproportionate Impacts During the COVID-19 Pandemic?

This section explores the underlying causes of why Black, Latinx, and Asian business owners experienced disproportionate losses in the pandemic. I take a two-step approach to answering this question. The first step is simply to examine racial differences in business, owner, and geographic characteristics. Are there any characteristics that differ substantially by race, suggesting they might explain why some groups experienced larger COVID-19–induced business earnings losses? For example, are Black-owned businesses concentrated in industries that were hit hardest by COVID-19 in 2020? If Black-owned businesses, on the other hand, have roughly similar industry distributions as white-owned businesses, then industry exposure cannot be a major cause of disproportionate earnings losses among Black-owned businesses in the pandemic.

The second step is to examine the interaction between prepandemic business, owner, and geographic characteristics and pandemic-induced business earnings losses. Using a new decomposition technique, I estimate direct contributions from racial differences in prepandemic characteristics to the change in the racial business earnings gap from 2019 to 2020. The technique directly answers the question, for example, of how much of the disproportionate loss in Black business earnings (relative to whites' earnings) is the result of Black-owned businesses being concentrated in the industries hardest-hit by the pandemic.

Racial or Ethnic Differences in Owner, Business, and Geographic Characteristics

Table 4.6 reports owner, business, and geographic characteristics for each racial and ethnic group prior to the pandemic. Among business owners, there are major differences across racial and ethnic groups. Starting with owner's education, Latinx are the least educated group. Only 21 percent of Latinx have a college degree, whereas 43 percent of whites have a college degree. The percentage of high school dropouts among Latinx is 28 percent, which is considerably higher than for whites (4 percent). Blacks also have lower levels of education, with 8 percent high school dropouts and 33 percent with a college degree. Asians have the highest levels of higher education degrees, with 62 percent having a college degree. Racial differences in education levels are large and might have placed less educated groups at a higher risk of business earnings losses in the pandemic.

Industry distributions differ across racial and ethnic groups. Table 4.6 reports industry distributions for business owners in 2019. Latinx business owners are more concentrated in Construction (29 percent) than white business owners (17 percent). Black business owners are less concentrated in Construction but more concentrated in Transportation (12 percent) and Other Services (14 percent).[9] Asian business owners have the most dissimilar industry distribution, with much higher concentrations in Wholesale and Retail Trade (13 percent), Leisure and Hospitality (12 percent), and Other Services (17 percent) and a much lower concentration in Construction (5.1 percent). All minority groups have fewer business owners in Agriculture than whites.

Another major difference across racial and ethnic groups is their geographic concentrations across the country. More than one-half of Black

Table 4.6
Business, Owner, and Geographic Characteristics by Race and Ethnicity, 2019

	Percentage of business owners with characteristic			
Characteristic	Black	Latinx	Asian	White
High school dropout	7.7	28.3	6.0	4.3
High school graduate	26.7	30.6	17.8	24.5
Some college	32.4	20.4	14.4	28.2
College graduate	33.3	20.7	61.8	43.0
Agriculture	1.5	1.4	0.3	6.6
Construction	10.8	28.7	7.8	17.3
Manufacturing	1.7	3.7	2.0	3.7
Wholesale and Retail Trade	8.3	7.8	12.8	9.4
Transportation	12.0	7.5	5.9	4.6
Information	2.3	1.7	1.4	2.1
Financial Activities	6.3	4.6	8.3	8.4
Professional and Business Services	21.3	22.7	20.1	21.8
Educational and Health Services	12.3	7.2	12.7	10.2
Leisure and Hospitality	9.9	6.6	11.9	6.9
Other Services	13.7	8.2	16.9	8.9
Northeast	18.6	11.4	21.9	17.7
Midwest	14.4	6.4	10.2	25.0
South	53.5	44.1	28.7	33.0
West	13.5	38.0	39.2	24.4
Central city	41.5	41.4	39.9	22.4
Suburbs	41.8	47.3	52.2	44.7
Rural	6.7	4.3	2.1	17.8
Not identified geographically	10.0	7.0	5.8	15.0
Female	39.9	33.5	43.7	36.6
Male	60.1	66.5	56.3	63.4
Age	43.95	43.36	45.46	47.00
Sample size	438	1041	444	4270

Notes: Author's calculations from compiled annual Current Population Survey microdata.

owners and 44 percent of Latinx owners live in the South, whereas only one-third of white owners live in the South. Roughly 40 percent of Asian and Latinx owners live in the West. The Midwest captures one quarter of the white population, the highest proportion of all groups. Turning to central city status, Black, Latinx, and Asian owners are more concentrated in central cities but less concentrated in rural areas than are white owners.

Among white owners, 37 percent are female. Black owners are more likely than white owners to be female (40 percent), and similarly, Asian owners are more likely to be female (44 percent). Latinx owners have the lowest share of female business ownership (34 percent). Black and Latinx owners are younger on average than white owners.

Previous research indicates that many of these characteristics are important in determining business ownership and outcomes.[10] The results reported in table 4.6 demonstrate that many of these characteristics are also associated with business earnings losses in the pandemic. I turn to estimating how much racial differences in each of these characteristics contributed to the disproportionate impacts of COVID-19 on minority business earnings.

Did Business and Owner Characteristics Place Minority Business Owners at Risk During the COVID-19 Pandemic?

It is useful to focus directly on the interaction between racial differences in prepandemic owner, business, and geographic characteristics and pandemic business earnings losses. The goal is to identify factors that contributed to the changes between 2019 and 2020 in business earnings and differ by race. Another goal is to identify how much each factor contributed to disproportionate losses in business earnings by race. For example, how much did the Black industry distribution relative to the white industry distribution contribute to larger Black business earnings losses during the pandemic? The equations used for this technique are reported in appendix 4.B.

Table 4.7 reports estimates for each business, owner, and geographic characteristic and each racial and ethnic group. The disproportionate business earnings loss from 2019 to 2020 among Black owners was −12.7 log points. The largest contributing factor to this disproportionate loss was prepandemic industry differences. In other words, the industry concentrations of Black business owners relative to the industry concentrations of white business owners placed them at a higher risk of business earnings losses in the pandemic. This factor alone contributed −6.3 log points to the

Table 4.7
Decomposition of Changes in Log Business Earnings Gaps, 2019 to 2020

Mean levels and contributions to losses	Black-white	Latinx-white	Asian-white
Mean levels:			
Minority log business income 2020	9.952	9.987	10.437
Minority log business income 2019	10.229	10.177	10.645
Minority loss	–0.277	–0.191	–0.209
White log business income 2020	10.361	10.361	10.361
White log business income 2019	10.510	10.510	10.510
White loss	–0.150	–0.150	–0.150
Minority disproportionate loss	–0.127	–0.041	–0.059
Contributions to disproportionate losses from 2019 racial differences in:			
Education	–0.008	–0.018	0.015
	(0.005)	(0.011)	(0.009)
Industry	–0.064	–0.020	–0.066
	(0.025)	(0.008)	(0.026)
Region	–0.009	–0.011	–0.013
	(0.009)	(0.011)	(0.013)
Central city status	–0.011	–0.013	–0.013
	(0.013)	(0.014)	(0.014)
Age	0.008	0.008	0.004
	(0.006)	(0.006)	(0.003)
Female	–0.001	0.001	–0.003
	(0.002)	(0.001)	(0.003)
All included variables	–0.085	–0.052	–0.076
	(0.042)	(0.026)	(0.038)

Notes: Author's calculations from compiled annual Current Population Survey microdata. Standard errors of contribution estimates in parentheses.

disproportionate loss, which was roughly half the total. Specifically, Black businesses were more concentrated in Transportation, Leisure and Hospitality, and Other Services, industries that were also hit hard by the pandemic. Additionally, Black business owners were less concentrated in Agriculture, which experienced earnings growth during the pandemic. Disproportionate business earnings losses among Black business owners might also have been partly due to prepandemic geographic differences. The relative distribution by central city status contributes –1.1 log points to the disproportionate loss in business earnings and the relative regional distribution contributes an additional –0.9 log points (although neither contribution is statistically significant).

Latinx owners experienced a disproportionate business earnings loss of –4.1 log points due to the pandemic. The largest contributing factor to this disproportionate loss was prepandemic industry differences. The industry concentrations of Latinx business owners contributed –2.1 log points to the disproportionate business earnings losses. Latinx businesses were more concentrated in Transportation, which experienced large business earnings losses, and less concentrated in Agriculture, which experienced positive earnings growth.

The disproportionate business earnings loss among Asian owners from 2019 to 2020 was –5.9 log points. Again, the largest contributing factor to this disproportionate loss was prepandemic industry differences. The industry concentrations of Asian business owners contributed –6.5 log points to the disproportionate business earnings losses. Asian businesses are concentrated in Leisure and Hospitality and Other Services but less concentrated in Agriculture and Construction. Interestingly, higher education levels among Asian owners relative to white owners shielded them from larger disproportionate business earnings losses. The contribution estimate of a positive 1.8 log points implies that all else equal, Asian business earnings would have increased relative to white business earnings from 2019 to 2020 if only education mattered.

Using levels instead of log business earnings, I found similar overall results. For example, I found that an unfavorable industry distribution placed Black business owners at a higher risk of earnings losses in the pandemic. Similarly, industry distributions placed Asian business owners at a higher risk of losses and higher educational levels for Asian business owners reduced their exposure to losses in the pandemic.

Focusing the decompositions to show the impacts of differential exposure to pandemic losses is important. Standard Blinder-Oaxaca decompositions reveal the importance of educational differences for point-in-time differences. Instead, the new decomposition technique isolates the part of the contribution from factors that placed racial groups at higher or lower risk of business earnings losses during the pandemic and reveals the importance of industry differences to business earnings losses during the pandemic.

Differential Exposure to COVID-19 and Policy Responses

Chapter 2 provided evidence on how states varied in the spread of COVID-19 and in imposing early social distancing restrictions and mask mandates.

Table 4.8
Geographic Differences in COVID-19 Cases and Policy Variables

	Average value for business owners			
Case nos. and policy variables	Black	Latinx	Asian	White
COVID-19 cases per capita	0.059	0.061	0.057	0.061
Early state business restrictions	0.991	0.984	0.992	0.942
Mask mandates (Dec. 2020)	0.755	0.763	0.886	0.788
Sample size	438	1,041	444	4,270

Notes: Author's calculations from compiled annual Current Population Survey microdata.

Did geographic differences in exposure to COVID-19, social distancing restrictions, and mask mandates contribute to larger minority-owned business earnings losses? To explore whether business owners of color were differentially exposed to COVID-19 and state policies, table 4.8 reports average values of COVID-19 cases per capita, social distancing restrictions on businesses early in the pandemic, and mask mandates across states by race. COVID-19 cases are measured for the entire year 2020 and are sourced from the CDC. Early social distancing restrictions refer to the first few months of the pandemic and are sourced from *The New York Times*. Mask mandates are also sourced from *The New York Times* and refer to polices as of the end of 2020.[11] All measures are at the state level.

Differences in number of COVID-19 cases and restrictions are either nonexistent or not large across ethnic and racial groups. Per capita COVID-19 cases were roughly the same for each group, at 6 percent in 2020. White business owners tended to live in states with fewer early pandemic social distancing restrictions than minority groups. The largest differences are found for state-level mask mandates (which were implemented near the end of 2020). Asian business owners were exposed the most to these restrictions (0.886). Blacks had the lowest likelihood of living in states in which mask mandates were imposed (0.755). Seventy-nine percent of whites lived in states with mask mandates near the end of 2020.

Table 4.9 explores the contributions of these state-level differences to racial inequality in business earnings during the pandemic. I find that racial differences in exposure to COVID-19 per capita does not contribute to disproportionate business earnings losses from 2019 to 2020. Similarly, racial differences in exposure to social distancing restrictions and mask mandates

Table 4.9

Decomposition of Changes in Log Business Earnings Gaps: Additional State COVID-19 Cases and Restriction Variables

Mean levels and contributions to losses	Black-white	Latinx-white	Asian-white
Mean levels:			
Minority log business income 2020	9.952	9.987	10.437
Minority log business income 2019	10.229	10.177	10.645
Minority loss	–0.277	–0.191	–0.209
White log business income 2020	10.361	10.361	10.361
White log business income 2019	10.510	10.510	10.510
White loss	–0.150	–0.150	–0.150
Minority disproportionate loss	–0.127	–0.041	–0.059
Contributions to disproportionate losses from 2019 racial differences in:			
Education	–0.008	–0.018	0.015
	(0.005)	(0.011)	(0.009)
Industry	–0.064	–0.020	–0.066
	(0.025)	(0.008)	(0.026)
Region	–0.004	–0.009	–0.015
	(0.005)	(0.010)	(0.016)
Central city status	–0.011	–0.012	–0.012
	(0.012)	(0.014)	(0.014)
Age	0.008	0.008	0.004
	(0.006)	(0.006)	(0.003)
Female	–0.001	0.001	–0.003
	(0.002)	(0.001)	(0.003)
COVID-19 cases per capita in 2020	0.000	0.000	0.001
	(0.004)	(0.001)	(0.008)
Early state business restrictions	–0.002	–0.002	–0.002
	(0.006)	(0.005)	(0.006)
Mask mandates (Dec. 2020)	–0.002	–0.002	0.006
	(0.002)	(0.002)	(0.006)
All included variables	–0.084	–0.053	–0.073
	(0.044)	(0.028)	(0.038)

Notes: Author's calculations from compiled annual Current Population Survey microdata. Standard errors for contribution estimates in parentheses.

do not contribute to differential business earnings losses by race. In all cases, racial differences in exposure to state-level COVID-19 cases, business restrictions, and mask mandates do not contribute to changes in racial inequality in business earnings.[12]

Additional Evidence

The impacts of COVID-19 on racial inequality in business activity and earnings are clear using the CPS microdata presented here. Additional research using these data and other data sources provides a similar picture of disproportionate impacts by race at the start of the pandemic. Also using CPS data but focusing on year-over-year (YOY) changes, Wilmoth (2020) found that Blacks experienced the largest YOY decline, at 37.6 percent, with Asians experiencing only a slightly smaller decline, at 37.1 percent. The decline for Latinx business owners was smaller (26.0 percent) but also larger than the national average (20.2 percent). Amuedo-Dorantes, Borra, and Wang (2024) found that COVID-19 disproportionately hurt Asian entrepreneurship especially for Asian immigrants, who saw business earnings decline by 17 percent relative to those of non-Latinx whites. Farrell, Wheat, and Mac (2020) examined data from the transactions of financial accounts at JPMorgan Chase for a few states and found that by the end of March 2020, Black firms had cash balances that were 26 percent lower, compared with a 12 percent decrease for all firms. Also, the Stanford Latino Entrepreneurship Initiative (2020) surveyed 224 high-revenue Latinx-owned businesses and found that 86 percent of respondents reported immediate negative effects, such as delayed projects and closures from the pandemic.

Appendix 4.A: Regression Equations That Adjust for Prepandemic Trends

To more formally test whether COVID-19 had disproportionate impacts on business owner earnings for different groups, I estimated regressions in which log business earnings was the dependent variable. The regressions control for trends prior to COVID-19 and prepandemic differences in business, owner, and geographic characteristics. Controlling for prior trends in business earnings or racial gaps in business earnings might be especially important for identifying the effects of COVID-19. To start, I estimated the following base equation:

$$\begin{aligned} Y_{it} = {} & \alpha + \gamma^{B}\, Black_i + \gamma^{L}\, Latinx_i + \gamma^{A}\, Asian_i + COVID20_t \\ & + \delta^{B}\, Black_i * COVID20_t + \delta^{L}\, Latinx_i * COVID20_t \\ & + \delta^{A}\, Asian_i * COVID20_t + \beta' X_{it} + \lambda_t + Black_i * \lambda_t \\ & + Latinx_i * \lambda_t + Asian_i * \lambda_t + \varepsilon_{it}, \end{aligned} \tag{4.1}$$

where Y_{it} is annual log business earnings for owner i in calendar year t, $COVID20_t$ is a dummy variable for the post-COVID-19 year 2020, X_{it} includes owner, business, and geographic characteristics, λ_t is a linear time trend, and ε_{it} is the error term. The analysis sample covers seven years, with five pre-COVID-19 years (2015–2019) and one post-COVID-19 year (2020). As noted earlier, 2020 captures the months of January and February, which were prior to social distancing restrictions, and March only partially captures those restrictions. Estimates of *annual* losses in the pandemic will be downward biased because of this limitation.

The parameters of interest are the δ_j, which capture the estimates of COVID-19 effects on business earnings for each minority group, j, relative to the left-out group, non-Latinx white business owners. The regressions control for business (industry), owner (education/skill level, age, gender), and geographic (region, central city status) characteristics. The main specification includes a linear time trend and linear time trends interacted with each minority group. All specifications are estimated with OLS using CPS sample weights.

Equation (4.1) is in the nature of a "difference-in-difference" estimator of the impact of COVID-19 on racial gaps in business earnings. For the Black-white gap for example, the first "difference" is white business earnings minus Black business earnings, and the second "difference" is postpandemic business earnings minus prepandemic business earnings. But unlike with most difference-in-difference applications, however, I am not evaluating the impact of a specific policy but am estimating whether there are disparate impacts of COVID-19 relative to prepandemic levels and trends. There is no control group as all groups were affected by the pandemic.

Equation (4.1) implicitly calculates the second or post-pre difference from a comparison of 2020 business earnings with mean business earnings from 2015 to 2019 (detrended). Although this approach provides more precise estimates because of a longer pre-COVID-19 time period, it has the disadvantage of including years that are more distant in time from the beginning of the pandemic in the calculation of COVID-19 effects. One method of addressing this issue is to focus the prepandemic period comparison on 2019 only. The simplest way to do so is to include a dummy variable that equals one for the entire 2015–2018 time period and include its interactions with the race dummies. Pre-2019 is a dummy variable equal to one if the year is in the 2015–2018 period and zero otherwise.

Another approach is to include a full set of year dummies and their interactions with race instead of combining all pre-COVID-19 years prior to the base year, 2019. This event-study–style regression is specified as follows:

$$Y_{it} = a + \sum_{s=-5}^{1} \delta_s^B Black_i + \sum_{s=-5}^{1} \delta_s^L Latinx_i + \sum_{s=-5}^{1} \delta_s^A Asian_i + \beta' X_{it} + \lambda_t + \varepsilon_{it}, \quad (4.2)$$

where the reference year is $s = 0$ (2019), and λ_t are now year fixed effects. This event-study regression estimates racial disparities in the pre-COVID-19 years to directly examine whether there were racial differences in any years prior to the pandemic (i.e., to test the common trends assumption). There might be differential trends in business earnings, but examining years prior to 2019 should not reveal big jumps in earnings, at least not at the level created by COVID-19 in 2020.

Appendix 4.B: Pandemic Decomposition Technique

The new decomposition technique differs from the standard Blinder-Oaxaca decompositions because it focuses on identifying factors contributing to the changes from 2019 to 2020 in business earnings instead of identifying factors that contributed to each year's earnings separately. The estimates provide a direct answer to the question, for example, of how much the Black industry distribution relative to the white industry distribution contributed to larger Black business earnings losses in the pandemic.

The following equation is calculated:

$$\left[\left(\bar{X}_{2019}^{W} - \bar{X}_{2019}^{M}\right)\left(\hat{\beta}_{2020}^{*} - \hat{\beta}_{2019}^{*}\right)\right], \quad (4.3)$$

where 2019 or 2020 is the sample year, $\bar{X}_t^j$ is the mean for group j (either white or minority) and year t (either 2019 or 2020), and $\hat{\beta}_t^*$ is the set of regression coefficient estimates for the pooled (all-group) sample and for the sample year t (either 2019 or 2020). All decomposition specifications use pooled coefficient estimates from regressions using the full sample of all races to estimate $\hat{\beta}_t^*$. A full set of race dummy variables is included in the underlying regression. CPS-provided sampling weights are used in the regression and to calculate means by group and year.

This equation provides an estimate of the disproportionate effects of the pandemic that captures all the effects of COVID-19 on business earnings, such as demand shifts, mandated closures, and social distancing restrictions. Different sets of variables can be used to define $\bar{X}_t^j$ and $\hat{\beta}_t^*$. For example, for the contribution of education, $\bar{X}_t^j$ and $\hat{\beta}_t^*$ would include the three dummy variables for different, mutually exclusive education levels included in the regression (i.e., graduated from high school, completed some college, and graduated from college).

The modified decomposition equation is useful for studying the question of how different population groups' prepandemic jobs, businesses, or personal characteristics placed them at higher risk of negative outcomes from COVID-19. For example, the new decomposition technique could be used to study how different education levels placed some groups at higher risk of becoming unemployed in the pandemic. Many college-educated workers were able to shift to remote work and not lose their jobs, which has implications for disproportionate employment losses by race. The decomposition technique can quantify the importance of this factor, especially when compared with other factors. The technique is not limited to examining racial differences. It can be used to study disproportionate impacts for any group relative to a base group. For example, young workers could be compared with middle-aged workers to examine the causes of disproportionate impacts from COVID-19.

5 The Paycheck Protection Program at the Beginning of the Pandemic: The First and Second Rounds

The foregoing chapters have provided unmistakable evidence that COVID-19 was spreading, and small businesses and the broader economy were struggling. From February to April 2020 business activity dropped by more than 20 percent, and from 2019 to 2020 business earnings dropped by slightly less than 20 percent. Small businesses were closing storefronts, discontinuing service to customers, and halting production; they were clearly in need of help. If small businesses were to survive and retain their employees, a large aid package was needed. In response, the federal government provided more aid than ever seen before in terms of financial assistance targeted at small businesses. As part of the larger $2 trillion Coronavirus Aid, Relief, and Economic Security (CARES) Act, the Paycheck Protection Program (PPP) was born. The PPP provided roughly $800 billion to small businesses over three rounds of fundings running from April 2020 to May 2021.[1] The PPP was the largest relief program ever provided to small businesses.

The PPP targeted small businesses with employees. Small businesses could qualify for funds by retaining employees. The three main goals of the PPP were (1) to keep small businesses afloat in the early stages of the pandemic, (2) to limit layoffs of employees, and (3) to limit spillover disruptions in the economy. Loan amounts were generally equal to 2.5 months of average payroll costs, and loans could be forgiven if the business retained its employees.

Saving small businesses, which are often seen as the driver of job growth and innovation, was a clear priority of the PPP. Limiting job losses for those small businesses was also very important. The basic idea was that it was better to have workers remain employed at businesses through aid than to have workers be laid off from their jobs and move onto state unemployment insurance rolls. Retaining existing employer-employee relationships would certainly minimize disruptions, but it might also save the government money from reduced unemployment insurance claims. As noted by the Small Business Administration (SBA), the goal of the PPP was that it "helps businesses keep their workforce employed during the COVID-19 crisis." Additionally, aid to small businesses might prevent defaults on mortgages and equipment loans, tenants falling behind on rent, and the gutting of downtown commerce, all of which could reduce the chances of a fast recovery from the mandated shutdowns. The disruptions caused by the unprecedented closures of small businesses owing to COVID-19 were expected to have large negative spillover effects on the broader economy—something the federal government wanted to avoid.

The PPP was part of the larger $2 trillion CARES Act signed into law on March 27, 2020. In addition to the original $350 billion in funding for the PPP, the CARES Act provided stimulus payments to households and expanded unemployment insurance benefits, estimated to total $560 billion at the time. The CARES Act also provided $500 billion in loans for large corporations and $340 billion to state and local governments. Funds were also allocated to education, public health, and the safety net.

This chapter explores how PPP funds were disbursed to small businesses, focusing on the first two rounds of funds provided in 2020. During the first year of the PPP it ran for roughly four months, from April 3, 2020, to August 8, 2020. A discussion and analysis of the rebooted and revised program, which ran from January 2021 to May 2021, are provided in chapter 9.

The PPP Basics

The PPP was administered and backed by the U.S. SBA, but banks, credit unions, and other financial institutions provided the loans to small businesses. The World Health Organization (WHO) declared COVID-19 a pandemic on March 11, 2020. The restrictions that shut down businesses followed very quickly. Only five days later, the San Francisco Bay Area had imposed the first shelter-in-place restrictions, followed shortly by the States of California and New York. By early April most states had imposed social distancing restrictions that shut down businesses. In response to worries about the negative effects of these mandated shutdowns for owners and workers and the speed at which everything was happening at the time, Congress rushed to provide a massive aid package to help small businesses. The PPP started providing loans to small businesses on April 3, 2020. PPP fund disbursement stopped after only a couple of weeks. The program provided 1.7 million loans for a total of roughly $342 billion from April 3 to April 16, 2020. The allocated money ran out quickly.

Because of the rush to get aid to small businesses at the beginning of the pandemic Congress and the SBA reached out primarily to large banks in the first round of the program in the spring of 2020. PPP loans were guaranteed by the SBA, removing any risk to banks of providing loans because the SBA would buy the loan if the borrower defaulted. Borrowers of PPP loans were also given up to five years to apply for forgiveness of the loan if they retained employees and compensation levels. Even with these guarantees and forgiveness plans backed by the federal government, financial institutions had to provide the PPP loans to small businesses, and the haste with which the program was created resulted in larger banks taking a lead role. The decision had consequences for minority-owned businesses and communities, as examined later in this chapter.

Although large banks provided the bulk of loans early on, a wide variety of lender types became involved in providing PPP loans to small businesses. The U.S. SBA (2020c) reports, for example, that roughly three hundred Community Development Financial Institutions (CDFIs) were involved, providing 115,000 loans, and more than seven hundred credit unions were involved, providing 70,000 loans. There were also 175 Minority Depository Institutions (MDIs) providing 125,000 loans.

The First Round of PPP Funding

To get a sense of the size and scope of the program, table 5.1 reports the number of loans, total dollars, and number of different lenders involved in the PPP. In the first round of the PPP, which ran from April 3 to April 16, 2020, 1.7 million loans were provided to small businesses. Nearly five thousand different financial institutions provided loans to these small businesses, for a massive $342 billion disbursed.

Table 5.1
Summary of PPP Funding

Round	No. of loans approved	Total net dollars disbursed	Total no. of lenders	Dates
First	1,661,367	342,277,999,103	4,975	April 3, 2020–April 16, 2020
Second	3,550,761	182,734,202,021	NA	April 17, 2020–Aug. 8, 2020
Total	5,212,128	525,012,201,124	5,460	April 3, 2020–Aug. 8, 2020

Source: U.S. Small Business Administration (2020c) PPP report.

Lenders During the First Round

The PPP provided loans to small businesses through thousands of different financial institutions in the country. To better understand how the PPP worked, I downloaded and compiled loan data. The version of loan microdata used here was posted by the SBA on October 11, 2024.[2] The SBA released complete loan-level microdata for the PPP in response to a FOIA request by the media. The PPP microdata cover the universe of loans provided through the program and provide information on loan amounts, lenders, and characteristics of businesses receiving the loans.[3] The approval date of the loan, the loan approval amount at origination, and the name of the financial institution are first used here.

The top fifteen lenders in the first round of the PPP were mostly large, well-known national banks. Table 5.2 reports the top fifteen lenders in total dollars in the first round of the PPP in 2020 (April 3 to April 16, 2020). These fifteen lenders accounted for a total of nearly $88 billion in PPP loans in the first two weeks of the program and 334,000 loans. As expected, many of the largest banks in the country are listed in the top fifteen PPP lenders in the first round.[4] JPMorgan Chase provided the most total dollars, a staggering $13.5 billion, through 32,406 loans to small businesses. Truist Bank provided $9.4 billion in loans, and PNC Bank provided roughly $8.8 billion in loans to small businesses in those first two weeks of the program.

The list of top lenders in terms of the number of loans provided to small businesses changes somewhat but mostly continues to include the largest banks. Table 5.3 reports the top fifteen lenders in total number of loans in the first round of the PPP in 2020. The top three banks providing loans to small businesses in the first round were Manufacturers and Traders Bank, providing 36,636 loans, Readycap Lending, providing 34,115 loans, and

Table 5.2
Top Fifteen Lenders in Total Dollars in the First Round of PPP Funding in 2020

Rank	Originating lender	Total dollars disbursed	Total no. of loans
1	JPMorgan Chase Bank, National Association	13,515,820,566	32,406
2	Truist Bank	9,356,447,894	30,653
3	PNC Bank, National Association	8,846,693,268	20,562
4	Manufacturers and Traders Trust Company	8,139,960,845	36,636
5	KeyBank National Association	6,981,771,355	32,669
6	The Huntington National Bank	6,957,529,556	28,167
7	TD Bank, National Association	5,769,591,552	25,904
8	BMO Bank National Association	4,928,813,801	13,925
9	Zions Bank, A Division of	4,111,823,230	13,913
10	City National Bank	3,781,894,926	11,419
11	Bank of America, National Association	3,644,422,791	9,056
12	Citizens Bank, National Association	3,623,521,809	24,414
13	Fifth Third Bank	3,232,135,304	9,440
14	Frost Bank	2,718,607,560	10,378
15	Readycap Lending, LLC	2,639,071,765	34,115

Notes: Author's calculations from compiled loan microdata provided by the U.S. Small Business Administration (posted on October 11, 2024). The first round of PPP funding covered April 3 to April 16, 2020.

KeyBank, providing 32,669 loans. JPMorgan Chase and Truist Bank also provided more than 30,000 PPP loans to small businesses in the first two weeks of the PPP. There is a lot of overlap between the two top fifteen lists in tables 5.2 and 5.3.

Overall, the types of financial institutions involved varied. Although a lot of dollars were provided by large banks, many other financial institutions provided loans. Figure 5.1 displays the distribution of the number of lenders that provided different numbers of loans to small businesses in round one. For example, 34 percent of all lenders provided one to forty-nine loans to small businesses, and 6 percent of all lenders provided one

Table 5.3
Top Fifteen Lenders in Number of Loans in the First Round of PPP Funding in 2020

Rank	Originating lender	Total no. of loans	Total dollars disbursed
1	Manufacturers and Traders Trust Company	36,636	8,139,960,845
2	Readycap Lending, LLC	34,115	2,639,071,765
3	KeyBank National Association	32,669	6,981,771,355
4	JPMorgan Chase Bank, National Association	32,406	13,515,820,566
5	Truist Bank	30,653	9,356,447,894
6	The Huntington National Bank	28,167	6,957,529,556
7	TD Bank, National Association	25,904	5,769,591,552
8	Citizens Bank, National Association	24,414	3,623,521,809
9	PNC Bank, National Association	20,562	8,846,693,268
10	U.S. Bank, National Association	17,371	2,279,783,667
11	BMO Bank National Association	13,925	4,928,813,801
12	Zions Bank, A Division of	13,913	4,111,823,230
13	Cross River Bank	13,615	1,060,936,839
14	SouthState Bank, National Association	12,324	1,943,182,386
15	First National Bank of Pennsylvania	11,670	2,224,752,457

Notes: Author's calculations from compiled loan microdata provided by the U.S. Small Business Administration (posted on October 11, 2024). The first round of PPP funding covered April 3 to April 16, 2020.

thousand or more loans to small businesses. The distribution indicates that a large share of lenders provided fewer than two hundred PPP loans to small businesses.

The Second Round of PPP Funding, Summer 2020

The first $342 billion allocated to the PPP was exhausted just two weeks after the time the funds were made available to small businesses. As the pandemic continued and the negative economic impacts to small businesses

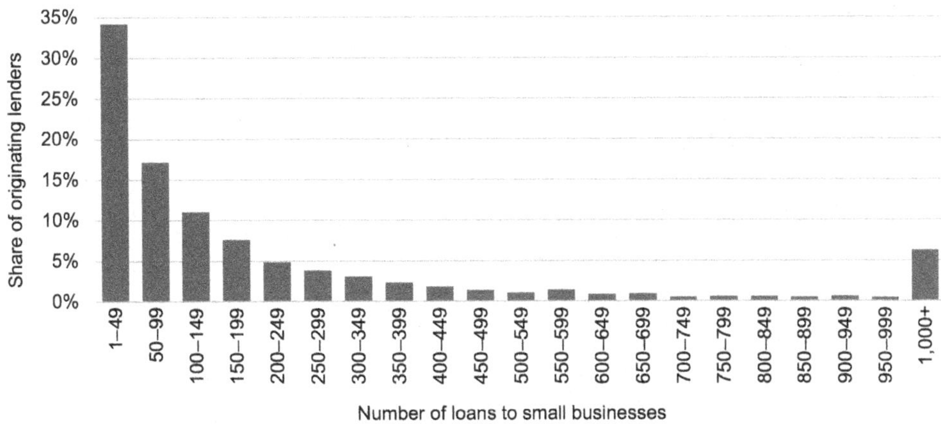

Figure 5.1
Distribution of number of PPP loans by lenders, first round of funding.

became increasingly clear, as also did the unmet need by small businesses for assistance, Congress appropriated additional funds and the PPP started up again on April 17, 2020. At the time, Congress approved an additional $310 billion, but not all of the allocated funds were spent. The second round ran from April 17 to August 8, 2020, and included more than 3.5 million loans for a total value of roughly $180 billion. Table 5.1 reports loan numbers for the second round of PPP funding in 2020.

Several changes occurred in the second round of the PPP. First, in the rush of getting PPP funds out to small businesses at the very beginning of pandemic Congress relied heavily on the largest banks in the country. But in the second round much of the early money flowed through smaller community banks, which were often in rural areas, because these banks were nimbler at accessing the aid (Grotto, Mider, and Sam 2020). Second, fintech and other online lenders were brought in and approved by the SBA (Liu and Parilla 2020). Third, smaller businesses caught up in applying for funds. Smaller businesses typically took longer to complete required paperwork because they often did not have in-house accountants, legal help, or other support.

The list of top lenders in the second round of PPP funding changed somewhat from the first round. Table 5.4 reports a list of the top fifteen lenders in total dollars in the second round of PPP funding in 2020 (April 17 to August 8, 2020). In this round, Bank of America topped the list, providing $21.7

Table 5.4
Top Fifteen Lenders in Total Dollars in the Second Round of PPP Funding in 2020

Rank	Originating lender	Total dollars disbursed	Total no. of loans
1	Bank of America, National Association	21,740,174,511	334,431
2	JPMorgan Chase Bank, National Association	17,855,554,419	257,575
3	Wells Fargo Bank, National Association	10,277,508,455	192,014
4	Cross River Bank	5,335,629,791	179,430
5	U.S. Bank, National Association	5,326,822,423	90,659
6	PNC Bank, National Association	4,218,184,417	53,349
7	Celtic Bank Corporation	3,811,135,298	146,189
8	Truist Bank	3,714,509,197	49,792
9	Kabbage, Inc.	3,052,750,498	161,032
10	BMO Bank National Association	2,931,748,327	26,052
11	Zions Bank, A Division of	2,879,547,164	33,835
12	TD Bank, National Association	2,804,201,943	59,807
13	Customers Bank	2,265,278,008	67,612
14	Comerica Bank	2,263,129,299	13,250
15	Regions Bank	2,227,906,788	40,870

Notes: Author's calculations from compiled loan microdata provided by the U.S. Small Business Administration (posted on October 11, 2024). The second round of PPP funding covered April 27 to August 8. 2020.

billion in loans to small businesses. The next two top lenders in terms of total dollars were JPMorgan Chase, which provided $17.9 billion in loans, and Wells Fargo, which provided 10.3 billion in loans.

A notable change in the top fifteen lists from round one to round two was that Cross River Bank became the number fourth-ranked provider of total loan amounts ($5.3 billion in PPP loans). Cross River Bank is also a fintech lender. In terms of types of financial institutions, the second round was different from the first round of the PPP. Fintechs became major providers of PPP loans to small businesses, Celtic Bank provided $3.8 billion (no. 7), Kabbage provided $3.1 billion (no. 9), and Customers provided $2.3 billion (no. 13).

Table 5.5

Top Fifteen Lenders in Number of Loans in the Second Round of the PPP in 2020

Rank	Originating lender	Total no. of loans	Total dollars disbursed
1	Bank of America, National Association	334,431	21,740,174,511
2	JPMorgan Chase Bank, National Association	257,575	17,855,554,419
3	Wells Fargo Bank, National Association	192,014	10,277,508,455
4	Cross River Bank	179,430	5,335,629,791
5	Kabbage, Inc.	161,032	3,052,750,498
6	Celtic Bank Corporation	146,189	3,811,135,298
7	U.S. Bank, National Association	90,659	5,326,822,423
8	WebBank	72,237	1,985,055,937
9	Customers Bank	67,612	2,265,278,008
10	TD Bank, National Association	59,807	2,804,201,943
11	PNC Bank, National Association	53,349	4,218,184,417
12	Truist Bank	49,792	3,714,509,197
13	Regions Bank	40,870	2,227,906,788
14	Zions Bank, A Division of	33,835	2,879,547,164
15	Fifth Third Bank	30,478	2,220,233,858

Notes: Author's calculations from compiled loan microdata provided by the U.S. Small Business Administration (posted on October 11, 2024). The second round of PPP funding covered April 27 to August 8, 2020.

Turning to lenders ranked by the number of loans instead of total dollars provides additional evidence of the arrival of fintech in the provision of PPP loans. Table 5.5 lists the top fifteen lenders in total number of loans in the second round of the PPP in 2020. Some of the large banks remain on the list of top number-of-loans providers, such as Bank of America, JPMorgan Chase, and Wells Fargo, but there are several newcomers to the list, and these newcomers are primarily fintech lenders. Cross River Bank, Kabbage, Celtic Bank, WebBank, and Customers Bank all made the top fifteen list, providing a combined 626,500 loans totaling $16.4 billion.

Figure 5.2 displays the distribution of the number of lenders that provided different numbers of loans to small businesses in round two. The

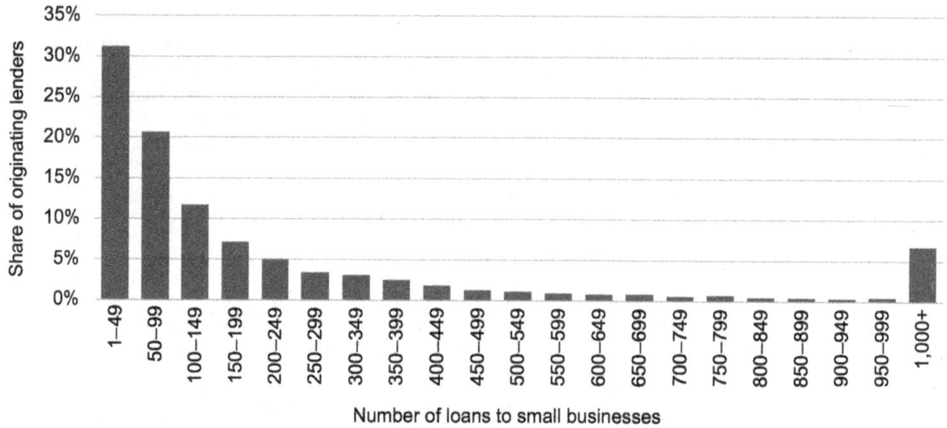

Figure 5.2
Distribution in number of PPP loans by lenders, second round of funding.

distribution spread is fairly similar in round two to that in round one. For example, 31 percent of all lenders provided one to forty-nine loans to small businesses, and 7 percent of all lenders provided one thousand or more loans to small businesses. The distribution indicates that a large share of lenders provided fewer than two hundred PPP loans to small businesses in round two, as was the case in round one.

PPP and Related Tax Breaks for Employment

In 2020, the PPP provided a total of $525 billion (see table 5.1). More than five million loans were provided to small businesses from April 3, 2020, to August 8, 2020. Over the year, 5,460 different lenders provided loans through the program. The PPP was the largest aid program ever provided to small businesses. The PPP would rise again as COVID-19 continued to spread and small businesses struggled through 2020, but small businesses would have to wait several months, until the beginning of 2021.

In 2020, the federal government also provided a tax break and additional debt relief for small businesses with employees. The Employee Retention Tax Credit provided a refundable tax credit of 50 percent in qualified wages paid per employee in 2020. The credit was relatively small compared to the PPP, imposing a maximum of $10,000 in wages per employee or a maximum tax credit of $5,000 per employee for the year. To qualify, businesses must have experienced at least a partial shutdown due to government mandates or a quarterly loss of at least 50 percent in gross receipts.

The SBA also offered debt relief to small businesses that already had SBA loans as another part of the CARES Act. If small businesses with previous loans were struggling during the pandemic, they could apply for debt relief on these loans to provide a break. The SBA would pay six months of principal, interest, and associated fees that borrowers owed for SBA 7(a), 504, and microloans. If an SBA loan was not on deferment, the SBA initially would make the monthly payments up to six months, but the SBA later expanded this time period as the pandemic continued.

Did PPP Funds Get Disbursed Evenly to Minority Communities?

One of the stated goals of the CARES Act was to prioritize serving "underserved markets" and businesses owned by "socially and economically disadvantaged individuals" (U.S. Congress 2020). In light of the larger negative effects of COVID-19 on business activity among minority businesses, targeting PPP funds through the CARES Act to minority communities might be especially important. Another concern was that the focus on providing PPP loans through large banks meant that loans would not get distributed evenly to minority communities even conditional on similar numbers of qualified small businesses with employees. If the clientele of larger, national banks were disproportionately white-owned small businesses, then at the least the first round of PPP funds may not have been evenly distributed.

Did PPP funds get disbursed evenly to minority communities, thus benefiting the businesses and employees in those communities? I explore this question using the microdata on the universe of PPP loans in 2020. Fairlie and Fossen (2022a) provide more details on the analysis. The findings were also presented in testimony before the U.S. House of Representatives Committee on Small Business, February 4, 2021 (Fairlie 2021a), and the California State Assembly Committee on Jobs, Economic Development, and the Economy on February 23, 2021 (Fairlie 2021b).

To explore the question, I examined the relationship between loan receipt and the minority share of the population across every zip code in the United States. Figure 5.3 displays PPP loan receipt per employer business establishment by minority share of the population at the zip code

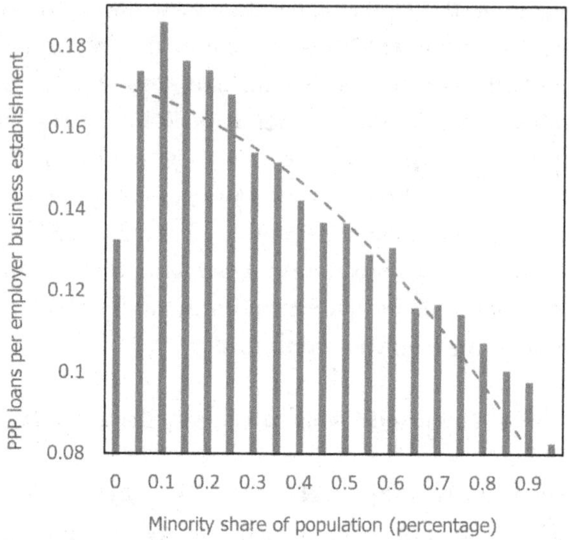

Figure 5.3
Number of PPP loans per employer business establishment by minority share of the population, round one of funding.

level.[5] I used the universe of PPP loans and administrative data on employer firms based on the Census Business Register. In total, the average number of PPP loans per employer business establishment is roughly 0.5, implying that about half of employer business establishments received a PPP loan. The relationship between PPP loan receipt and minority share of the population is shown without controlling for other factors because the goal is to capture only the racial composition of the community and not to capture other correlated characteristics such as income levels and population density. The number of loans per employer business establishment implicitly controls for differences in business density across communities.

The two rounds of PPP funds disbursed in 2020 are separated because of the differences in the speed at which funds were rolled out and the differences in the types of financial institutions involved (as shown above). Figure 5.3 displays the first-round relationship. In the first round, loan receipt per business went disproportionately to nonminority communities. The figure shows a strong negative relationship, with a decline of 0.05 loans per business between the twenty-fifth and seventy-fifth percentiles in minority shares.

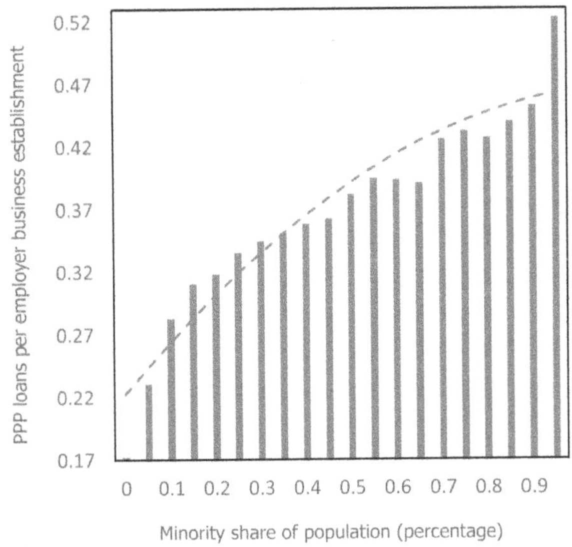

Figure 5.4
Number of PPP loans per employer business establishment by minority share of population, round two of funding

Did the relationship between PPP loans per business and minority share of population change after funds ran out in the initial two weeks of the program? Did the second round of PPP funds become more equitably distributed to communities of color? Figure 5.4 displays the relationship between PPP loans per business and the minority share of the population for the second round. In the second round of PPP loans running from April 17 to August 8, 2020, the relationship reversed. For this round, there is a clear positive relationship between loan receipt and minority share of the population. Moving from the first quartile to the third quartile in minority share of the population is associated with an increase of 0.08 PPP loans per firm.

Another way to measure whether funds were evenly distributed is examine the relationship between PPP loan receipt and the minority share of businesses in the community. The minority share of PPP fund receipt on the *y*-axis is thus compared with the number of minority businesses relative to the total number of businesses on the *x*-axis instead of the number of people of color being compared with the total number of people in an area. Data from the Annual Business Survey (ABS) on employer businesses at the county level are used to measure the minority share of businesses. Unfortunately, data are not available at the zip code level. Counties are much larger geographic areas than zip codes: there are 3,143 counties in the United States compared with 41,704 zip codes.

Figure 5.5 displays the relationship between PPP loan receipt and the minority business share in the first round. Similar to the finding using the minority share of the population displayed in figure 5.3, there is a negative relationship between PPP loan receipt and minority business share in the first round. Changing the measure from minority share of the population to minority share of businesses thus does not change the conclusion of a negative relationship with PPP loans per business in the first two weeks of the program.

Figure 5.6 displays the relationship between PPP loan receipt and minority business share in the second round. The relationship changes direction between the first and second rounds of the PPP. The relationship is positive, indicating that the share of PPP loans per employer business establishment generally increased with the minority share of businesses in the county.

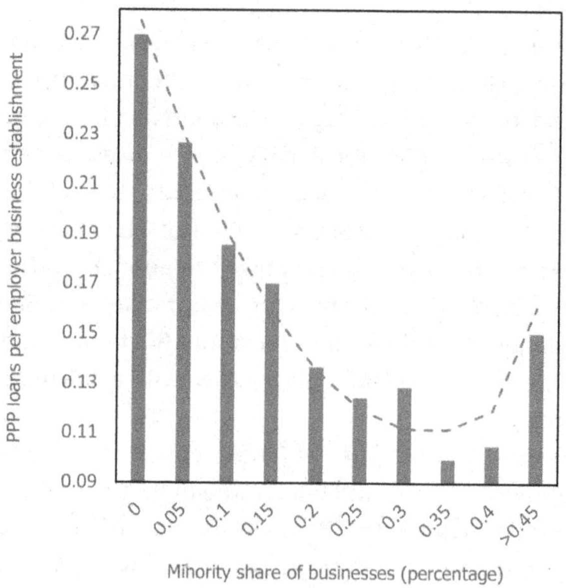

Figure 5.5
Number of PPP loans per employer business establishment by minority share of businesses, first round of funding.

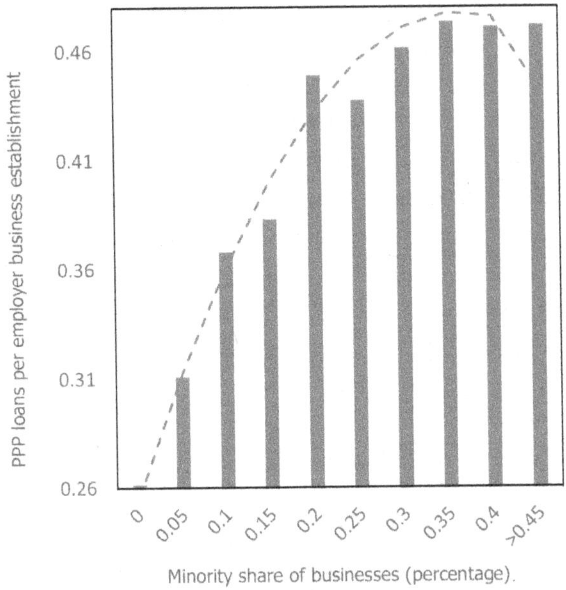

Figure 5.6
Number of PPP loans per employer business establishment by minority share of businesses, second round of funding.

The positive relationship between PPP receipt and minority share is consistent regardless of whether the focus is on the minority share of the population or the minority share of businesses.

The evidence is clear. In the first round there was a negative relationship between PPP funding and minority share, and in the second round there was a positive relationship. The reversal of patterns is evident no matter what measures are used for both rounds. One factor that likely contributed to the switch from a negative relationship in the first round of the PPP to a positive relationship in the second round is the expansion of different financial institutions involved. As presented above, a much wider range of lenders participated in the second round. Fintech and other online lenders were brought in and approved by the SBA, and these lenders were often active in minority areas (Liu and Parilla 2020). Early on, banks prioritized existing customers, long-established relationships, and large loans, which placed the smallest businesses and those without a banking relationship at the end of the line for receiving loans (Mills 2024). All of these factors limited the ability of minority-owned businesses and businesses located in minority communities to receive funds in the first round of PPP funding. There was also a shift from rural banks, which were nimbler at accessing the aid, to urban banks, which took longer to catch up (Grotto, Mider, and Sam 2020). Minority-owned businesses tend to be smaller than nonminority-owned businesses (Fairlie and Robb 2008; U.S. Census Bureau 2016), and smaller businesses typically took longer to complete required paperwork because they often did not have in-house accountants, legal help, or other support. The patterns were especially worrisome because of the lack of risk assumed by financial institutions in providing PPP loans because the leans were backed by the federal government (Mills 2024).

Differential Exposure to PPP Loans and Business Earnings Losses

The measure of the number of PPP loans per employer business establishment can be used to build on the analysis in chapter 4 of identifying what contributed to disproportionate impacts of COVID-19 on minority business earnings. Black business earnings dropped by 12–14 percent more than white business earnings dropped in 2020. Chapter 4 examined whether racial differences in state health status, such as COVID-19 cases per capita, and in exposure to state-level policies, such as early social distancing restrictions and mask mandates, contributed to racial gaps in COVID-19 impacts on business earnings. Did state-level differences in total PPP loan receipt per business establishment contribute to racial gaps in COVID-19 impacts on business earnings?

To answer this question, I first examine whether minority business owners live in areas with lower per employer business receipt of PPP loans. The analysis builds on the analysis at the zip code and country level provided above, but unfortunately, the CPS data limit the focus to states. Table 5.6 reports state-level differences in the number of PPP loans received per employer business establishment. Business earnings data are measured for calendar year 2020, and thus PPP loans are measured for 2020. State-level differences in PPP loan receipt per business capture both supply and demand factors and thus are difficult to interpret but potentially demonstrate some useful variation in access to loans through differing financial institution composition, information provision, and local small business development assistance. Differences in state-level PPP loans per establishment for 2020 are very small across racial groups.

Table 5.6
State Differences in PPP Loan Receipt per Employer Business Establishment by Race and Ethnicity, 2020

	Average value for business owners			
	Black	Latinx	Asian	White
Number of PPP loans per business establishment	0.651	0.655	0.644	0.644
Sample size	438	1,041	444	4,270

Notes: Author's calculations from compiled annual Current Population Survey microdata. PPP loan data are from the SBA and the number of employer establishments data are from the U.S. Census Bureau.

Black business owners lived in states where, on average, 65.1 percent of business establishments with employees received a PPP loan. The PPP loan to business establishment ratio was very similar at 0.655 for the states where Latinx business owners reside. It is important to note here that these data do not capture loans to business owners of a specific race. That information is not generally available and cannot be linked to the CPS microdata that measure business earnings by owner. Asian and white business owners live in states that on average have 0.644 PPP loans per business on average. These differences are small.

I next use the pandemic-focused decomposition technique from chapter 4 to test whether these relatively small racial differences at the state level contributed to disproportionate losses in business earnings. Table 5.7 adds PPP loans per employer business establishment to the previous decomposition model reported in chapter 4 (see table 4.9). State-level differences in PPP receipt per business do not appear to contribute to racial differences in business earnings losses. Similar to the findings for racial differences in exposure to state-level COVID-19 cases, business restrictions, and mask mandates, I do not find evidence that racial differences in PPP loan receipt per business contribute to changes in racial inequality in business earnings, at least as measured at the state level.

The analysis is useful but somewhat disappointing in that it is restricted to state-level variation instead of more local geographic variation. Another problem is that the measure of state-level variation in PPP loan receipt is not based on the race of the business owner. I discuss these important issues and limitations next.

Table 5.7

Decomposition of Changes in Log Business Earnings Gaps with Added PPP Variable

Mean levels and contributions to losses	Black-white	Latinx-white	Asian-white
Mean levels:			
Minority log business income 2020	9.952	9.987	10.437
Minority log business income 2019	10.229	10.177	10.645
Minority loss	–0.277	–0.191	–0.209
White log business income 2020	10.361	10.361	10.361
White log business income 2019	10.510	10.510	10.510
White loss	–0.150	–0.150	–0.150
Minority disproportionate loss	–0.127	–0.041	–0.059
Contributions to disproportionate losses from 2019 racial differences in:			
Education	–0.008	–0.018	0.015
	(0.005)	(0.011)	(0.009)
Industry	–0.064	–0.020	–0.066
	(0.025)	(0.008)	(0.026)
Region	–0.005	–0.009	–0.015
	(0.005)	(0.009)	(0.016)
Central city status	–0.011	–0.012	–0.012
	(0.012)	(0.014)	(0.014)
Age	0.008	0.008	0.004
	(0.006)	(0.006)	(0.003)
Female	–0.001	0.001	–0.003
	(0.002)	(0.001)	(0.003)
COVID-19 cases per capita	0.001	0.000	0.001
	(0.009)	(0.002)	(0.018)
Early state business restrictions	–0.002	–0.002	–0.002
	(0.006)	(0.005)	(0.006)
Mask mandates (Dec. 2020)	–0.002	–0.002	0.007
	(0.002)	(0.002)	(0.007)
PPP loans per business	0.001	0.001	0.000
	(0.003)	(0.005)	(0.000)
All included variables	–0.084	–0.052	–0.071
	(0.045)	(0.028)	(0.039)

Notes: Author's calculations from compiled annual Current Population Survey microdata. Standard errors of contribution estimates in parentheses.

Evidence on the Receipt of PPP Loans by Minority-owned Businesses

Unfortunately, information on the owner's race for small businesses receiving PPP loans in the data is incomplete. The PPP loan application did not ask for owner's race. Only 10 percent of loans have race information, and that information is concentrated among a few banks that provided information on race. It is unlikely that these banks are representative of all financial institutions providing PPP loans. Noting these concerns, Atkins, Cook and Seamans (2022a) used different comparison groups with and without missing race information, and statistical methods to adjust for selection bias from missing race information to examine disparities in PPP loan amounts. They found that Black-owned businesses received loans that were approximately 50 percent smaller than white-owned businesses that were observationally similar. They also found that Black-white disparities in PPP loans appeared (marginally) greater in areas with fewer bank branches. The Black-white disparities in PPP loans decreased during the second round of funding when more nonbank entities were approved by the SBA to participate in the program. In a related paper, Atkins, Cook, and Seamans (2022b) found that while Black-owned businesses received loans that were approximately 50 percent lower than observationally similar white-owned businesses, the differential narrowed considerably when fintechs were involved in providing loans. Erel and Liebersohn (2020) found that fintech was disproportionately used to disburse PPP funds in high-minority-share zip codes.

Garcia and Darity (2022) found evidence of benefits from not reporting race by black-owned businesses on PPP loan applications early in the pandemic. Using hand-collected information from small businesses that concealed their race on PPP applications, they found evidence that it was advantageous to not disclose race information on those applications. Black-owned businesses that concealed their race obtained 52 percent more in PPP funding.

A few studies have addressed the lack of race information by imputing the race of the small business owner receiving the PPP loan. For example, Howell et al. (2021) predicted a business owner's race and ethnicity using information such as the owner's name and location. Owner names were obtained from business registrations in collaboration with a data analytics firm. A random forest model trained by using the subset of PPP loans with owner's race information was used to improve prediction accuracy. They found that many conventional banks did not serve Black-owned firms in proportion to those firms' share in the PPP borrower population, and that among conventional lenders, small banks had a particularly low rate of lending to Black-owned firms (even with the 100 percent guarantee from the federal government). They find instead that it was fintech lenders that made a disproportionate share of loans to Black-owned firms, accounting for over half of PPP loans. Another interesting finding is that after conventional lenders automated their lending processes, rates of lending to Black-owned businesses increased.

Another example is provided by Fei and Yang (2021), who examined PPP lending to small businesses in the Food Services and Drinking Places sector. Using Yelp listings, they proxied for minority ownership of businesses based on listed food types. They found that minority-owned businesses were more likely to use fintech lenders, and that the racial disparity in using fintech versus traditional lenders was likely related to racial gaps in the small business lending market. Chernenko and Scharfstein (2021) also examined lending in restaurants. They identified race and ethnicity and other information about owners of restaurants in Florida by using state administrative data on restaurant licenses, corporate records, voter registration, lien filings, mortgage records, and Yelp listings. They found that minority-owned firms were more likely than observationally similar white-owned firms to receive PPP loans from nonbank lenders than from banks. Importantly, however, they found only partial substitution between bank lending and nonbank lending, resulting in lower PPP loan receipt rates among minority-owned firms, particularly Black-owned firms.

Another approach to studying the question is to use survey data that directly provide information on the race of business owners and PPP loan receipt. The Survey of Small Business Finances (SSBF) of more than nine thousand employer firms was conducted in 2020, six months after the start of the pandemic. Using survey data instead of the PPP loan data released by the SBA, U.S. Federal Reserve Banks (2021) found racial disparities in both applications for PPP loans and receipt of the full amount applied for in loans. Among Black-owned businesses, 61 percent applied for PPP loans, compared with 82 percent of white-owned businesses. The percentages of Latinx-owned businesses and Asian-owned businesses applying for loans were 73 percent and 85 percent, respectively. The most common reason provided for not applying for a loan for all groups was "Business would not qualify for the loan or loan forgiveness." The study also found that Black-owned businesses were only half as likely as white-owned businesses to receive the entire PPP funding amount they requested, and they were nearly five times as likely to receive none. The percentages of businesses receiving all the PPP funding sought were 79 percent for white-owned businesses, 68 percent for Asian-owned businesses, 61 percent for Latinx-owned businesses, and 43 percent for Black-owned businesses.

Lederer et al. (2020) examined whether there were differential barriers to applying for PPP loans. To conduct the analysis, they used matched-pair audit testing of financial institutions in Washington, D.C., for PPP loans. Matched-pair audit testing uses a pair of applicants with similar profiles but of a different race to test for discrimination through different treatment from financial institutions. Black and white applicants with similar credit characteristics who applied to a lender in the same time period were found to receive differential treatment in encouragement to apply for a loan, products offered, and information provided by the bank representative.

More general research that does not focus on race provides interesting findings. Granja et al. (2022) found that the first round of PPP funds flowed to areas more adversely affected by the economic effects of the pandemic but that the early PPP receipt did not have a substantial effect on local economic outcomes. Humphries, Neilson, and Ulyssea (2020) reported, based on survey data, that the smallest businesses were less aware of the PPP, less likely to apply, and, conditional on applications filed later, faced longer processing times and were denied more often.

The Economic Injury Disaster Loan Program (EIDL)

Another large program targeted at helping small businesses that provided massive amounts of funds during the pandemic was the Economic Injury Disaster Loan (EIDL) program. Similar to the PPP, it was administered by the SBA and provided funds very early in the pandemic. The program was designed to provide either loans or advances to small businesses that were losing sales and revenues as a result of COVID-19. As of November 2020, 3.6 million EIDL loans had been approved, for a total of $194 million, and as of July 2020, 5.8 million EIDL advances had been approved, for a total of $20 million (U.S. SBA 2020a, 2020b).

EIDL loans could be used to cover up to six months of a wide array of working capital and normal operating expenses, such as continuation of health care benefits and rent, utilities, and fixed debt payments, up to a maximum of $2 million. Unlike PPP loans, EIDL loans did not have a forgiveness condition. The loans had a fixed interest rate and a term of thirty years. Businesses applying for EIDL loans of more than $25,000 had to provide collateral. EIDL advances were grants and did not have to be repaid, but were for smaller amounts ($1,000 per employee up to a maximum of $10,000). EIDL advances were subtracted from the forgiveness amount of a business's PPP loan if they were received in addition to the PPP loan.

Fairlie and Fossen (2022a) studied the distribution of EIDL funds using the universe of data on loans and advances released by the SBA. The study explored the question of whether EIDL loans were evenly distributed to minority communities. The average number of EIDL loans per employer business establishment was roughly 0.25, indicating that one out of four establishments received funding. In contrast to PPP loans in the first round of funding, EIDL loans and advances, in both number per business and amounts per employee, were provided positively to minority communities. There was a strong positive relationship in the receipt per business of these loans and advances by the minority share of the population. The program was intended to help hard-hit communities.

6 The Partial Rebound from May 2020 Through the End of the Year

Did small businesses rebound immediately after the initial shock to the economy in April 2020? As shown in the previous chapter, the number of new COVID-19 cases in the country continued to increase in the months following April 2020. The social distancing restrictions slowed the rapid growth in the number of cases that resulted from the initial waves of new coronavirus cases in March and April, but the effectiveness of these restrictions in containing the disease did not last for long. In the last full week in April, there were 220,769 new COVID-19 cases. Even with social distancing restrictions in place, new COVID-19 cases continued to increase throughout May. For the last full week in May, which ended May 30, there were substantially more cases, at 427,463. The increase in the number of new COVID-19 cases started to level out in June and lessened over the month. By the last full week in June, which ended June 27, there were 543,697 reported cases. How did the inability to contain the spread of the disease and continued social distancing restrictions affect business activity in the next few months of the pandemic?

The effects of COVID-19 were devastating for small business activity in the first full month of social distancing mandates and health- and economic-driven demand shifts. The number of working business owners plummeted by 22 percent, which was the largest drop on record. Patterns were even more alarming when distinguished by race. Black business activity dropped by 41 percent in the first month. Latinx business activity fell by 32 percent, and Asian business activity fell by 26 percent. Building on these findings for April 2020, the analysis of COVID-19 impacts by race is extended into the second and third full months of social distancing restrictions in the pandemic—May and June 2020. Were there further closings of small businesses, or instead was there a partial rebound as small business owners tried to reopen or partially reopen, and importantly, were there racial differences in these patterns?

The analysis is further extended to examine July through December 2020. How did restrictions and demand shifts in the summer and fall alter these patterns? Social distancing restrictions were relaxed in the summer as people tired of staying in place and warmer weather made it easier to be outside. Also, the end of 2020 represented a potential turning point as vaccines would be available soon and presidential power would be changing hands in January.

Impacts on Total Business Activity in May and June 2020

To examine what happened in the next two months, figure 6.1 displays trends in the number of active business owners from January 2019 through the end of 2020. The dramatic drop in the number of active business owners in April 2020 rebounds partially in May and again in June. The number of working business owners dropped by 3.3 million from February to April. May 2020 shows a partial rebound from April 2020, adding back 1.1 million active business owners. Thus the rebound in May brought back 1.1 million of the 3.3 million business owners who had become inactive in the first full month of pandemic restrictions.[1]

The bounce back was far from complete, but one-third of business owners scrambled to figure out ways to reopen or at least work in their business behind the scenes. The losses due to COVID-19 measured from February to May remained high, at 15 percent, but the rebound suggests that not all the losses of active business owners in April 2020 represented permanent closures. Unfortunately, there is no way to determine from these data whether the business owners that reactivated operations had any sales or profits in May 2020. Many of these owners were likely scrambling to figure things out instead of selling products and services.

June saw a further rebound in business activity. In June another 984,000 business owners became active again. The month restored close to another third of the initial losses to business owner activity from February to April. But business activity was down 8 percent, or 1.2 million active business owners, from the February level just prior to the start of the pandemic.[2]

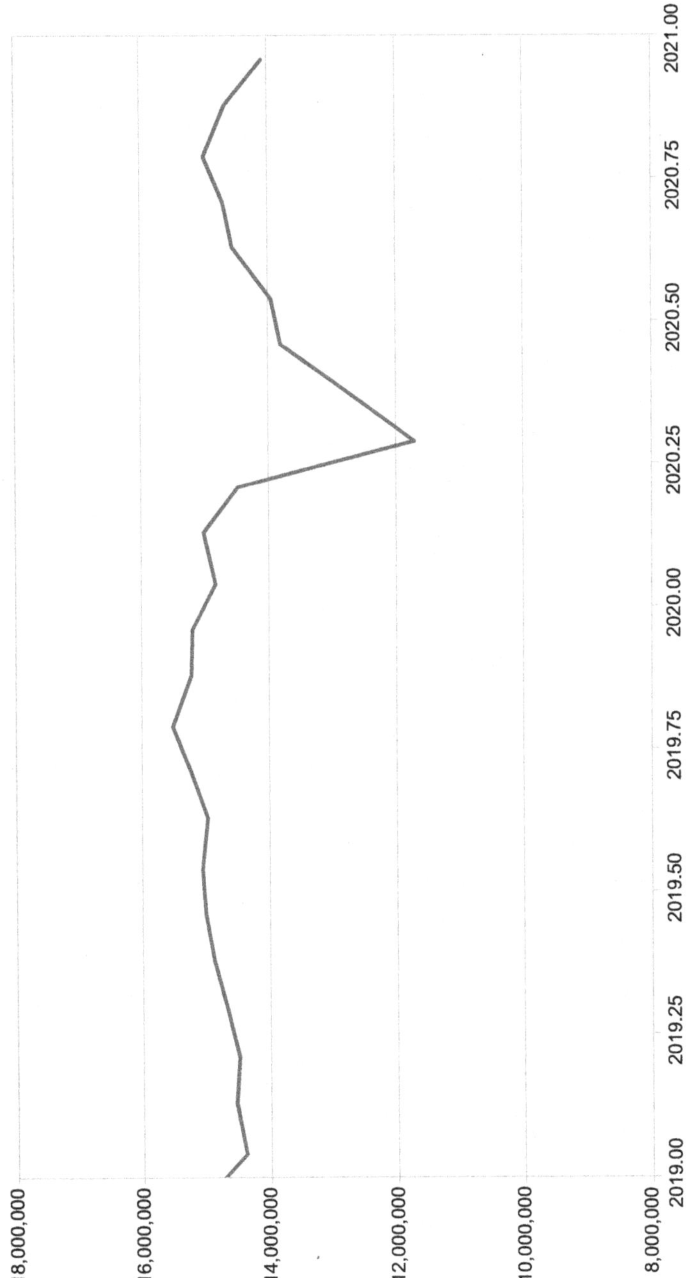

Figure 6.1
Number of active business owners in the United States, January 2019–December 2020.

Partial Rebounds in May and June 2020 by Race

Were there differential rebounds in business activity in May and June 2020 by race? Figure 6.2 displays the number of active business owners by major racial groups. The number of Black business owners plummeted from 1.1 million in February 2020 to 640,000 in April. Although there was a partial rebound, the number of actively working Black business owners remained 26 percent lower in May than in February 2020, which is the largest drop for any major racial/ethnic group. Moving on to June, the number of active Black business owners remained lower than prepandemic levels. Black business activity moved slight upward but remained 19 percent lower than in February 2020.

Latinx business owners also suffered major losses in business activity. The number of active Latinx business owners dropped from 2.1 million to 1.4 million (32 percent) from February to April. These losses in business activity from COVID-19 continued into the second and third months after widespread shelter-in-place restrictions were imposed. The number of active Latinx business owners dropped by 19 percent from February to May and by 10 percent from February to June. Although there was a partial rebound from April, these losses continued to be large and resulted in lost income for owners not operating their businesses.

Asian business owners suffered losses in business activity of 230,000, representing 26 percent of February levels. Even with the rebounds in May and June, the number of Asian business owners who were actively running their businesses dropped by 21 percent and 10 percent, respectively. Consumer discrimination against Asian-owned businesses was a concern because of the coronavirus's first appearance in China.

White business owners also experienced a drop in business activity but at smaller levels of losses. The drop in business activity from February to April for white business owners was 1.8 million business owners, representing 17 percent of original levels. White business owners experienced declines in operating businesses of 11 percent in May and 5 percent in June.

Differential Early Rebounds by Industry

Were there differential rebounds to small businesses in different industries in May and June 2020? Table 6.1 reports estimates of business activity losses

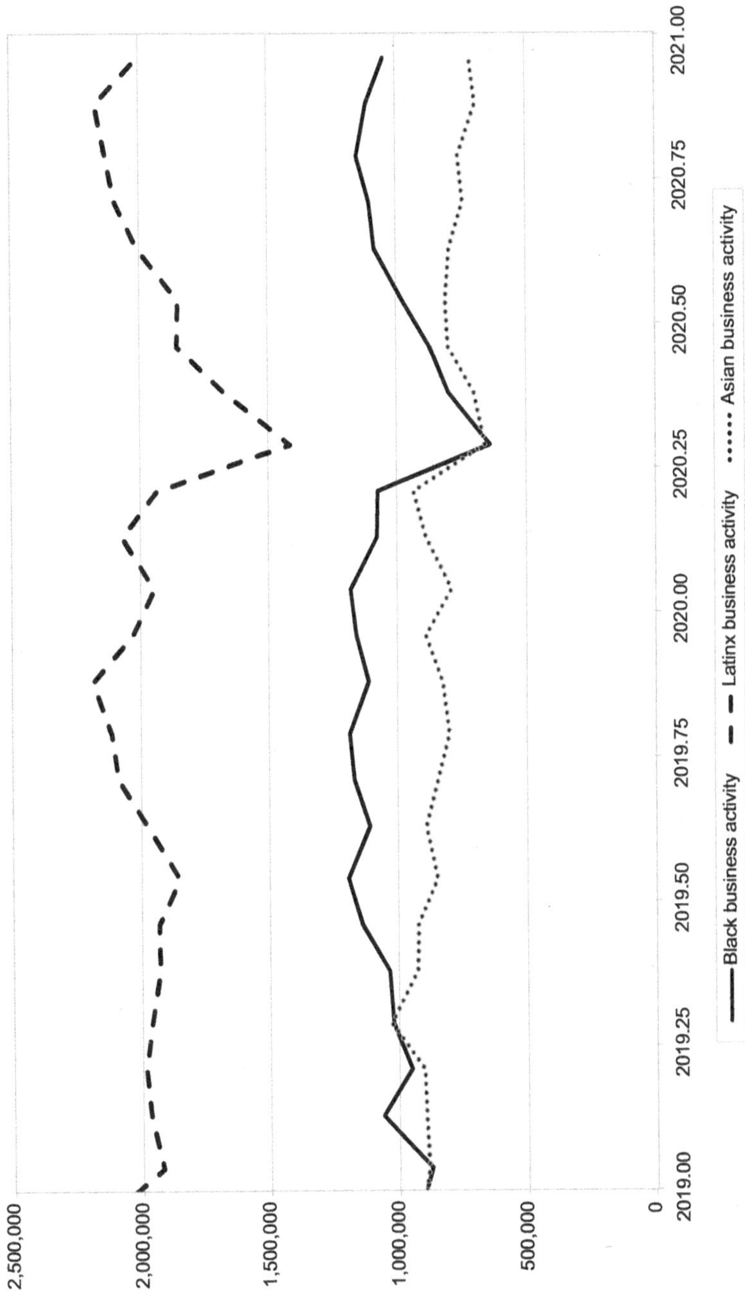

Figure 6.2
Number of active business owners by race, January 2019—December 2020.

Table 6.1
Business Owner Activity Losses by Industry in Early 2020

	Percent changes in no. of active business owners (estimated)		
Industry	February to April 2020	February to May 2020	February to June 2020
Agriculture	7	16	14
Construction	–27	–19	–8
Manufacturing	–11	–26	–2
Wholesale Trade	–14	1	5
Retail Trade	–10	–2	–1
Transportation	–22	–12	–1
Information	–10	–19	–20
Financial Activities	–12	–6	–1
Professional and Business Services	–18	–10	–7
Educational Services	–39	–10	–25
Health Services	–16	–18	–8
Arts, Leisure, and Accommodations	–35	–35	–31
Restaurants	–22	–24	–13
Repair and Maintenance	–25	–22	–29
Personal and Laundry Services	–79	–48	–26
"Nonessential" industry	–38	–28	–17
"Essential" Industry	–17	–10	–5

Notes: Author's calculations from compiled monthly Current Population Survey microdata. Essential industries are defined using the classification provided by Delaware state for essential and nonessential businesses.

by major industry groups in April, May and June 2020. Almost every industry continued to experience sizable drops in the number of active business owners from February through May, with the exception of Agriculture. By June, many industry groups were experiencing only small losses from February levels, but others continued to experience large losses from prepandemic levels.

Construction, one of the largest industries for business ownership, experienced a major decline of nearly 19 percent in May, which represents a partial recovery of the 27 percent drop from February to April 2020. Construction continued to rebound in June, removing an additional 11 percentage points of losses. By June 2020, Construction was down only 8 percent from February 2020.

Retail Trade experienced a loss of 10 percent of business activity in April but rebounded strongly in May and June. Losses in business activity were only one to two percentage points relative to February levels. Restaurants experienced a decline of more than 20 percent in April and continued low levels of business activity over the next two months. The broad sector of Arts, Leisure, and Accommodations experienced essentially no rebound from the devastating losses of more than 30 percent in the first full month of economic damage from the pandemic.

Both high-skill and lesser-skill services continued to experience losses from COVID-19. Personal and Laundry Services regained part of the 79 percent loss of business owner activity in April, but losses were still large. Business activity in this industry group was 48 percent in May and 26 percent in June. Transportation Services, which includes taxi and some Uber drivers, partially rebounded in May and June from large losses in April. Higher-skill services such as Financial Activities rebounded strongly, but business activity in Professional and Business Services remained 7–10 percent lower in May and June. Health Services also continued to experience large losses in business activity in May and June.

As discussed in chapter 3, industries can be categorized into essential versus nonessential according to state or local government guidelines. Using the Delaware categorization, losses to the number of active business owners are lower for essential industries than for nonessential industries. Although both groups of business owners experienced partial rebounds, the number of active business owners in essential industries was down by 10 percent in May and 5 percent in June, while the number of business owners in nonessential industries was down by much more, 28 percent, in May and 17 percent in June.

Industry Distribution and Race

Did the industry distribution of businesses owned by different demographic groups place them at a higher or lower risk of COVID-19–related shutdowns through May and June? To explore this question, I simulate the total number of business owners for each demographic group by switching their industry distribution for the U.S. national industry distribution (as discussed in chapter 3). The industry distribution of Black business owners placed them at a higher risk of business activity losses due to COVID-19. Similar to the findings for the first month of the pandemic, the industry distribution also placed Black business owners at higher risk of sustained losses in May 2020. As Black business owner activity rebounded further in June, the industry distribution was not as responsible for these larger total losses.

A similar pattern is found for Latinx. When switching the Latinx industry distribution to the U.S. national industry distribution the predicted number of active Latinx business owners drops from 19 percent to 13 percent for May and from 10 percent to 6 percent for June. These findings imply that Latinx business owners had an "unfavorable" industry distribution, partly placing them at higher risk of sustained business activity losses in May and June.

Asian business owners show a similar pattern in April, but not in May and June. For April, I also find that Asian business owners were more concentrated in industries placing them at a higher risk of losses in business activity. But when the industry distribution is switched to the national industry distribution in May and June, Asian business owners are predicted to have larger losses in business activity, which implies the opposite pattern. In these months, business activity losses switched to industries in which Asian business owners were less concentrated.

The Next Six Months of 2020

July started to see more opening up of activities and removal of the strict social distancing restrictions in place in the spring and early summer. The summer weather was helpful for holding more activities outside, with the adviso that people should stay six feet apart in social settings and lines. At the same time, people were starting to socialize and interact again, even as the expected number of COVID-19 cases started to rise. The last full week in June saw 543,697 new cases, but by mid-July there were 750,631 new cases for the week ending July 18, 2020. The number of new cases finally reversed course when the week ending July 25 had 701,985 new cases. New case numbers mostly declined over the summer until another reversal, with new case numbers increasing for the week ending September 19. The number of new cases increased by more than 100,000 from the previous week, and new cases were nearly at the three-quarter-million mark again.

COVID-19 case numbers started to increase again, and numbers of new cases per week rose into unchartered territory. The fall brought people back inside, and Halloween parties might have accelerated the spread of the virus. On November 14, 2020, the nation witnessed more than one million new COVID-19 cases over the previous week. The following week, ending November 21, saw a peak number of 1,094,536 new cases of COVID-19. Weekly new case numbers remained high mostly through the end of 2020. People traveled and visited for Thanksgiving and the winter holidays, potentially accelerating the spread of COVID-19 across the country.

Business Activity in the Second Half of 2020

How did business owner activity trend over the second half of 2020? Did small businesses continue to reopen or did the rise in new COVID-19 cases result in retrenchment? Figure 6.1 shows that the number of active business owners increased in the next few months, starting in July 2020. The increases in the number of active business owners were much smaller than in May and June, but there was clear evidence of sustained rebounds in business activity. Through the summer and into the fall, small businesses were reopening, customers were returning, and there was a more positive outlook in general. By August the number of active business owners was higher than immediately before the pandemic. To be sure, business activity is typically higher in the summer than in the winter, but a comparison of business activity in August 2020 with that in August 2019 shows that business activity was only 3 percent lower in August 2020.

Business activity continued to increase in September and October. In October, business activity hit its postpandemic peak for the year. There were 15.0 million business owners actively working in businesses in the country. The total matched the prepandemic number of February 2020 but was lower than the October 2019 level of 15.5 million active business owners.

The number of active business owners started to fall from this peak in November and December. In December there were 14.1 million active business owners, representing a drop of nearly one million business owners from the October 2020 level. Because of the rapid increase in new COVID-19 cases in the late fall and early winter, social distancing restrictions were tightened and consumer fears ramped up. Compared to 2019 levels, business activity dropped by 1.1 million from December 2019 to December 2020.

Business activity experienced a rocky road over 2020. At no time during the year was the recovery complete. Additionally, the last couple of months of 2020 saw a retrenchment, with business activity levels ending the year at 1.1 million fewer active business owners (representing 7 percent) than at the end of 2019, before the start of the pandemic.

Racial Inequality in Business Activity

Were there differential trends in business activity through the rest of 2020 by race? Did all groups experience the rebounds in business activity in the summer and fall of 2020? Figure 6.2 shows that the number of Black business owners continually increased until hitting a peak in October, at 1.15 million. In October 2020, Black business activity was only 3 percent lower than the 2019 level. Similar to the U.S. total, Black business activity dropped during the last two months of the year. December 2020 levels for Black business activity were nearly 10 percent lower than December 2019 levels.

Latinx business owners experienced a similar pattern. The second half of 2020 showed a continual rebound in Latinx business activity. The peak level of business activity was in November, but December showed a similar drop. Latinx business activity essentially fully recovered when compared with2019 levels. The December 2020 level of 2.0 million active Latinx business owners was only 1 percent lower than the December 2019 level.

Asian business owner activity suffered sustained losses during the second half of 2020. The peak in business activity was 810,000 in July 2020. Asian business activity differed than business activity for other groups by declining through the end of the year. The number of active business owners in December 2020 was 713,000. The decline was roughly 20 percent from December 2019 to December 2020, much higher than for any other group or the U.S. total. There might have been continued discrimination against Asian-owned stores, restaurants, and other businesses (Amuedo-Dorantes, Borra, and Wang 2024; Huang et al. 2023; Ong, Cheng, and Ong 2021).

California Taxable Sales Data

COVID-19 resulted in a huge drop in sales among businesses in California in the second quarter of 2020. The analysis in chapter 3 revealed that taxable sales dropped by 15.4 percent from 2019Q2 to 2020Q2. Were there continued losses in the next two quarters of 2020? Or was there a rebound

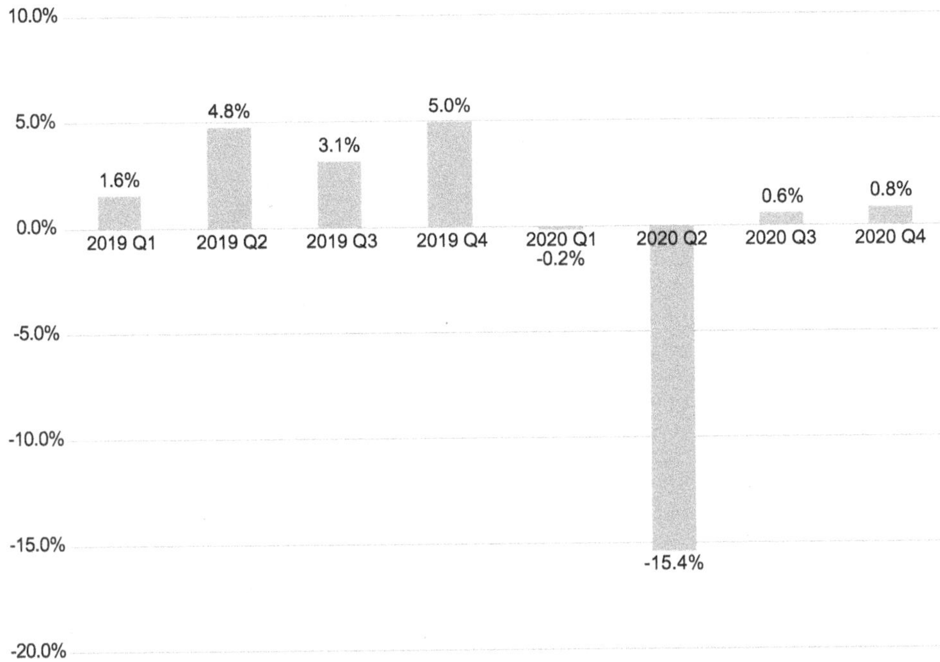

Figure 6.3
Year-over-year change in taxable sales in California.

in taxable sales commensurate with the rebound for business activity? Using data from the California Department of Tax and Fee Administration (CDTFA), figure 6.3 displays year-over-year changes in taxable sales by businesses reporting taxable sales in California through the end of 2020. Taxable sales decreased substantially in the second quarter of 2020 but rebounded partially in both the third and fourth quarters of 2020. The year-over-year growth rates of 0.6 percent in 2020Q3 and 0.8 percent in 2020Q4 were positive but much smaller than the comparable prepandemic year-over-year growth rates in 2019Q3 and 2019Q4. Growth in business sales did not recover fully to prepandemic growth rates.

GDP Trends

The pandemic created the largest quarter-to-quarter fall in GDP over the past century. GDP fell by 28.0 percent. What happened in the third and fourth quarters of 2020? Figure 6.4 displays quarterly GDP growth rates though

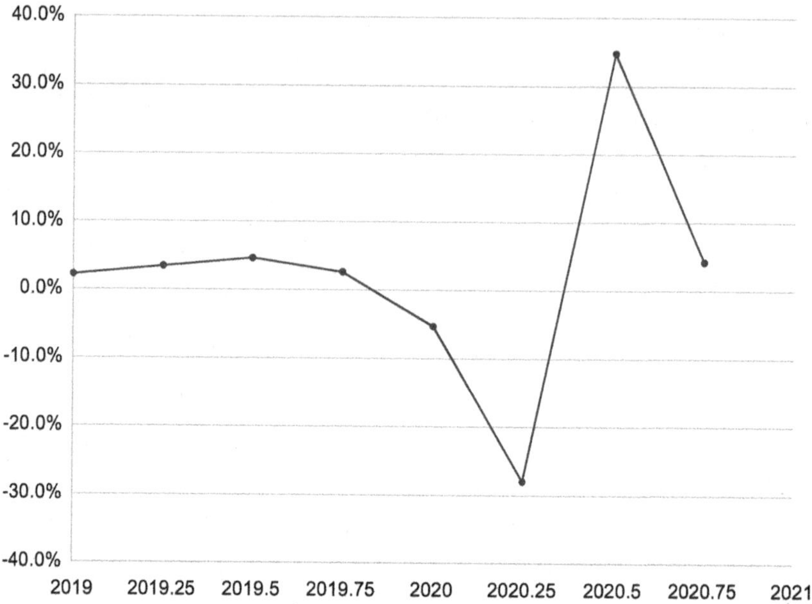

Figure 6.4
Quarterly GDP growth rate, 2019Q1–2020Q4.

the end of the year. The pandemic created an extremely severe but short recession. The GDP reversed course quickly after the free fall in 2020Q2 and grew by 34.8 percent in 2020Q3. The GDP also experienced positive growth in the fourth quarter of 2020 but was more in its normal range, growing by 4.2 percent in 2020Q4. The average growth rate over the four quarters of 2019, just prior the pandemic, was 3.2 percent for comparison.

Unemployment Through the End of 2020

The unemployment rate hit its long-term peak in April 2020, when it reached 14.8 percent. Did it rebound to lower levels quickly as business activity started to pick up after April? Figure 6.5 displays the national unemployment rate through the end of 2020. The drop in unemployment rates happened very quickly. In May 2020 the unemployment rate dropped by more than 1.5 percentage points, which was followed by an even larger drop of 2.2 percentage points in June. This two-month drop is the fastest two-month drop on record.

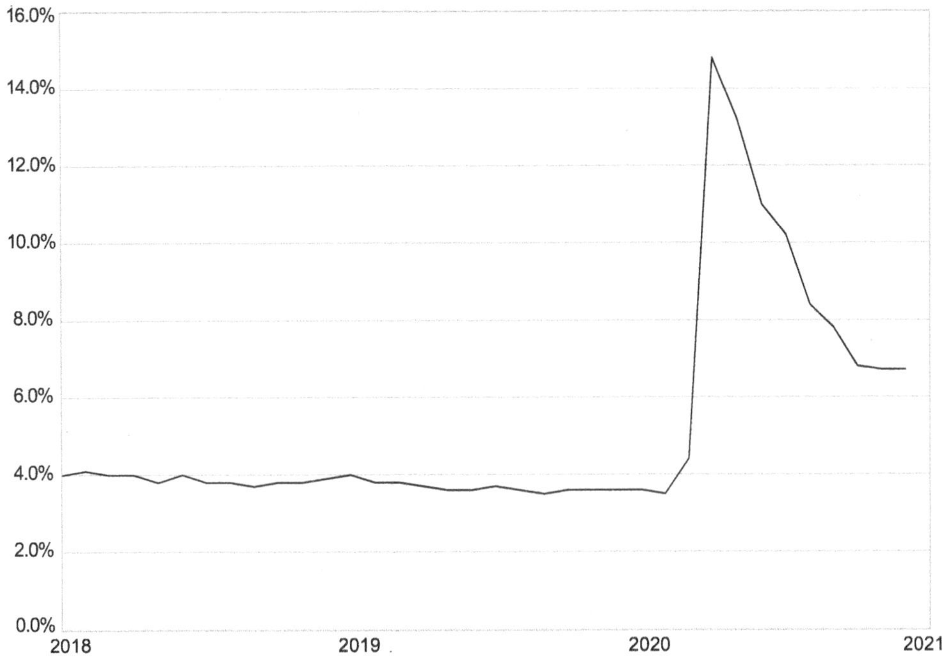

Figure 6.5
Unemployment rate, January 2018–December 2020.

The rapid descent of the unemployment rate continued through the summer and into the fall. In September 2020 the unemployment rate was at 6.8 percent, which was eight percentage points lower than the peak in April 2020. A drop of eight percentage points over such a short period of time is unprecedented. Over the next two months the unemployment rate remained essentially unchanged, ending the year at 6.7 percent. Although the decline from April's peak was exceptionally large, the unemployment rate ended the year more than three percentage points above prepandemic levels.

7 The Second Year of the Pandemic: 2021

Operation Warp Speed led to the rapid discovery of a COVID-19 vaccine. Normally it takes years to develop a new vaccine, but with the aid of $18 billion in federal funding and a public-private partnership, the vaccine was developed and ready before the end of 2020, less than one year after the pandemic was declared. In December 2020 the vaccine was approved under an emergency use authorization (EUA) by the Food and Drug Administration (FDA).[1] The Pfizer-BioNTech COVID-19 vaccine was available under an EUA on December 11, 2020, and by December 14 the first deliveries of the COVID-19 vaccines had begun. Only a few days later, on December 18, 2020, the FDA issued the second EUA, for use of the Moderna COVID-19 vaccine.

Although the vaccines were approved in December 2020, it took some time to get them out to the general public. The elderly received vaccines in January, while others often waited until March. Personally, my elderly mom received her first dose of the vaccine on January 17, 2021, and I received my first dose on March 6, 2021. A second dose of the vaccine was needed, which lengthened the waiting period before things could start to "get back to normal." The recommended interdose interval was three weeks for the Pfizer vaccine and four weeks for the Moderna vaccine. I received my second dose on March 27, for example. Most people were anxiously waiting to receive their two shots of either the Pfizer or the Moderna vaccine in the first few months of 2021. At the end of February 2021 a third option, the Johnson & Johnson vaccine, became available and required only one shot.

The optimism, however, was not shared by everyone and was short-lived in some sense. There was hesitancy, and even refusal, on some part of the population to get the vaccine. The hesitancy became partly political. There was much discussion about how it was a divided issue, with "red" states having much higher rates of choosing not to get vaccinated for COVID-19 in early 2021. Vaccines were required for work in many jobs, including health care and federal government work. Many large businesses required their workers to get vaccinated independent of any federal regulations. Vaccine requirements at jobs faced pushback by some people and concern among others who had already received the vaccine but who might get exposed to the disease through unvaccinated coworkers.

One problem that vaccines and public support for them faced was that viruses evolve. Unfortunately, "gamma," "beta," "alpha," "delta," and "omicron" became well-known names for the numerous variants of the mutating virus, and it was these mutations around the world that caused confusion over vaccine effectiveness and ultimately loss of confidence in a fast return to normal. In June 2021, the delta variant, which was first identified in India, became the most common variant. The variant surged over the summer. Then there were the breakthrough infections, in which vaccinated individuals were getting infected with COVID-19. As early as the end of April 2021, a total of 10,262 COVID-19 vaccine breakthrough infections had been reported in the country across forty-six different states (Centers for Disease Control 2021). Breakthrough infections increased even more, especially when the fast-spreading new omicron variant showed up. One reason is that with increasing time since the initial vaccination, the likelihood of a breakthrough infection also increases. Further, immunity against infection decreases with time as antibody levels fall. Vaccines are also created for specific variants, and thus their efficacy changed from the alpha to the delta to the omicron variant, for example. All in all, breakthrough infections eroded some of the support for getting vaccinated and optimism about a quick social and economic recovery from the pandemic.

This chapter examines business activity and earnings as the vaccines were rolled out and a new president took over at the helm. Chapter 3 provided estimates of the effects of COVID-19 on small business activity in the first month, April 2020, and chapter 6 provided estimates for the rest of 2020. The analysis revealed that the number of working business owners plummeted in April 2020 but rebounded partly, though not in a linear fashion, over the rest of the year. Here the analysis of COVID-19 impacts is extended to 2021, which was clearly a pivotal year in the pandemic in terms of the vaccine and a new presidential administration. Was there a grand-scale reopening of small businesses or instead a sluggish economic recovery during the second year of the pandemic?

COVID-19 Cases in 2021

The start of 2021 saw much optimism about the vaccine for COVID-19. Nurses and other health care professionals were receiving vaccines at the end of 2020. The rest of the United States was waiting. After an increase at the beginning of January 2021, the number of COVID-19 cases started to decline rapidly. Figure 7.1 displays the number of new COVID-19 cases per week through the end of 2021. There were 820,185 cases during the week ending January 9, 2021, dropping to 568,508 cases for the week ending February 6, 2021. As the vaccines rolled out, COVID-19 cases steadily declined until July 2021. The number of cases hit a low, at 244,708 cases, for the week ending July 3, 2021.

COVID-19 cases, surprisingly, started to rise quickly in the summer of 2021. A large share of the U.S. population was still not fully vaccinated by then and the delta variant was surging. But another cause of the rise in cases was that people were letting down their guard and returning to social activities. New COVID-19 case numbers rose to 670,309 during the week ending September 18, 2021. The weekly tally of new cases started to drop in the early fall and rose slightly at the end of the year. But these trends in the fall and early winter were small in comparison with the rapid decline in new case numbers early in 2021 and the sharp rise in the summer of 2021.

Business Activity in 2021

Did business activity follow a similar pattern as the number of new COVID-19 cases or did it gradually continue the rebound that started in 2020? Figure 7.2 displays monthly business activity rates through the end of 2021. Business activity dropped in November 2020 through February 2020. Then vaccines started to roll out, and there was a lot more optimism. Business activity turned around in March 2021 and started a march upward. Business activity increased through the spring and summer of 2021. It was not until the fall of 2021 that business activity dropped again, partly because of shutdowns related to the surge in the delta variant of COVID-19 and a return to the indoors and holiday gatheringss. By the end of 2021, however,

Figure 7.1
New COVID-19 cases in the United States per week for weeks ending March 14, 2020, to December 25, 2021.

Figure 7.2
Number of active business owners in the United States, January 2019–December 2021.

business activity had surpassed its level in 2019. The number of active business owners was 15.3 million in December 2021, compared with 15.2 million in December 2019.

The improvement in business activity through 2021 was strong. There was the continuation of the decline at the end of 2020 for the first two months, but the vaccine rollout created a lot of optimism. The combination of warmer weather in spring and summer also increased confidence in returning to shops and restaurants and in travel. Although the rise in business activity was promising, it is unclear whether business owners also recovered strongly in terms of take-home earnings from running their businesses.

Business Earnings in 2021

The losses to business earnings were severe in the first year of the pandemic. Although the 2020 calendar year only captures effects from April to December, with a partial rebound in business activity through the end of the year, there were large losses to annual business earnings in 2020. What happened in 2021 as vaccines were rolled out to the population and business activity continued to improve? Figure 7.3 displays trends in mean and mean log

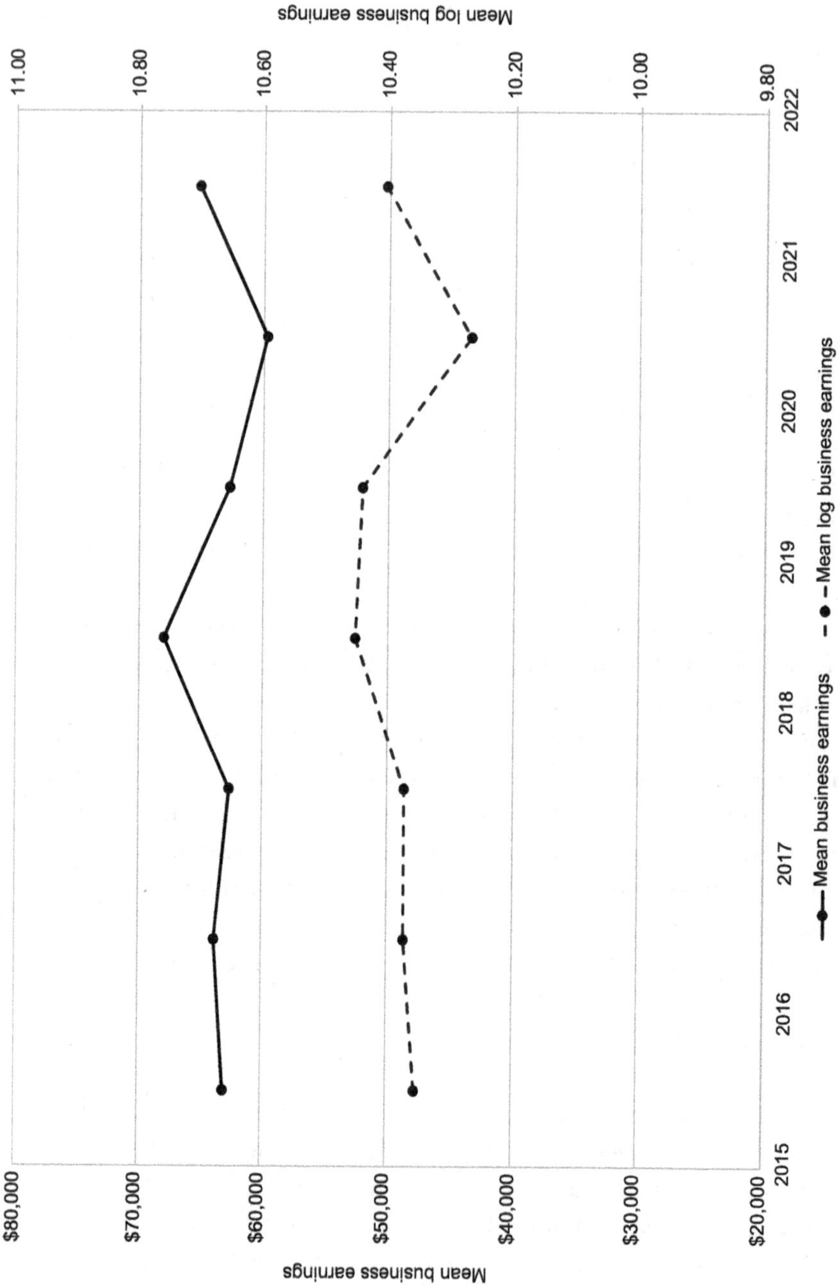

Figure 7.3
Business earnings trends, 2015–2021.

business earnings by calendar year through 2021. All estimates are adjusted for inflation and are measured in 2019 dollars.

The trends in business earnings are clear. Mean business earnings dropped by roughly $3,000 in 2020 from the previous year, then rebounded strongly in 2021. In fact, the rebound was so strong that mean business earnings were $2,500 higher than in the year before the pandemic. Turning to trends in mean log business earnings that reduce the influence of large outliers on comparisons between years, I find a similar trend, but a slightly different comparison between 2021 and prepandemic levels. Mean log business earnings dropped by 17 log points from 2019 to 2020 and rebounded strongly in 2021. From 2020 to 2021, business earnings increased by roughly 14 percent. The rebound, however, was incomplete, with business earnings ending roughly 4 percent lower in 2021 than in 2019.

Industry Rebounds in 2021

Did business owners in different industries vary in their rebound from the major, nearly across the board losses in 2020? As noted in chapter 3, Agriculture and Construction did not experience losses in 2020. Both industries experienced losses from 2020 to 2021 but remained in positive territory relative to the year prior to the pandemic, 2019 (table 7.1). The Information industry was the real winner, though. Information posted gains of 41 percent in mean business earnings in 2020 and an additional 53 percent gain in 2021, resulting in a total gain of 94 percent relative to prepandemic levels. Manufacturing experienced a partial rebound. Wholesale and Retail Trade cut roughly half of the losses to mean business earnings from 2020 to 2021. Transportation experienced a major loss in 2020 but turned things around strongly in 2021, posting an increase of 10 percent from prepandemic levels. Financial Activities also showed first-year losses in the pandemic but then gains in the second year of the pandemic. Leisure and Hospitality rebounded strongly from the huge losses that the industry suffered in 2020. Finally, Other Services experienced a sizable rebound in 2021 from losses in 2020.

Regression-Adjusted Losses

As in chapter 3, I explore the effects of the COVID-19–induced drop and rebound oi business earnings using regressions that control for trends that

Table 7.1
Business Earnings Losses by Industry, 2019–2020 and 2019–2021

	Mean business earnings			
Industry	2019	Percent change from 2019 to 2020	Percent change from 2019 to 2021	Average *N*
Agriculture	$42,262	53	7	377
Construction	$50,512	8	10	1095
Manufacturing	$70,465	−19	−17	220
Wholesale and Retail Trade	$66,539	−26	−12	572
Transportation	$51,185	−17	10	357
Information	$49,958	41	94	95
Financial Activities	$98,315	−11	25	489
Professional and Business Services	$73,437	4	−5	1252
Education and Health Services	$71,215	2	3	633
Leisure and Hospitality	$60,032	−43	6	416
Other Services	$40,154	22	−15	613

Notes: Author's calculations from Current Population Survey (CPS) microdata, 2019–2021. All estimates use CPS-provided sample weights. Sample includes only individuals with longest-held work activity as self-employed business owner in a calendar year.

existed prior to the start of the pandemic. The question becomes whether and how much COVID-19 knocked any preexisting trends in business earnings off of their predicted course from 2019 to 2020 and 2021. Table 7.2 reports estimates from equations (3.1) and (3.2) in appendix 3.B. The loss in business earnings in 2020 is reported as the "Post-COVID-19 2020" coefficient and the loss/rebound in 2021 is reported as the "Post-COVID-19 2021" coefficient.

Controlling for preexisting trends and demographic characteristics, the losses to business earnings are estimated to be from 16 to 19 percent in 2020. All estimates point to a strong but incomplete rebound in 2021. The regression estimates indicate that business earnings were 2–7 percent lower in 2021 than where they were predicted to be based on trends in business earnings prior to the pandemic.

Table 7.2
Regressions for Log Business Earnings, Current Population Survey, 2015–2021

Explanatory variables	(1)	(2)	(3)	(4)
Post-COVID-19 2020	−0.168 (0.023)	−0.191 (0.021)	−0.191 (0.022)	−0.164 (0.021)
Post-COVID-19 2021	−0.022 (0.023)	−0.072 (0.024)	−0.072 (0.024)	−0.018 (0.021)
Main controls	No	Yes	Yes	Yes
Industry controls	No	Yes	Yes	Yes
Time trend	No	Yes	Yes	Yes
Pre-2019 indicator	No	No	Yes	No
Full 2015–2019 indicators	No	No	No	Yes
Sample years	2019–2021	2015–2021	2015–2021	2015–2021
Sample size	18,357	46,498	46,498	46,498

Notes: Author's calculations from compiled monthly Current Population Survey microdata. The sample consists of business owners (ages 20–64) who worked in their business in the calendar year. Coefficient estimates and their standard errors (in parentheses) are reported. Main controls include race/ethnicity, female, age, education, region, and central city status indicator variables.

GDP Growth and Unemployment in 2021

Did the broader economy also rebound strongly in 2021? GDP growth in all four quarters of 2021 was strong. The GDP grew by 5.2 percent in the first quarter of 2021. It continued this pace with growth of 6.2 percent in 2021Q2 but slowed a little in 2021Q3, declining to 3.3 percent. The GDP finished the year strongly with 7.0 percent growth in the last quarter of 2021. In terms of the broader U.S. economy, the recovery in 2021 was exceptionally strong.

Trends in the unemployment rate in 2021 were surprising. Not only did the unemployment rate start to decline after stalling somewhat at the end of 2020 but it reached extremely low levels by the end of the year. Figure 7.4 displays trends in the national unemployment rate from January 2018 to December 2021. The unemployment rate ended 2020 at 6.7 percent. It dropped steadily over the entire year, ending 2021 at a surprisingly low 3.9 percent.

The rapid decline in the unemployment rate in 2021 was so surprising that the term "Great Resignation" was used to describe it. COVID-19 created

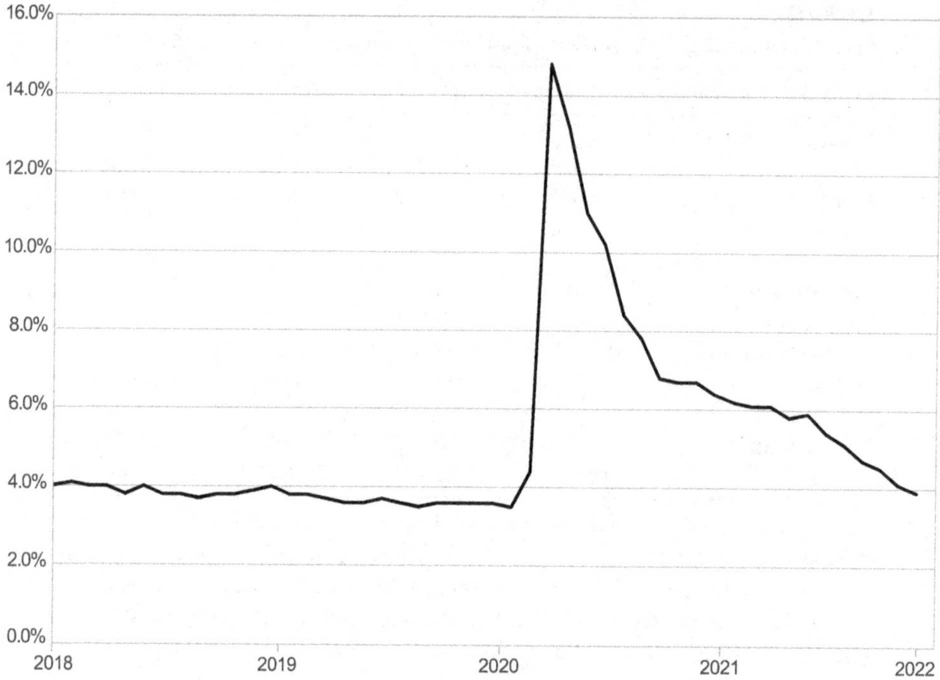

Figure 7.4
Unemployment rate, January 2018–December 2021.

a massive disruption to the labor market, and many workers simply quit their jobs instead of going back, while others left the labor force entirely. It was a disruptive period. Officially, however, the unemployment rate, which captures individuals not at work but actively seeking a job, was near historical lows by the end of 2021, only slightly more than one and a half years after the start of the social distancing restrictions of the pandemic.

8 Race and the Economic Rebound in the Year After the Start of the Pandemic

Although there was optimism at the beginning of 2021 because vaccines would soon be available to the general public and a new president promised to do more in the pandemic, small businesses were about to face a rocky road ahead that year. The vaccines turned out to be less effective than the public anticipated and there was substantial resistance to taking vaccines that was partly aligned by political lines. The year 2021 was nevertheless a turning point in the pandemic.

The previous chapter explored what happened to business activity in 2021 and found substantial improvement over the course of the year. But, as seen in chapter 4, there were very uneven effects of COVID-19 on business owners by race early in the pandemic. The losses to business activity were much higher, for example, among Black, Latinx, and Asian business owners than among white business owners, and these differences had not fully recovered to prepandemic levels by the end of 2020 for Black and Asian business owners. Black and Asian business activity ended 2020 roughly 10 percent and 20 percent lower than at the end of 2019, respectively. Building on these findings, this chapter extends the analysis of COVID-19 impacts by race through the end of 2021. What happened to business activity and earnings and racial inequality in those business outcomes in 2021? Was the reopening of small businesses strong or sluggishness for business owners of color?

Rebounds in Business Activity by Race

Figure 8.1 displays business activity by race from January 2019 to December 2021. The patterns for each group generally follow the total pattern for all groups discussed in the previous chapter. The drop in April 2020 and the rebound starting immediately afterward are the most distinctive business

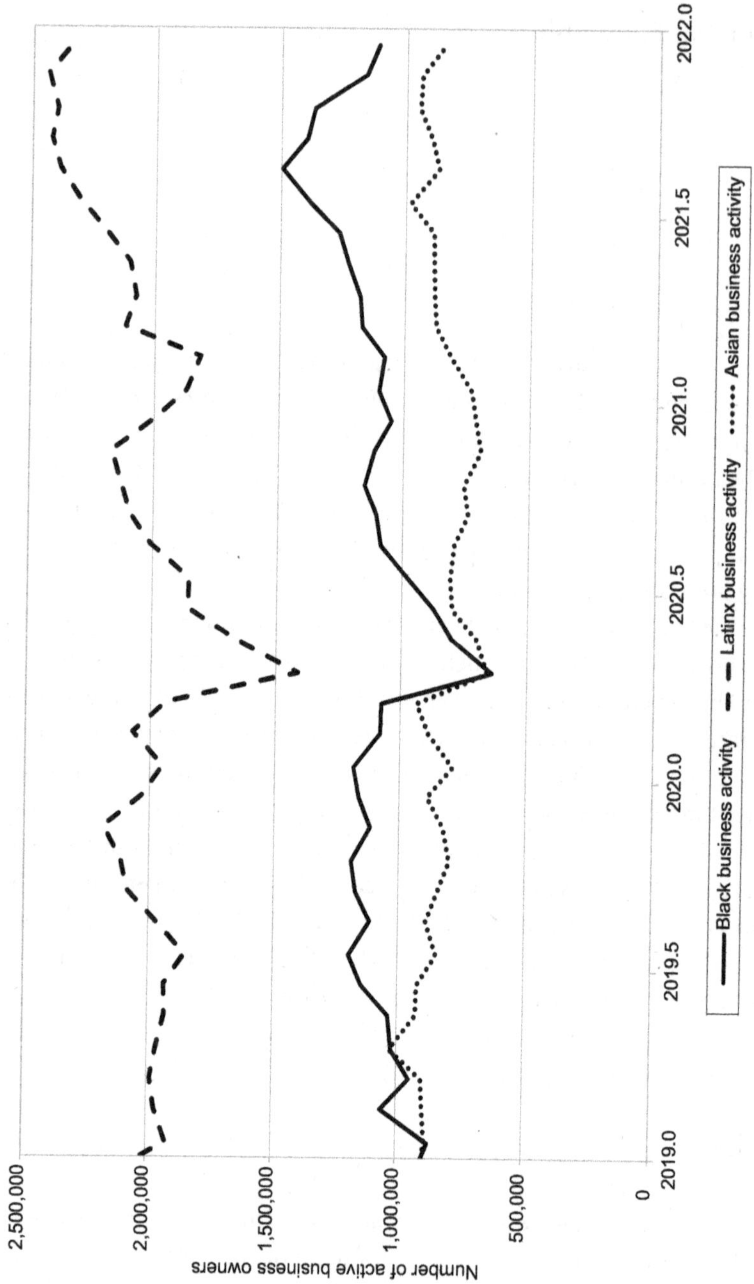

Figure 8.1
Number of active business owners by race, January 2019–December 2021.

activity patterns over the time period for each group. For all three minority groups, 2021 was a year of continued recovery.

Of the three groups, Latinx business owners experienced the strongest rebound and growth over the year. Latinx Americans ended 2020 with 2.0 million active business owners. By the end of 2021 the total had grown to 2.3 million active business owners. The growth rate of 16 percent over the year was quite strong. Compared with December 2019, just prior to the start of the pandemic, the growth in business activity was the same. There were 2.0 million active Latinx business owners at the end of 2019. The path to get there, however, was definitely not linear.

Black business activity also grew over 2021. There were 1.0 million active Black business owners at the end of 2020. That figure grew to 1.1 million in December 2021, for a growth rate of 6 percent over the year. Compared with December 2019, however, Black business activity was still 4 percent lower. Additionally, the month-to-month time pattern reveals a potential dip in the last few months of the year.[1] Again, Black business activity did not experience a clean, linear recovery over the year.

The patterns for Asian business activity also show both growth and ups and downs over the year. At the end of December 2021 there were 850,000 active Asian business owners. Asian business activity was up 19 percent relative to a year earlier but down 5 percent from December 2019. The path over the year was not linear but instead showed some fluctuations over the year.

Although not displayed in the figure, white business activity ended 2021 at 10.5 million active business owners. The total represents an increase of 5 percent from the end of 2020 but a decrease of 2 percent from the end of 2019. Of the groups, Latinx business owners were the only group that ended 2021 at a higher level of activity than just prior to the start of the pandemic.

Business Earnings in 2021

The analysis in chapter 4 revealed that business earnings took a large hit in 2020 relative to prepandemic levels. At the same time, business activity was much stronger in 2021 than in 2020. An important question is whether business earnings remained lower in 2021 than prepandemic levels or rebounded strongly from the drop in the first year of the pandemic. Trends through 2021 in mean log business earnings by race are displayed in figure 8.2.

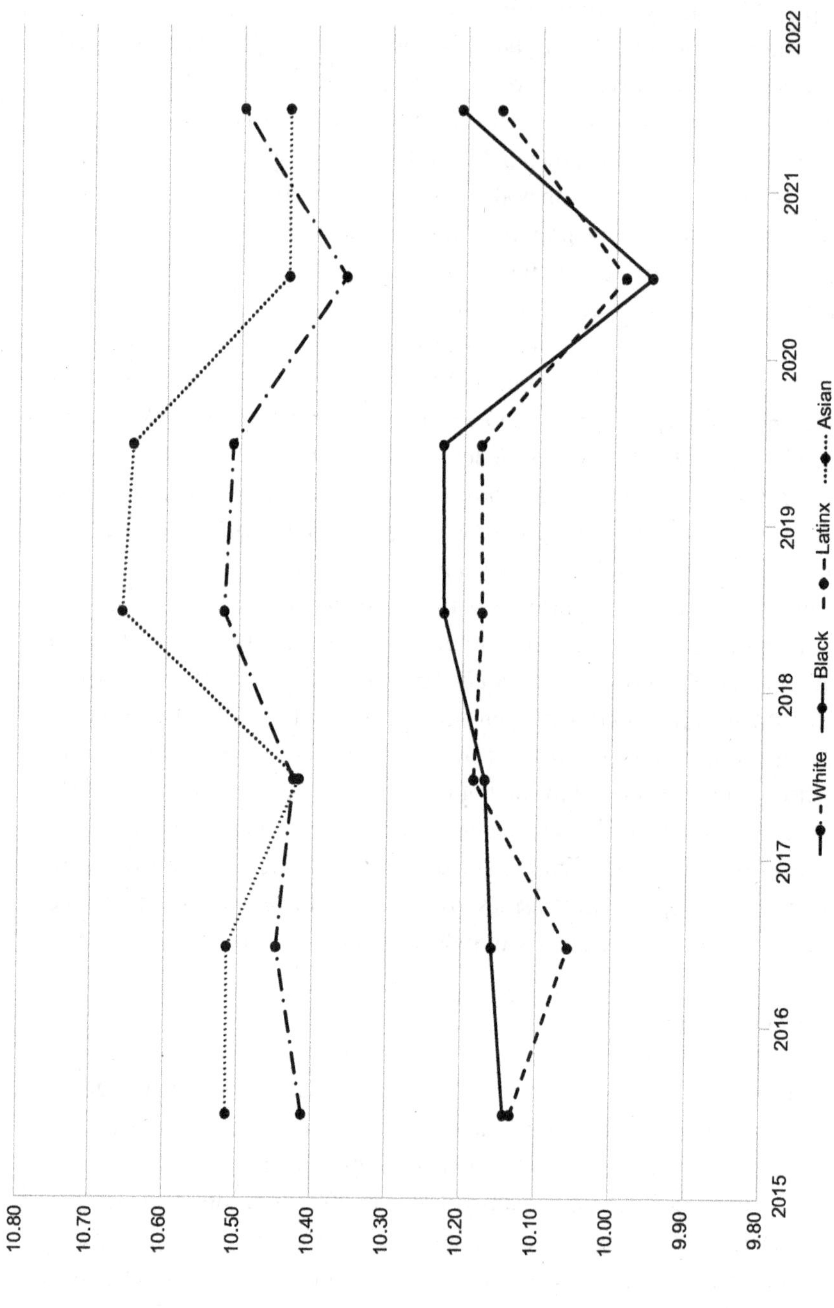

Figure 8.2
Mean log business earnings trends, 2015–2021.

As shown in the previous chapter, total mean log business earnings dropped by 17 log points from 2019 to 2020 but partly rebounded by 14 percent from 2020 to 2021. Following these patterns were each racial or ethnic group's trends in business earnings. From 2019 to 2020 business earnings dropped by 28 percent for Black business owners, which was considerably greater than the loss of 15 percent for white business owners. Asian business owners lost 21 percent and Latinx business owners lost 19 percent in the pandemic. In the economic recovery from 2020 to 2021, Black business earnings mostly returned to prepandemic levels, and Latinx business earnings returned to prepandemic levels. Asian business earnings, however, did not rebound in 2021. In contrast to these patterns, there is some evidence that white business earnings were higher in 2021 than prepandemic levels.

Prior to the pandemic there appears to be either a flat or slightly increasing upward trend in business earnings for all groups. The fluctuations from year to year make it difficult, however, to see a clear pattern. I next estimate regressions that control for preexisting trends for each group.

Disproportionate COVID-19 Impacts by Race and Ethnicity

To further explore the rebounds in business earnings in 2021 by race, I estimate regressions similar to equation (3.1). The regressions build on the underlying patterns displayed in figure 8.2 by controlling for pre-COVID-19 trends and owner, business, and geographic characteristics. Table 8.1 reports estimates from equations (3.1) and (3.2). Specification 1 starts with a stripped-down model that includes no additional variables except the race/ethnicity indicators and their interactions with 2020 or 2021 (i.e., the "Post-COVID-19 2020" or "Post-COVID-19 2021" by race interactions). The loss in business earnings for all groups in 2020 is captured by the "Post-COVID-19" coefficient, which was roughly –15 percent. As discussed in chapter 4, Black business owners disproportionately lost roughly 12 percent more than white business owner earnings in 2020, whereas estimates are not statistically significant for relative Latinx and Asian business earnings. Estimates of the business earnings effects in 2021 indicate that the main effect was a full recovery to 2019 levels (found in "Post-COVID-19 2021"). For both Black business earnings and Latinx business earnings there is no evidence of a differential rebound.

Table 8.1
Regressions for Log Business Earnings, Current Population Survey, 2015–2021

Explanatory variables	(1)	(2)	(3)	(4)
Post-COVID-19 2020	–0.146 (0.028)	–0.166 (0.026)	–0.166 (0.026)	–0.139 (0.025)
Post-COVID-19 2020 × Black	–0.121 (0.082)	–0.131 (0.076)	–0.136 (0.077)	–0.143 (0.073)
Post-COVID-19 2020 × Latinx	–0.035 (0.063)	–0.029 (0.057)	–0.023 (0.059)	–0.026 (0.056)
Post-COVID-19 2020 × Asian	–0.053 (0.094)	–0.071 (0.087)	–0.083 (0.088)	–0.092 (0.084)
Post-COVID-19 2021	–0.004 (0.028)	–0.049 (0.030)	–0.050 (0.030)	0.004 (0.025)
Post-COVID-19 2021 × Black	–0.016 (0.080)	0.014 (0.087)	0.016 (0.087)	0.003 (0.072)
Post-COVID-19 2021 × Latinx	–0.017 (0.061)	–0.045 (0.065)	–0.044 (0.065)	–0.050 (0.054)
Post-COVID-19 2021 × Asian	–0.200 (0.092)	–0.174 (0.099)	–0.171 (0.099)	–0.189 (0.083)
Main controls	No	Yes	Yes	Yes
Industry controls	No	Yes	Yes	Yes
Time trend	No	Yes	Yes	Yes
Pre-2019 interactions	No	No	Yes	No
Full 2015–2019 interactions	No	No	No	Yes
Sample years	2019–2021	2015–2021	2015–2021	2015–2021
Sample size	18,357	46,498	46,498	46,498

Notes: Author's calculations from compiled annual Current Population Survey microdata. Main controls include female, age, education, region, and central city status indicator variables. Coefficient estimates are reported with standard errors in parentheses.

The coefficient on Asian business earnings, however, is large, negative, and statistically significant. Asian business earnings are substantially lower in 2021 than in 2019. Asian business earnings did not rebound to 2019 levels.

Specification 2 reports regression estimates that include a time trend, and controls for owner, business, and geographic characteristics. Inclusion of the time trend and controls does not change the conclusions. Additionally, the coefficients from specification 3, which focuses the estimation of COVID-19 effects on using 2019 as the comparison year instead of the average, detrended level over 2015–2018, are similar. Finally, specification 4 reports estimates from an event-study regression and also finds similar estimates. Overall, the estimates are robust across different estimation strategies. In 2021, Asian business earnings suffered a substantially larger loss than white business earnings. The rebound did not occur for Asian business owners. In contrast, Black and Latinx business earnings rebounded in 2021. The rebound in the recovery from the pandemic was strong for business earnings for most groups except Asian business earnings, which remained low relative to prepandemic levels.

What Caused the Disproportionate Impacts in the Pandemic?

This section explores the underlying causes of why Black, Latinx, and Asian business owners experienced different patterns of losses and recovery in the pandemic. I take a two-step approach to answering this question. First, did racial differences in business, owner, and geographic characteristics exist prior to COVID-19 that might explain differential recoveries in 2021? Second, what is the interaction between prepandemic business, owner, and geographic characteristics and pandemic-induced business earnings losses? Using the decomposition technique used in chapter 4, I estimate direct contributions from racial differences in prepandemic characteristics to the change in the racial business earnings gap from 2019 to 2021. The technique directly answers, for example, how much of the lack of recovery in Asian business earnings (relative to white business earnings) can be attributed to the concentration of Asian businesses inindustries slowest to recover in the pandemic.

Chapter 4 provided a detailed comparison of owner and business characteristics by race prior to the pandemic. The highlights from that analysis are that Latinx are the least educated group. Blacks also have relatively low levels of education. Asians have the highest levels of education. Racial differences in education levels are large and might have placed less educated groups at a higher risk of business earnings rebounds in 2021.

Another potentially important factor contributing to differential rebounds in business earnings by race is industry. The analysis in chapter 4 indicates that industry distributions differ across racial and ethnic groups. For example, Latinx business owners are more concentrated in Construction than white business owners. Black business owners are less concentrated in Construction but more concentrated in Transportation and Other Services. Asian business owners have the most dissimilar industry distribution, with much higher concentrations in Wholesale and Retail Trade, Leisure and Hospitality, and Other Services and a much lower concentration in Construction. All minority groups have fewer business owners in Agriculture than whites. These industry differences might have contributed to why some groups experienced stronger or weaker business earnings rebounds in 2021.

Table 8.2 reports estimates for the COVID-19 decomposition for the 2019 to 2021 change. The white-Black gap in mean log business earnings

Table 8.2
Decomposition of Changes in Log Business Earnings Gaps, 2019 to 2021

Mean levels and contributions to losses	Black-white	Latinx-white	Asian-white
Mean levels:			
Minority log business income 2021	10.207	10.154	10.437
Minority log bus. income 2019	10.229	10.177	10.645
Minority loss	−0.022	−0.023	−0.209
White log business income 2021	10.499	10.499	10.499
White log business income 2019	10.510	10.510	10.510
White loss	−0.012	−0.012	−0.012
Minority disproportionate loss	−0.010	−0.012	−0.197
Contributions to disproportionate losses from 2019 racial differences in:			
Education	0.001	0.002	−0.002
	(0.005)	(0.011)	(0.009)
Industry	−0.001	0.005	−0.010
	(0.001)	(0.003)	(0.008)
Region	−0.014	−0.014	0.001
	(0.013)	(0.013)	(0.001)
Central city status	0.003	0.003	0.003
	(0.015)	(0.015)	(0.015)
Age	0.004	0.004	0.002
	(0.006)	(0.006)	(0.003)
Female	0.003	−0.003	0.006
	(0.002)	(0.001)	(0.003)
All included variables	−0.005	−0.003	0.000
	(0.004)	(0.003)	(0.000)

Notes: All decomposition specifications use pooled coefficient estimates from the full sample of all races (and include a full set of race dummies in the regressions). Sampling weights are used in all specifications. Standard errors in parentheses.

changed only slightly from 2019 to 2021, which is consistent with most business, owner, and geographic characteristics not placing Black businesses at a higher or lower risk of experiencing a stronger recovery in 2021. Of all the characteristics, a less favorable regional distribution is the only one appearing to contribute to a weaker recovery for Black business earnings, but this was offset by other factors.

Latinx owners experienced a disproportionate business earnings loss in 2020 and the largest cause of this loss was prepandemic industry differences. For the change from 2019 to 2021 in business earnings, the only factor contributing to a slightly weaker recovery for Latinx business owners is a less favorable regional distribution.

The largest contributing factor to disproportionate losses in 2020 for Asian business earnings was prepandemic industry differences. Asian businesses are concentrated in Leisure and Hospitality and Other Services but less concentrated in Agriculture and Construction. Interestingly, higher education levels among Asian business owners relative to white business owners shielded them from larger disproportionate business earnings losses. Dissimilar to other groups, Asian business earnings did not recover in 2021. The Asian-white gap was –0.20 log points. The industry composition placed Asian businesses at a higher risk of earnings losses from 2019 to 2021. The remaining gap is due to other unobservable factors, which might include consumer discrimination against Asian-owned stores, restaurants, and other businesses (Amuedo-Dorantes, Borra, and Wang 2024; Huang et al. 2023; Ong, Cheng, and Ong 2021).

Differential Exposure to COVID-19 and Policy Responses

As in chapter 4, I examine whether geographic differences in exposure to COVID-19 and state policies contributed to differential business earnings recovery by race, but in this case for 2021. The analysis in chapter 4 found that racial differences in exposure to state-level COVID-19 cases, business restrictions, and mask mandates did not contribute to changes in racial inequality in business earnings from 2019 to 2020. Table 8.3 explores the contributions of these state-level differences to racial inequality in business earnings in the second year of the pandemic, 2021. The decomposition equations that are estimated here are described in chapter 4, appendix 4.B.

Table 8.3

Decomposition of Changes in Log Business Earnings Gaps: Additional State COVID-19 Cases and Restriction Variables, 2019 to 2021

Mean levels and contributions to losses	Black-white	Latinx-white	Asian-white
Mean levels:			
Minority log business income 2021	10.207	10.154	10.437
Minority log business income 2019	10.229	10.177	10.645
Minority loss	–0.022	–0.023	–0.209
White log business income 2021	10.499	10.499	10.499
White log business income 2019	10.510	10.510	10.510
White loss	–0.012	–0.012	–0.012
Minority disproportionate loss	–0.010	–0.012	–0.197
Contributions to disproportionate losses from 2019 racial differences in:			
Education	0.001	0.003	–0.002
	(0.005)	(0.011)	(0.009)
Industry	–0.001	0.005	–0.010
	(0.001)	(0.003)	(0.008)
Region	–0.012	–0.012	0.002
	(0.013)	(0.013)	(0.003)
Central City Status	0.003	0.004	0.004
	(0.016)	(0.018)	(0.019)
Age	0.004	0.004	0.002
	(0.006)	(0.006)	(0.003)
Female	0.003	–0.003	0.006
	(0.002)	(0.001)	(0.003)
COVID cases per capita. in 2021	0.000	0.001	0.003
	(0.004)	(0.009)	(0.042)
Early state business restrictions	–0.005	–0.004	–0.005
	(0.006)	(0.005)	(0.006)
Mask mandates (Dec 2020)	–0.001	–0.001	0.003
	(0.002)	(0.002)	(0.007)
PPP loans per establishment in 2021	0.002	0.000	–0.001
	(0.007)	(0.001)	(0.004)
All included variables	–0.005	–0.004	0.002
	(0.005)	(0.004)	(0.002)

Notes: Author's calculations from compiled annual Current Population Survey microdata. Standard errors in parentheses.

State variation in COVID-19 cases and policy variables did not contribute to changes from 2019 to 2021. Racial differences in exposure to state-level COVID-19 cases, business restrictions, mask mandates, and PPP loan receipt did not contribute to changes in racial inequality in business earnings. The findings hold for all racial groups. Differential exposure to policies, at least as measured at the state level, do not appear to have contributed to racial differences in earnings losses for the 2019 to 2020 or the 2019 to 2021 comparisons.

9 The Paycheck Protection Program in the Second Year of the Pandemic: The Third Round

The Paycheck Protection Program (PPP) provided nearly half a billion dollars to small businesses in the first several months of the pandemic. The goal was to help small businesses "weather the storm" and retain their employees instead of laying them off in the pandemic. Small businesses, however, continued to struggle throughout 2020, and by the end of the year business activity remained lower than prepandemic levels. The effects of COVID-19 on business owners by race were also uneven during 2020. The losses to business activity were much higher among Black, Latinx and Asian business owners in the first few months. By the end of the year, Latinx business activity had essentially fully recovered from pre-pandemic levels, but Black business owners ended the year nearly 10 percent lower than 2019 levels and Asian business activity recovered the least, ending the year at a roughly 20 percent lower level than in 2019.

In light of these concerns, the PPP was restarted in January 2021. President Biden's administration vowed to provide more assistance to help small businesses recover. The administration was also aware of the inequities in the first round of rolling out PPP funds and was determined to make substantial changes to address these inequities. The program included several major changes, including a head start for community lenders, a two-week exclusivity period for very small employers, an expansion of loans to sole proprietors and independent contractors, and the possibility of second-draw loans by small businesses with a continued need for assistance. This chapter focuses on the rebooted and revised PPP, which ran from January 2021 to May 2021.

The Reboot

In the reboot of the program there was a strong emphasis on helping eligible borrowers in underserved and disadvantaged communities. To promote access for smaller lenders and their customers, the SBA imposed some restrictions on lenders. One restriction was that the 2021 PPP had to include a head start for applications through Community Development Financial Institutions (CDFIs) at the beginning of the third round in January 2021 before more broadly opening up the program to other lenders. Another new restriction the PPP imposed was a two-week exclusivity application period for businesses with fewer than twenty employees in February 2021. Additionally, part of the funds from the PPP were set aside for low- or moderate-income businesses, and some exclusionary restrictions were eliminated (U.S. SBA 2021a). Another major change was that small businesses that were continuing to struggle in the pandemic were allowed to obtain a second loan. In this third and final round of funding, PPP loans were also more focused on sole proprietors, self-employed individuals, and independent contractors without employees than on employer businesses. There was an emphasis on helping to preserve the owner's job.

During the third round of the PPP, a total of $278 billion through 6.7 million loans was provided to small businesses from January 2021 to May 2021. Table 9.1 reports numbers of loans, total dollars, and number of different lenders for 2021 and the total for both 2020 and 2021. Over the two years, the PPP provided nearly 12 million loans for $800 billion from more than 5,000 lenders. The PPP covered two different presidential administrations, time periods with and without social distancing restrictions in place, and time periods with and without vaccines for COVID-19. The PPP was by far the largest program ever providing assistance to small businesses.

Table 9.1
Summary of PPP Funding, Third Round

Year	No. of loans approved	Net dollars disbursed	No. of lenders	Dates
2021	6,681,929	$277,700,108,079	5,242	Jan. 2021–May 2021
Total	11,823,594	$799,832,866,520	5,467	April. 3, 2020–May 2021

Source: U.S. Small Business Administration (2021b) PPP report.

The numerous changes to the program led to different types of lenders. The SBA (2021b) reports that more than 850 different credit unions provided nearly two million loans to small businesses, and more than four thousand different banks and savings and loan institutions provided nearly two million loans. There were also forty-one different fintechs providing 1.2 million loans, forty-seven different farm credit lenders providing 36,000 loans, and thirty-four different microlenders providing 530,000 loans.

Similar to the analysis presented in chapter 5, I downloaded and compiled PPP loan data for 2021. The top fifteen lenders in the third and final round of the PPP in 2021 were somewhat different from those in the first two rounds (both in 2020). However, large, well-known national banks were still represented. Table 9.2 lists the top fifteen lenders in total dollars in the third round of the PPP, covering from January to May 2021. JPMorgan Chase continued to provide the most total dollars, at $12.9 billion in 2021, and Bank of America provided $8.9 billion in loans.

Table 9.2
Top Fifteen Lenders in Total Dollars in the Third Round of the PPP, 2021

Rank	Originating lender	Total dollars disbursed	Total no. of loans
1	JPMorgan Chase Bank, National Association	$ 12,932,625,259	162,911
2	Bank of America, National Association	$ 8,934,348,167	147,547
3	Harvest Small Business Finance, LLC	$ 6,936,199,669	402,965
4	Prestamos CDFI, LLC	$ 6,823,260,998	443,855
5	Cross River Bank	$ 6,512,122,597	285,821
6	Capital Plus Financial, LLC	$ 6,213,716,102	395,359
7	Itria Ventures LLC	$ 4,799,555,410	169,737
8	PNC Bank, National Association	$ 4,325,443,971	45,441
9	Benworth Capital	$ 4,200,937,136	310,443
10	Manufacturers and Traders Trust Company	$ 3,969,296,873	36,708
11	BSD Capital, LLC dba Lendistry	$ 3,888,503,916	203,207
12	Fountainhead SBF LLC	$ 3,755,421,161	269,466
13	TD Bank, National Association	$ 3,716,997,261	47,429
14	Customers Bank	$ 3,699,568,691	180,896
15	Truist Bank	$ 3,656,915,878	37,511

Notes: Author's calculations from compiled loan microdata provided by the U.S. Small Business Administration (posted on October 11, 2024). The third round of the PPP covers January 21 to May 21, 2021.

The third-ranked lending institution is Harvest Small Business Finance. Attesting to the shift in the provision and outreach of the rebooted 2021 PPP, Harvest was a newcomer to the lending scene and is not a large bank. Instead, Harvest Small Business Finance is a Small Business Lending Company that originates, owns, sells, and services small business loans in accordance with the SBA's 7(a) loan program. Harvest provided $6.9 billion in loans to small businesses in 2021. Additional evidence of the wider range of types of financial institutions involved in 2021 PPP lending is provided by Prestamos, a CDFI, which provided $6.8 billion in loans (ranked no. 4), and Cross River Bank, a fintech, which provided $6.5 billion in loans (ranked no. 5). The sixth-ranked lender in total dollars disbursed was another CDFI, Capital Plus Financial ($6.2 billion), and the seventh-ranked lender was a fintech, Itria Ventures ($4.8 billion).

Ranking the number of loans provided by each bank shows some similarities to the total dollar ranking but also some dissimilarities. Table 9.3 reports the top fifteen lenders in number of loans for the third round of the

Table 9.3
Top Fifteen Lenders in Number of Loans in the Third Round of the PPP, 2021

Rank	Originating lender	Total no. of loans	Total dollars disbursed
1	Prestamos CDFI, LLC	443,855	6,823,260,998
2	Harvest Small Business Finance, LLC	402,965	6,936,199,669
3	Capital Plus Financial, LLC	395,359	6,213,716,102
4	Benworth Capital	310,443	4,200,937,136
5	Cross River Bank	285,821	6,512,122,597
6	Fountainhead SBF LLC	269,466	3,755,421,161
7	BSD Capital, LLC dba Lendistry	203,207	3,888,503,916
8	Customers Bank	180,896	3,699,568,691
9	Itria Ventures LLC	169,737	4,799,555,410
10	JPMorgan Chase Bank, National Association	162,911	12,932,625,259
11	Bank of America, National Association	147,547	8,934,348,167
12	Wells Fargo Bank, National Association	87,699	3,497,289,331
13	Square Capital, LLC	72,564	681,844,008
14	Readycap Lending, LLC	72,029	2,258,955,011
15	U.S. Bank, National Association	66,792	3,228,098,076

Notes: Author's calculations from compiled loan microdata provided by the U.S. Small Business Administration (posted on October 11, 2024). The third round of the PPP covers January 21 to May 21, 2021.

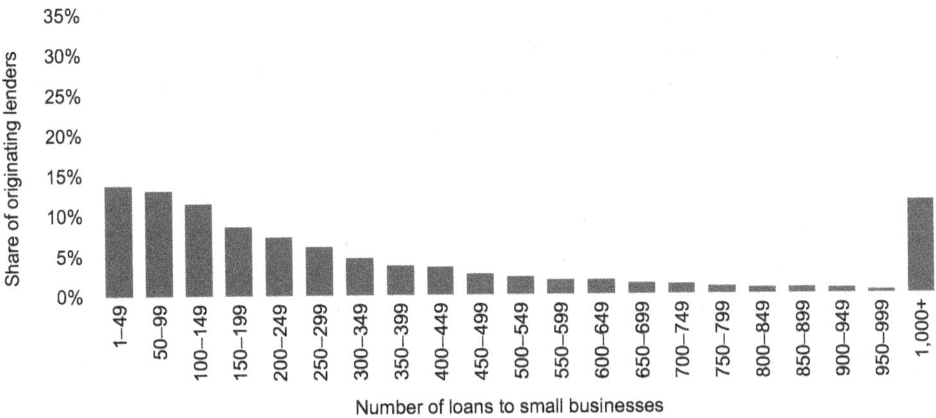

Figure 9.1
Distribution of number of PPP loans by lenders: third round.

PPP. Prestamos led the way, with 443,855 loans, followed by Harvest Small Business Finance, with 402,965 loans, and Capital Plus, with 395,359 loans. There were several newcomers to the top fifteen list compared to the 2020 lists, and these financial institutions were not the standard large banks.

Figure 9.1 displays the distribution of the number of lenders that provided different numbers of loans to small businesses in round three. The distribution is spread more than in the first two rounds in 2020 at the bottom of the distribution but not at the top. For example, 14 percent of all lenders provided one to forty-nine loans to small businesses, compared with 31–34 percent in earlier rounds. But a larger percentage of lenders provided one thousand or more loans to small businesses (12 percent, compared with 6–7 percent in the earlier rounds).

Second-Draw Loans in 2021

A major change to the PPP in 2021 was allowing small businesses to apply for a second loan, referred to as second-draw loans. Eligible borrowers that had previously received a PPP loan in 2020 or 2021 could now apply for a second-draw loan with the same general terms as the terms of their first-draw loan. The second-draw PPP loans could be used to help fund payroll costs, including benefits. The loans could also be used to help pay mortgage interest, rent, utilities, worker protection costs related to COVID-19, uninsured property damage costs caused by looting or vandalism during 2020, and certain supplier costs and expenses for operations. For most borrowers, the maximum loan amount of a second-draw loan was two and a half times average monthly payroll costs as measured in 2019 or 2020. The maximum amount that any small business could receive was capped at $2 million. Because restaurants and hotels were continuing to struggle at the end of 2020, which was before vaccines became available, exceptions were made for these businesses. In the Accommodation and Food Services sector, the maximum second-draw loan amount was higher, at three and a half times average monthly payroll costs, although with the same $2 million cap.

For a small business to be eligible for a second-draw PPP loan the business had to have received a first-draw loan. The small business also had to have used the full amount of the first-draw loan for its intended purposes. The small business also had to remain under 300 employees, and had to have experienced revenue losses. The small business had to demonstrate that it lost 25 percent or more in gross receipts between comparable quarters in 2019 to 2020. For example, it could show revenue losses from the second quarter of 2019 (April, May, June) to the second quarter of 2020 (April, May, June). Given the timing of social distancing restrictions that shut down nonessential businesses, the second quarter of 2020 included the most difficult months of the pandemic for small businesses.

Table 9.4 reports aggregate first- and second-draw loan numbers in 2021. During the third round of the PPP there were 3.8 million first-draw loans and 2.9 million second-draw loans. The total amount provided in loans, however, skewed toward second-draw loans. The total provided in second-draw loans was $209 million, compared with $69 million in first-draw loans. The number of different lenders providing first-draw and second-draw loans was similar. More than five thousand different financial institutions provided each type of loan to small businesses in 2021.

Table 9.4
First- and Second-Draw PPP Loans in 2021

Draw	No. of loans approved	Net dollars disbursed	Average loan size (in dollars)	Total no. of lenders
First-draw loans	3,768,309	68,915,276,574	18,288	5,168
Second-draw loans	2,913,620	208,784,831,505	71,658	5,216

Source: U.S. Small Business Administration (2021b) PPP Report.

Did PPP Funds Get Disbursed Evenly to Minority Communities in 2021?

Were PPP funds from the new revised program disbursed evenly to minority communities in the United States? One of the goals for the new administration was to address inequities: "Putting equity at the center of its policies and programs, the Biden-Harris Administration launched a comprehensive plan to engage small businesses and nonprofits, focusing on building trust in underserved communities" (U.S. SBA 2021a, 1). Using data on the universe of PPP loans in 2021, I explore whether PPP funds were evenly distributed or not using administrative microdata covering the universe of PPP loans to small businesses. The analysis of 2021 PPP loans builds on the analysis of 2020 PPP loans presented in chapter 5. More details on the loan data are provided in chapter 5. A separate analysis of 2021 PPP loan data is important because of the major changes that were made to the program, such as the implementation of second-draw loans and the emphasis on small businesses with employees.

The U.S. Senate was particularly interested in what was happening in this round of the PPP. The Senate reached out to me to find out more, which prompted early work on studying the 2021 PPP. The U.S. Senate was concerned at the time about the economic impacts of the pandemic and how these impacts had been especially severe for small businesses, workers, and communities of color, a concern that in part grew out of findings early in the pandemic (e.g., Couch, Fairlie and Xu 2020a, 2020b; Cowan 2020; Fairlie 2020a, 2020b; Montenovo et al. 2020). Findings from the original analysis of these patterns as they emerged for the 2021 PPP rounds were presented in testimony before the U.S. House of Representatives Committee on Small Business, Subcommittee on Oversight, Investigations, and Regulations, on March 16, 2022 (Fairlie 2022). The analysis and further details are reported in Fairlie and Fossen (2022c, 2022d) and noted by Senator Ben Cardin (Cardin 2022), then chair or the Senate Small Business and Entrepreneurship Committee.

Three main questions are explored here. First, did PPP funds in the rebooted program in 2021 get disproportionately disbursed to minority communities as intended or did the program struggle with equitable loan disbursement? Second, how did the disbursement of second-draw loans compare with the disbursement of first-loan draws? Demand for second-draw loans was likely to be higher in disadvantaged communities as small business continued to struggle, but second-draw loan receipt was conditional on receiving a prior loan, which might have been from the unequally distributed first round of the PPP. Third, did disbursement to minority communities differ between loans to small businesses with employees and loans to businesses without employees (nonemployers)? Nonemployer businesses were increasingly targeted in 2021, which has implications for the equitable disbursement of loans to owners of different groups.

The program in 2021 distinguished between businesses with employees and businesses without employees. Business entities without employees include sole proprietors, self-employed individuals, consultants, and independent contractors. Results are presented for employer businesses first and then for nonemployer businesses. Average loan numbers per business in the zip code or county are examined. The raw relationship between PPP loan receipt and minority share of the population without controlling for other factors is examined because the goal is to capture only the racial composition of the community and not to capture other correlated characteristics such as income levels or population density. The number of loans per business (either employer or nonemployer) implicitly controls for differences in business density across communities.

I begin with PPP loan receipt per employer business establishment by minority share of the population at the zip code level. Figure 9.2 displays the relationship in the third round of the PPP in 2021 for businesses receiving their first draw PPP loan.[1] Loan receipt per business can be interpreted as the percentage of employer businesses receiving PPP loans in each zip code, but it is important to note that not all employer businesses qualify or apply for loans. There is a positive relationship between loan receipt per employer business and the minority share of the population across zip codes in the United States. For first draw loans, moving from the first quartile in minority share of the population (16 percent minority) to the third quartile (59 percent minority), loan receipt increases from 0.06 to 0.09 PPP loans to employer businesses per employer business in the zip code.

Figure 9.3 displays the relationship in the third round of the PPP in 2021 for second-draw loans. Small businesses could not receive a second-draw loan unless they had previously received a first-draw loan. For second-draw PPP loans there is evidence of a positive relationship between loan receipt and minority share of the population, but it is less pronounced than the positive relationship for first-draw loans. Second-draw loans were conditional

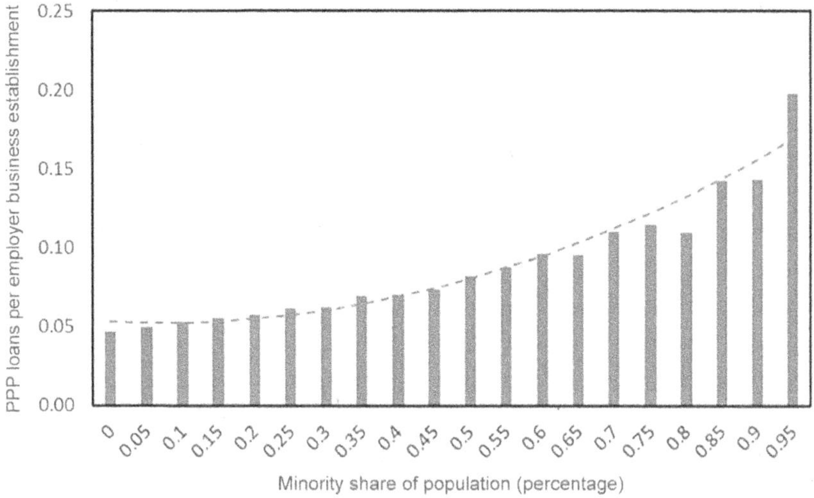

Figure 9.2
Number of PPP loans per employer business establishment by minority share of the population in 2021: first-draw loans in third round of the PPP.

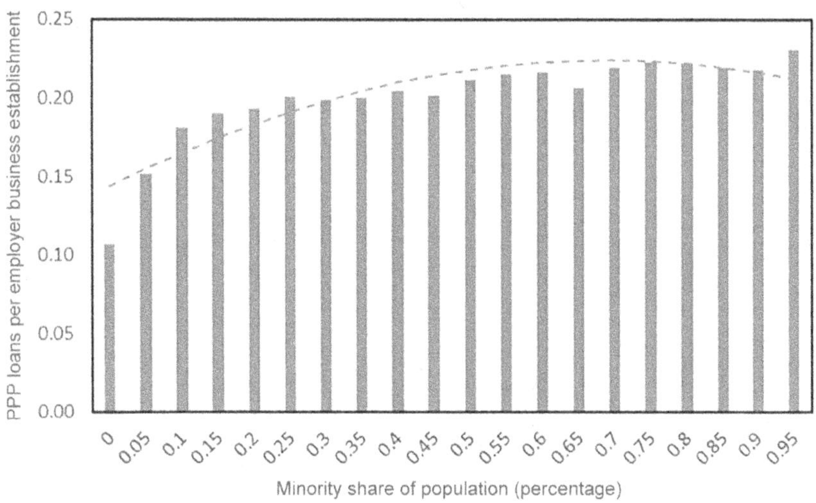

Figure 9.3
Number of PPP loans per employer business establishment by minority share of the population in 2021: second-draw loans in third round of the PPP.

on receiving a first draw PPP loan *and* conditional on needing additional aid. The analysis in chapter 5 reveled a negative relationship in the first round in 2020 and a positive relationship in the second round in 2020.

Another method of measuring the level of receipt of PPP funds is to compare the number of PPP loans per business with the minority share of businesses in a community. The minority share of businesses by zip code is used on the *x*-axis instead of the minority share of the population by zip code. Figure 9.4 displays the relationship between PPP loans per employer business and the minority share of businesses in zip codes for first-draw loans in the third round of the PPP (2021). Similar to the findings from using the minority share of the population, there is a positive relationship between loan receipt and minority business share in the third round of the PPP.

There is also a positive relationship for second-draw loans. Figure 9.5 displays the relationship between PPP loans per employer business and the minority share of businesses in zip codes for second-draw loans in the third round of the PPP. The positive relationship is found for both first-draw loans and second-draw loans in 2021, consistent with the stated goals of the rebooted program. Although eligibility for second-draw loans required

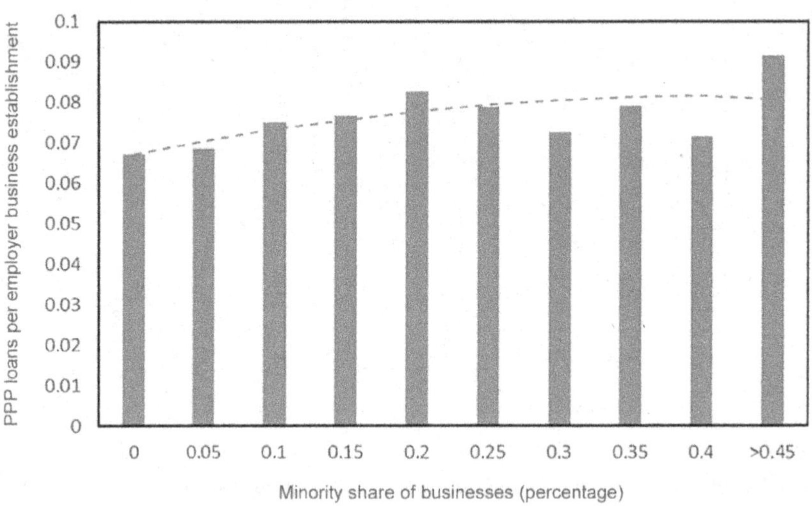

Figure 9.4
Number of PPP loans per employer business establishment by minority share of businesses in 2021: first-draw loans in third round of PPP.

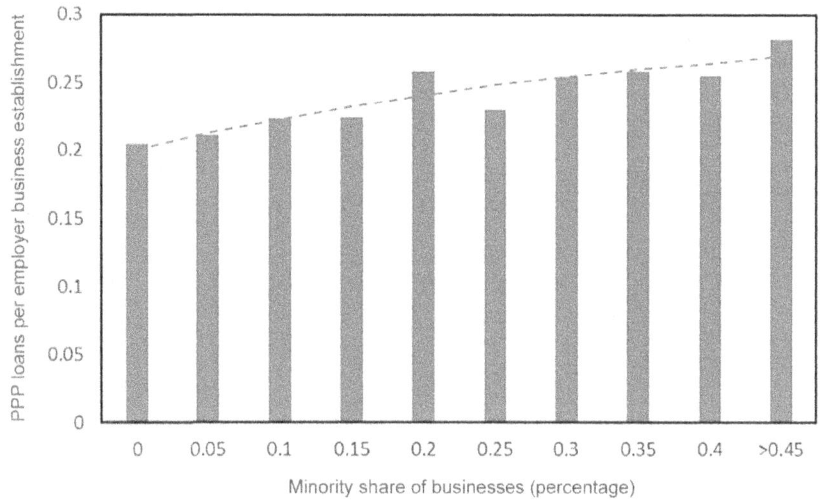

Figure 9.5
Number of PPP loans per employer business establishment by minority share of businesses in 2021: second-draw loans in third round of the PPP.

receiving a first-draw loan, that conditionality does not appear to have affected the positive relationship between PPP loan receipt per business and the minority share of businesses in the geographic area.

Business Owners Without Employees

The 2021 reboot of the PPP emphasized supporting sole proprietorships, self-employed individuals, and independent contractors with no employees. The goal was to provide PPP loans to these businesses without employees and possibly save owners' jobs. The partial shift in emphasis from employees to owners was a major change in the program. Were loans to these nonemployer business entities disbursed evenly to minority communities?

To explore this question using the PPP loan microdata, I classified all self-employed individuals and independent contractors as nonemployer businesses, as well as sole proprietorships that reported only one person working in the business. To normalize the number of PPP loans and loan amounts to nonemployer businesses, I used data from the 2018 Nonemployer Statistics (NES) series provided by the U.S. Census Bureau. These data are available only at the county level, which is a larger geographic area

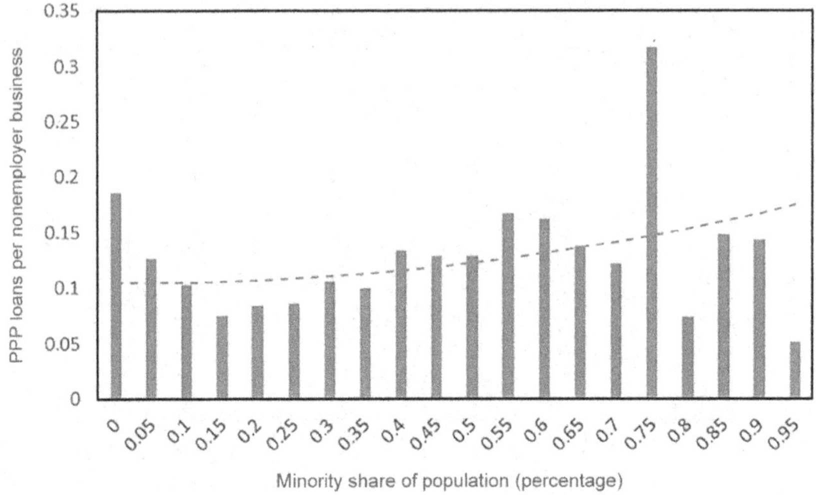

Figure 9.6
Number of PPP loans per nonemployer business by minority share of the population in 2021: first-draw loans in third round of the PPP.

than the zip code areas used in the previous figures. The definition of nonemployer business entities is overly inclusive for nonemployer businesses eligible for PPP funds.[2]

Figure 9.6 displays the relationship between the number of PPP loans to nonemployer businesses per nonemployer business by minority share of the population in counties. The number of PPP loans per nonemployer business has a positive relationship with the minority share of the population for first-draw loans.

Figure 9.7 displays the relationship for nonemployer businesses for second-draw loans. There is also a positive relationship with the minority share of the population. The positive relationship is also strong for second-draw loans, which might reflect continuing struggles to find work among minority independent contractors and small sole proprietors in the pandemic.

A similar analysis of nonemployer businesses in the two rounds in 2020 reveals that the relationship between nonemployer loans per nonemployer business in the county was essentially flat in the second round, but clearly negative in the first round. This pattern of results is similar to what was found for employer businesses in chapter 5. The PPP evolved over time

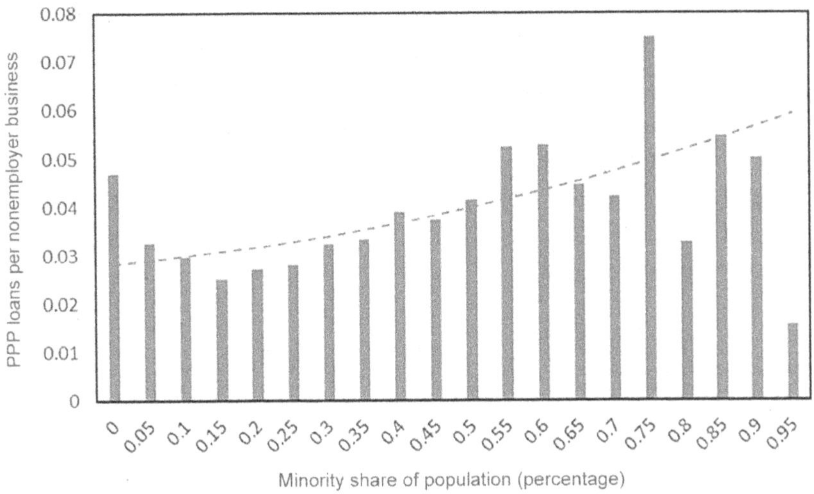

Figure 9.7
Number of PPP loans per nonemployer business by minority share of the population in 2021: second-draw loans in the third round of the PPP.

not just for employer businesses but also for much smaller, nonemployer businesses.

There is a clear evolution of PPP funding to minority communities across subsequent rounds of the PPP from a negative relationship in the first round in 2020 to the strong positive relationship in the rebooted program (i.e., the third round) in 2021. Why did the slope of the relationship change over time? Applying for PPP loans very early in the pandemic favored having long-established relationships with banks, which minority businesses were less likely to have (Mills and Battisto 2020). Minority-owned businesses also tend to be smaller than nonminority-owned businesses (Fairlie and Robb 2008; U.S. Census Bureau 2016), and smaller businesses often took longer to complete the required paperwork owing to a lack of resources and experience. An analysis of new Census Bureau data, presented in the next chapter, indicates that the smallest small businesses received PPP funds later than midsize small businesses. To counter this pattern, the 2021 PPP included the fourteen-day exclusivity application period for businesses with fewer than twenty employees.

Another major change from 2020 to 2021 in the program was a shift in the types of financial institutions providing loans. In particular, there was an increase in the involvement of fintech lenders, which resulted in more loans to minority-owned businesses (Fei and Yang 2021; Howell et al. 2021; Liu and Parilla 2020; Mills 2024). In 2021, the SBA also explicitly promoted involvement of CDFIs by providing a head start for applications through CDFIs at the beginning of the third round in January 2021. The rankings of lenders by total dollars in table 9.1 or total loans in table 9.2 show the rising importance of fintechs and CDFIs in providing loans to small businesses in the third round of the PPP.

10 New Evidence on PPP Receipt and Outcomes for Small Businesses

Over the three rounds of providing funds, the Paycheck Protection Program (PPP) provided twelve million loans to small businesses totaling $800 billion and involving 5,500 different financial institutions providing those loans. The Small Business Administration (SBA) provided information on the program and help for small businesses through sixty-eight district offices across the country. The SBA also organized help through local organizations such as SCORE mentors, Women's Business Centers, Small Business Development Centers, and Veterans Business Outreach Centers. For the PPP, financial institutions handled the actual loan applications and would submit them to the SBA for approval. Financial institutions also provided information and assistance to small businesses in applying for PPP loans. Even with the assistance from the SBA, its partners, and financial institutions, many small businesses that were eligible for PPP loans did not apply for loans or ultimately did not receive loans.

What percentage of eligible small businesses received PPP loans? How did loan receipt differ across the three rounds of the PPP, and how did it differ between first-draw loans and second-draw loans? Did the smallest of small businesses receive funds, or was it primarily larger small businesses? Did the program satisfy its intended goal of helping small businesses retain employees? Did survival and job retention differ by whether small businesses received a PPP loan or when small businesses received their first PPP loan? The answers to all these questions are important in light of the unprecedented magnitude of government expenditures on aid to small businesses during the pandemic.

To help address these questions, a new, exciting administrative data source providing information on PPP loan receipt, survival, and job destruction among small businesses recently became available. The new data source, the Business Dynamics Statistics of SBA COVID Response recipients (BDS-SBA COVID) database, links data on the universe of employer businesses to data on the universe of small businesses receiving PPP loans. In this chapter, I compile and analyze tabulations from the BDS-SBA COVID data to examine the percentage of small businesses receiving PPP loans. The data are also used to examine the relationships between PPP receipt and timing of PPP loan receipt and business survival and job destruction.

Some Measurement Issues

The intention of the BDS-SBA COVID data is to capture all employer businesses receiving PPP loans. However, not all PPP loans are successfully matched to the U.S. Census Bureau's employer business microdata as there is some slippage in matching. To measure PPP loan receipt by a business, there must be a positive match with the loan data. Otherwise the business will appear not to have received a PPP loan. The U.S. Census Bureau (2025) provides more details on the methodology of creating the new data source and these matching issues.[1] A key takeaway from the Census Bureau's report is that with regard to examining PPP loan receipt rates, the reported percentages are likely underreporting receipt rates because of the nonperfect matching between the datasets (U.S. Census Bureau 2025). Another limitation is that nonemployer businesses are not captured in the data because they are not represented in the BDS data. Even in light of these concerns, the BDS-SBA COVID data provide the most comprehensive source of data available on PPP loan receipt among small businesses and represent an extremely useful new source of information.

In addition to PPP receipt, the timing of firms receiving their first PPP loans is potentially important. As shown in chapter 5, for example, both the types of financial institutions involved in making loans and the relationship between loan receipt per business and the minority share of the population changed markedly over the first two rounds of the PPP, both of which occurred in 2020. The BDS-SBA COVID tabulated data distinguish between loans made under the CARES Act and loans made under the subsequent Paycheck Protection Program and Health Care Enhancement Act (U.S. Census Bureau 2025). "Early" first-draw loans are defined as first-time PPP loans made between March 27 and April 23, 2020, and "later" first-draw loans are defined as first-time PPP loans made between April 24, 2020, and May 2021, aligning with the two acts. The timing in the data is roughly similar to the definitions used by the SBA in published reports on PPP expenditures, noted in chapter 5 as the first round of the PPP, from April 3, 2020 to April 16, 2020, and the second round of the PPP, from April 7, 2020, to August 8, 2020. The BDS-SBA COVID data also delineate second-draw PPP loans, all of which occurred in 2021 because they did not exist in 2020.

PPP Loan Receipt Rates by Small Businesses

Table 10.1 reports the percentage of small businesses receiving PPP loans during the length of the program. Among the small businesses qualifying for PPP loans and in scope in 2020, 25 percent received a PPP loan in the early part of the first year of the program.[2] The table entry "Total in scope in 2020" captures the number of businesses or establishments possibly receiving PPP funds in 2020. These are active firms with employment in March 2020 or exiting firms that had employment in March 2019 but not in 2020 (U.S. Census Bureau 2025). The percentage of small businesses receiving PPP funds in the later period that captures 2020 and 2021 increased to 41

Table 10.1
First PPP Loan Receipt by Employer Businesses

Timing of loan receipt	Firms		Establishments		Employees	
	No.	Percent	No.	Percent	No.	Percent
Received first PPP loan before April 24, 2020	1,343,928	25.2	1,886,789	26.2	41,159,842	31.0
Received first PPP loan on or after April 24, 2020	2,180,561	40.8	2,593,503	36.0	35,016,726	26.4
Received first PPP loan in either time period	3,524,489	66.0	4,480,292	62.2	76,176,568	57.4
Total in scope in 2020	5,340,972		7,206,748		132,737,246	

Notes: Author's compilation and analysis of tabulations of the BDS-SBA COVID data (U.S. Census Bureau 2025).

percent. Combining both time periods of the PPP, 66 percent of small businesses received PPP funding.

Firms often have multiple establishments with different physical locations. Common examples include chain restaurants, retail franchises, branch offices, and different factories. However, the BDS-SBA COVID data were created from firm-level matches with PPP loans and not from establishment-level matches with PPP loans. Thus measurement of separate establishment-level PPP loan receipt within firms is not possible. Instead, the businesses receiving PPP loans that have multiple establishments are repeated in the counts. For example, if a firm has three establishments, then the data record three establishments receiving PPP loans instead of tracking which (or all) of three establishments received separate PPP loans.[3] Using this method of counting, the total number of business establishments receiving PPP loans is 4.4 million. The reported percentage of establishments receiving PPP loans in the tabulations, however, is roughly similar to the percentage of businesses receiving PPP loans, which is consistent with the method of counting establishment receipt.

Table 10.1 also reports PPP loan receipt by the number of employees working at each business. If the business has multiple establishments, then employees at all establishments are included. In the "Employees" column, PPP receipt is weighted by the number of employees potentially affected or the number of jobs potentially saved by the PPP loan. In this case, the per employee receipt of PPP loans is higher in the early period but lower in the later period and in total. Small businesses with fewer employees might have higher loan receipt rates, which is explored directly with the data below.

Table 10.2 reports PPP loan receipt by the employment size of the business. PPP loan receipt at any point in time is 64 percent among small businesses with 1–9 employees. Note that the underlying business data used in the BDS-SBA COVID data include only employer businesses. Unfortunately, there is no similar information currently available for the large number of nonemployer businesses that received PPP loans in the revised program in 2021. The percentage of small business receiving PPP loans is higher for the 10–499 employees firm size, at 84 percent. The difference in receipt rates could reflect variation in the need for loans to retain employees, ability to apply for loans, survival rates, or other factors. For the qualifying businesses in the largest size class, 500+ employees, the receipt rate was much lower, at 36 percent.

Table 10.2
PPP Loan Receipt by Employer Businesses by Size of Firm

Timing of loan receipt by firm size	Firms		Establishments		Employees	
	No.	Percent	No.	Percent	No.	Percent
Firm size: 1–9 employees						
Received first PPP loan before April 24, 2020	1,012,144	21.5				
Received first PPP loan on or after April 24, 2020	1,983,643	42.2				
Received first PPP loan at any time	2,995,787	63.8	3,043,065	64.0	16,771,908	76.2
Total in scope in 2020	4,698,657		4,758,486		22,020,844	
Firm size: 10–499 employees						
Received first PPP loan before April 24, 2020	329,042	52.7				
Received first PPP loan on or after April 24, 2020	194,506	31.1				
Received first PPP loan at any time	523,548	83.8	870,007	79.7	31,293,870	78.4
Total in scope in 2020	624,770		1,091,986		39,897,297	
Firm size: 500+ employees						
Received first PPP loan before April 24, 2020	4,371	20.6				
Received first PPP loan on or after April 24, 2020	3,286	15.5				
Received first PPP loan at any time	7,657	36.1	567,220	41.8	28,110,790	39.7
Total in scope in 2020	21,203		1,356,276		70,819,105	

Notes: Author's compilation and analysis of tabulations of the BDS-SBA COVID data (U.S. Census Bureau 2025).

Shifting the focus to employees does not change PPP receipt rates with the exception of the smallest firms. The receipt rate is higher among small businesses with 1–9 employees when weighting by the number of employees. The general pattern of the highest PPP receipt rates among midsize firms also holds.

The newly released data can also help answer the question of which small businesses received first-draw loans in the early period, March through April 23, 2020, relative to receiving first-draw loans in the later period, April 24 through May 2021. However, there is no information on why small businesses first received PPP funds in either time period. Note that all businesses in the data existed in 2020 and were within the scope of businesses that could have received funds in the first time period of the program. Figure 10.1 displays how PPP receipt rates changed over time by firm size. The evidence is clear: larger small businesses were more likely to receive first-draw PPP loans before April 24, 2020, instead of receiving first-draw PPP loans later in 2020 or in 2021. Twenty-two percent of small businesses with 1–9 employees received first-draw PPP loans in early 2020, a figure that jumps to 42 percent receiving first-draw loans later in 2020 or in 2021. The pattern was opposite for small businesses with 10–499 employees: 53 percent of these small businesses received first-draw loans early in 2020, compared with 31 percent receiving first-draw loans later in 2020 or in 2021.

As noted earlier in the chapter, eligible small businesses were allowed to apply for a second-draw PPP loan in 2021. The first-draw loan could have been received in either 2020 or 2021. The loans had the same general terms as the terms of the small business's first-draw loan and could be used for payroll costs, mortgage interest, rent, utilities, and certain other expenditures. Small businesses that received second-draw loans were likely ones that continued to struggle in 2021. Table 10.3 reports second-draw PPP loan receipt. In total among employer small businesses, 42 percent of firms receiving first-draw PPP loans also received second-draw PPP loans. As a share of the total of all small businesses, 28 percent ultimately received two loans from the program.

Small businesses of 10–499 employees were slightly more likely to receive second-draw loans (conditional on receiving a first-draw loan) than were very small businesses. Unconditionally, small businesses of the middle size had the highest likelihood of receiving two PPP loans, with 38 percent

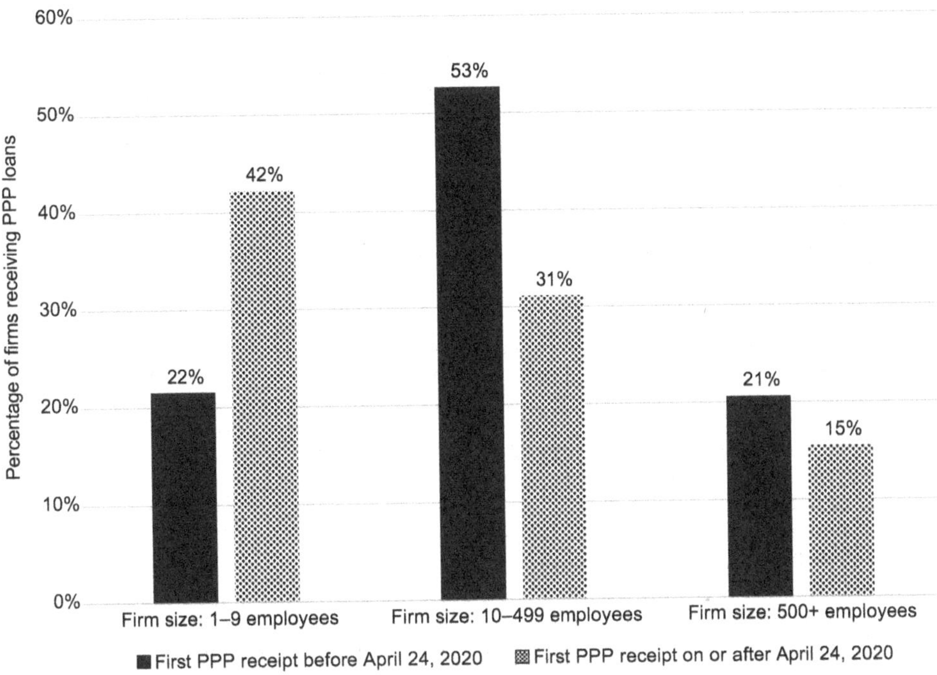

Figure 10.1
First-draw PPP loan receipt rates by firm employment size.

receiving both. The patterns of receipt of second-draw PPP loans are generally similar using establishment or employment counts.

Did PPP Loans Help Small Businesses Survive and Retain Employees?

Whether the PPP helped small businesses survive and retain employees during the pandemic is an important but very difficult question to answer. From a research perspective, it is a difficult question to answer because the program was widely available across the country. As discussed in chapter 2, there was not a natural control group, such as a region unaffected by COVID-19, to use in a comparison with the treatment group. Another major problem in trying to answer the question is that COVID-19 affected so many different aspects of the economy, health, education, and broader society that it is very difficult to isolate the effectiveness of one program among so many other new programs, regulations, and changes happening

Table 10.3

Second-Draw PPP Loan Receipt by Employer Businesses by Size of Firm

Timing of loan receipt by firm size	Firms		Establishments		Employees	
	No.	Percent of	No.	Percent of	No.	Percent of
Total: All firm sizes						
Received second-draw PPP loan	1,471,511		1,766,142		29,338,797	
Total received first PPP loan	3,524,489	42	4,480,292	39	76,176,568	39
Total in scope in 2020	5,340,972	28	7,206,748	25	132,737,246	22
Firm size: 1–9 employees						
Received second-draw PPP loan	1,234,878		1,254,717		7,435,383	
Total received first PPP loan	2,995,787	41	3,043,065	41	16,771,908	44
Total in scope in 2020	4,698,657	26	4,758,486	26	22,020,844	34
Firm size: 10–499 employees						
Received second-draw PPP loan	235,732		348,310		11,877,435	
Total received first PPP loan	523,548	45	870,007	40	31,293,870	38
Total in scope in 2020	624,770	38	1,091,986	32	39,897,297	30
Firm size: 500+ employees						
Received second-draw PPP loan	1,717		163,115		10,025,979	
Total received first PPP loan	7,657	22	567,220	29	28,110,790	36
Total in scope in 2020	21,203	8	1,356,276	12	70,819,105	14

Source: Author's compilation and analysis of tabulations of the BDS-SBA COVID data (U.S. Census Bureau 2025). Percentages are number receiving second-draw loans relative to either number receiving first-draw loans or total in scope in 2020.

at the time. Finally, a simple comparison between businesses that received PPP loans and those that did not receive PPP loans faces concerns over selection bias. Perhaps the businesses that received loans were the ones that could benefit the most from them (upward bias), or perhaps the businesses not receiving loans were the ones that were confident they could survive without them (negative bias). Selection bias is notoriously difficult to address in estimating the effects of government policies.

A comparison of businesses receiving loans with those that did not, however, is a useful first step to better understand the effects of the PPP on small businesses. Although the comparison is straightforward, it requires the ability to follow businesses over time after they have received loans, and information on business outcomes such as survival and retaining employees. I use the new BDS-SBA COVID data to explore this question. Table 10.4 reports business establishment exit rates in 2022 by PPP loan receipt. Exit rates are defined similarly to the Census Bureau's standard definition, which uses the average number of establishments in 2021 and 2022. As noted earlier in the chapter, establishment PPP receipt is defined by firm receipt and is not separately identified for each establishment within the

Table 10.4
Establishment Exit Rates by PPP First-Draw Loan Receipt by Employer Businesses

	No. of establishments			
Timing of loan receipt	2021	2022	Exits (no.)	Exit rate (%)
Total: All firm sizes				
Received early first-draw PPP loan	1,804,051	1,705,096	116,242	6.6
Received later first-draw PPP loan	2,430,184	2,287,582	202,476	8.6
Received any first-draw PPP loan	4,234,235	3,992,678	318,718	7.7
Did not receive PPP (in scope in 2020)	2,348,527	2,198,424	237,278	10.4

Notes: Author's compilation and analysis of tabulations of the BDS-SBA COVID data (U.S. Census Bureau 2025). Early first-draw PPP loans were received before April 24, 2020, and later first-draw loans were received on or after April 24, 2020. Exit rates are calculated using the average of 2021 and 2022 establishment levels for the denominator.

firm (Beem and Stinson 2025; U.S. Census Bureau 2025). The distinction between early first-draw loans and later first-draw loans is made because of concerns over the timing of loan receipt. The total is also reported for any PPP receipt. I do not, however, distinguish by receipt of second-draw PPP loans because the receipt is conditioned on receiving a first loan and surviving to that point, which could bias the comparison of business survival by PPP loan receipt versus no receipt.

In 2022, 318,718 business establishments that received any first-draw PPP funds exited. Calculated using the average number of establishments in 2021 and 2022, the exit rate was 7.7 percent. In comparison, 237,278 business establishments that did not receive any PPP funds exited in 2022, implying an exit rate of 10.4 percent. These were businesses that also existed in 2020 and were in the scope of ones for comparison with PPP receipt based on Census Bureau definitions. Therefore the main finding is that small businesses receiving PPP loans were less likely to exit than small businesses not receiving PPP loans. Although this finding does not necessarily imply that PPP loan receipt caused the lower exit rate, it is consistent with a causal impact.

Table 10.4 also reports exit rates by receipt of PPP loans early or later in the pandemic. Early receipt is defined as before April 24, 2020, and later receipt is defined as on or after April 24, 2020. The exit rate is lower for small businesses receiving PPP loans earlier, at 6.6 percent. For small businesses receiving PPP loans later, the exit rate is 8.6 percent. Again, these findings do not necessarily imply that earlier receipt of PPP funds caused the lower exit rate, but the descriptive evidence is consistent with this argument. The early scramble to provide loans may have had longer-term consequences for small business survival in the pandemic.

The relationship between survival and PPP receipt is explored further by the employment size of the firm. Table 10.5 reports business establishment exit rates in 2022 by PPP loan receipt and employment size. Exit rates are higher for small businesses not receiving PPP loans relative to small businesses receiving PPP loans for the two smaller employment size groups. Among firms with 1–9 employees, the establishment exit rate was 12.7 percent without PPP receipt compared with 9.0 percent with PPP receipt. The differential in exit rates is even larger when focusing on early versus later PPP loan receipt.

Table 10.5
Establishment Exit Rates by PPP First-Draw Loan Receipt by Employer Businesses by Size of Firm

Timing of first-draw loan by firm size	No. of establishments 2021	2022	Exits (no.)	Exit rate (%)
Firm size: 1–9 employees				
Received early first-draw PPP loan	994,732	937,144	76,763	7.9
Received later first-draw PPP loan	1,878,875	1,764,360	174,479	9.6
Received any first-draw PPP loan	2,873,607	2,701,504	251,242	9.0
Did not receive PPP (in Scope in 2020)	1,413,374	1,322,359	174,265	12.7
Firm size: 10–499 employees				
Received early first-draw PPP loan	567,126	539,110	21,120	3.8
Received later first-draw PPP loan	270,651	260,565	9,033	3.4
Received any first-draw PPP loan	837,777	799,675	30,153	3.7
Did not receive PPP (in scope in 2020)	198,566	186,808	11,199	5.8
Firm size: 500+ employees				
Received early first-draw PPP loan	242,193	228,842	18,359	7.8
Received later first-draw PPP loan	280,658	262,657	18,964	7.0
Received any first-draw PPP loan	522,851	491,499	37,323	7.4
Did not receive PPP (in scope in 2020)	736,587	689,257	51,814	7.3

Source: Author's compilation and analysis of tabulations of the BDS-SBA COVID data (U.S. Census Bureau 2025). Early first-draw PPP loans were received before April 24, 2020, and later first-draw loans were received on or after April 24, 2020. Exit rates are calculated using the average of 2021 and 2022 establishment levels for the denominator.

Among firms with employment sizes of 10–499 employees, there is also a large differential in exit rates by PPP receipt. The establishment exit rate is 5.8 percent for firms not receiving PPP loans and 3.8 percent for firms receiving PPP loans. Interestingly, there is no additional decline in exit rates from receiving the PPP loan earlier than later. Table 10.5 also reports establishment exit rates for firm sizes of 500 or more employees. For this group, the patterns by PPP receipt are less clear and do not point to lower exit rates with PPP receipt.

Another stated goal of the PPP was to save jobs. The BDS-SBA COVID data can be used to examine job destruction rates. The Census Bureau measures job destruction by adding the level of employment losses from establishments that are contracting (reducing their workforce) and from establishments that are shutting down completely. Job destruction rates can be calculated using average employment in the two years as the denominator. Table 10.6 reports job destruction rates in 2022 by PPP loan receipt. Among business establishments with PPP loans, nearly eight million jobs were lost through employment reductions or shutdowns. PPP loan receipt was associated with a job destruction rate of 11.3 percent.

The job destruction rate was slightly lower among business establishments not receiving PPP funds, at 10.9 percent. The difference in job destruction rates between businesses receiving and not receiving PPP loans is smaller when the analysis focuses on early receipt of PPP loans. Among small businesses receiving loans before April 24, 2020, the job destruction rate was 10.6 percent, compared with 10.9 percent for small businesses not receiving loans.

Table 10.6

Job Destruction Rates by PPP First-Draw Loan Receipt by Employer Businesses, All Firm Sizes

	No. of employees				
Timing of loan receipt	2021	2022	Denominator	Job destruction	Job destruction rate (%)
Received early first-draw PPP loan	38,154,913	38,738,866	38,399,136	4,058,361	10.56
Received later first-draw PPP loan	32,148,141	32,392,533	32,242,247	3,924,044	12.16
Received any first-draw PPP loan	70,303,054	71,131,399	70,641,383	7,982,405	11.29
Did not receive PPP (in scope in 2020)	51,935,444	52,267,845	52,073,426	5,681,915	10.91

Notes: Author's compilation and analysis of tabulations of the BDS-SBA COVID data (U.S. Census Bureau 2025). Early first-draw PPP loans were received before April 24, 2020, and later first-draw loans were received on or after April 24, 2020.

Additional Studies of PPP Impacts

Several studies have used empirical approaches that build on the simple comparison of businesses receiving or not receiving PPP loans to estimate the impacts of the PPP program on small business outcomes. A few examples are discussed here. In an early study, Bartik, Cullen, Glaeser, et al. (2020) used firm-level data from a survey of 5,800 small businesses through a network-based platform for small businesses. To address potential selection problems and the general endogeneity of PPP loan approvals, they used an instrumental variables approach with information about preexisting banking relationships of businesses. Individual banks varied in their loan approval rates: the largest banks had lower approval rates. They found that PPP loans led to an increase in a business's expected survival and a positive but imprecise effect on employment.

Humphries, Neilson, and Ulyssea (2020) compared small businesses receiving PPP loans with small businesses not receiving PPP loans early in the pandemic. They used daily surveys from March 28 to May16, 2020, and follow-up surveys from April 19 to May 16, 2020, of small businesses owners, who were recruited through social media ads. Small businesses receiving PPP loans reported having more employees, lower probabilities of closure or bankruptcy, and higher probabilities of recovering in the next two years than small businesses not receiving PPP loans. The comparisons held after controlling for business and owner characteristics and the geographic location of the business, and the associations with PPP loans were stronger for small businesses with fewer than ten employees.

Autor et al. (2022) used high-frequency administrative payroll data from ADP to study the effects of the PPP on employment. To identify effects, they took advantage of firm-size eligibility cutoffs that were specific to industries. The employment threshold is generally 500 employees for most industries, but not for all industries. They compared PPP-eligible firms with ineligible firms in a range above the industry-specific threshold. They found that the PPP increased employment at eligible firms by 2–5 percent in mid-May 2020 but generally had no or smaller effects after that period. They estimated that an additional 3.6 million jobs were retained as of mid-May 2020 and 1.4 million jobs at the end of 2020 because of the PPP. They also estimated that the annual cost of retained employment was high, at $169,000 to $258,000 per job.

Chetty et al. (2024) used a similar research design but a different large payroll processor to study the question. The analysis is part of a larger research project that builds a public database to measure spending, employment, and other outcomes at a high-frequency, granular level using anonymized transaction data collected by companies in the private sector. They took the same general approach of comparing employment changes at firms with fewer than 500 employees with firms in the same sector that had more than five hundred employees. They found that employment increased by 2.5 percentage points after the PPP was enacted in April 2020 (relative to employment at larger firms that were ineligible for PPP). Their estimates imply that the cost per job saved by the PPP was $301,863.

Granja et al. (2022) studied the role banks played in employment effects of the PPP program. To study the question, they used regional variation in lending relationships and individual firm-loan matched data. They found that the short- and medium-term employment effects of the program were small compared with the size of the PPP. They also found evidence that many firms used PPP loans for expenses or to build up savings instead of for employee payroll. Another factor potentially limiting employment effects is that many inframarginal firms likely received PPP loans and that there was a low correlation between regional PPP funding and the severity of local shocks.

Hubbard and Strain (2020) used Dun & Bradstreet data to study the early effects of the PPP on business outcomes. They used event-study and difference-in-difference models to estimate the effect of a small business applying for larger PPP loans and of a small business being eligible for PPP based on size. They found evidence of positive effects of the PPP on employment, financial health, and survival rates.

Recent studies build on these earlier studies. For example, Cole (2024) examined the impacts of PPP funding on very small businesses (median of five employees) using administrative data from a payroll processing firm. Using various identification strategies, they found that very small firms that received PPP funding increased employment by reducing layoffs but that costs per job retained were high. Staples and Krumel (2023) examined the impacts of the PPP on a specific type of business hit hard in the pandemic, craft breweries. They found that PPP loans increased survival rates and lessened reductions in annual production, and that earlier receipt of funding played a key role in these outcomes. In another example of recent research, Agarwal et al. (2024) examined the broader economic effects of the PPP. Looking at the performance of securitized commercial mortgages, they found that the PPP reduced mortgage delinquencies, limiting disruptions to small businesses.

Two New Programs in 2021 to Help Restaurants and Theaters

As businesses struggled to recover fully in the pandemic, a few industries were hit especially hard. The federal government created two additional programs that targeted businesses in the struggling food and entertainment industries. In May 2021, the Restaurant Revitalization Fund (RRF) was launched to provide emergency loans to a wide range of food and beverage retail businesses. These included restaurants, food trucks, caterers, snack bars, bakeries, bars, breweries, wineries, and inns that had on-site sales accounting for at least one-third of total sales. Eligible businesses received funding up to $10 million per business, and loans were forgivable if the funds were used for eligible purposes. More than 100,000 applicants to the program received a total of $28.6 billion in assistance.

Receipt of RRF loans among small businesses in the eligible industries varied by firm size. Table 10.7 reports RRF loan receipt by firm employment size.[4] Overall, 12 percent of eligible small businesses received RRF

Table 10.7
Restaurant Revitalization Fund Loan Receipt by Employment Size

Loan receipt	Firms, total		1–9 Employees		10–499 Employees		500+ Employees	
	No.	Percent	No.	Percent	No.	Percent	No.	Percent
Received RRF loan	74,214	12.0	57,362	9.4	16,782	12.2	70	2.2
Applied for RRF but did not receive loan	61,059	9.9	42,868	7.0	17,942	13.1	254	7.9
Total in scope for RRF	617,345		612767		137359		3206	

Notes: Author's compilation and analysis of tabulations of the BDS-SBA COVID data (U.S. Census Bureau 2025).

loans. The highest level of receipt was among small businesses with 10–499 employees, at 12.2 percent. The smallest small businesses, 1–9 employees, had a receipt rate of 9.4 percent. For firms of all sizes, a share of them, roughly 10 percent overall, did not receive RRF loans even though they applied for the loans.

Another targeted program was the Shuttered Venues Operator Grants (SVOG) program. The program was launched in April 2021 and provided aid to specific entertainment businesses that were especially struggling to bring customers back. These businesses included operators of live venues, theaters, live performing arts organizations, museums, motion picture theaters, and talent representatives. The maximum grant was for $10 million, and eligible loans were forgivable. New businesses, defined as born after February 2020, were not eligible for SVOG loans, and there were some restrictions and reductions associated with PPP receipt. As of July 5, 2022, SVOG had provided $14.6 billion in grants to about 23,000 small businesses (U.S. SBA 2022b).

More on EIDL

The Economic Injury Disaster Loan (EIDL) program discussed in chapter 5 provided additional loans to struggling small businesses in 2021 and into spring 2022. The EIDL program provided 3.9 million loans and 6.8 million advances for a total of $378 billion and $27.5 billion, respectively, as of April 23, 2022 (U.S. Government Accounting Office 2023). By the end of 2020, roughly $200 billion had been spent on EIDL loans, an amount that grew by another roughly $125 billion in 2021 and by another $50 billion in 2022, according to reports by the SBA (U.S. Small Business Administration 2022a).

Combining all EIDL funds provided during the pandemic, table 10.8 reports EIDL receipt rate among eligible small businesses. Among all eligible small businesses, 16 percent received EIDL funding. Nearly 20 percent, however, applied for loans but did not receive them. The percentages of firms receiving EIDL funds were similar for the smallest small businesses and the medium-size small businesses. Receipt rates were substantially lower for the largest small businesses.

Compared with the PPP, the EIDL program provided much less in number of loans and total funding even though it started around the same time

Table 10.8
Economic Injury Disaster Loan (EIDL) Receipt by Employment Size

Loan receipt	Firms, total		1–9 Employees		10–499 Employees		500+ Employees	
	No.	Percent	No.	Percent	No.	Percent	No.	Percent
Received EIDL	902,692	16.24	795,256	16.17	105,237	17.05	2,233	8.57
Applied for EIDL but did not receive loan	1,069,706	19.25	911,066	18.53	148,917	24.13	9,851	37.81
Total in scope for EIDL	5,557,612		4,917,601		617,255		26,056	

Source: Author's compilation and analysis of tabulations of the BDS-SBA COVID data (U.S. Census Bureau 2025).

in the pandemic and lasted longer. EIDL, however, was not designed to provide as extensive aid to small businesses in the pandemic as the PPP. EIDL loans did not have the forgiveness condition of PPP loans, and small businesses were required to provide collateral for loans over $25,000. Many businesses received both types of financial assistance during the pandemic.

Fraud in the PPP

Capturing the headlines numerous times was fraud in receipt of PPP loans. Pictures and videos of fraudulent claimants in expensive cars, lavish houses, and taking extravagant vacations were shown in the news. There was public outcry over concerns that government relief aid was going to people and organizations scamming the system instead of to legitimate small businesses struggling to survive in the pandemic. Numerous people have been charged with fraud schemes connected to COVID-19 aid programs such as the PPP (U.S. Department of Justice 2024).

The potential scope for fraud with the PPP is large. The U.S. Government Accounting Office (2023) analyzed PPP and EIDL loan and administrative wage data and identified over 3.7 million unique recipients with fraud indicators out of a total of 13.4 million. Fraud indicators included no wage data, different employee totals, different payroll costs, received multiple loans, reused information, and/or provided different information to each program. The unique recipients identified include potentially nonexistent businesses or businesses that may have misrepresented employee counts to obtain more funds. The U.S. GAO is careful to note, however, that these fraud indicators can be used to identify potential fraud but are by no means proof of fraud. The cases with fraud indicators were referred to the SBA Office of Inspector General (OIG) for further review and investigation.

The SBA OIG conducted one of the most comprehensive studies of potential fraud in pandemic assistance loan programs (U.S. Small Business Administration, Office of Inspector General 2023). The OIG notes that in the rush to swiftly disburse COVID-19 EIDL and PPP funds, the SBA calibrated its internal controls. The agency weakened or removed the controls necessary to prevent fraudsters from easily gaining access to these programs and provide assurance that only eligible entities received funds. However, the allure of "easy money" in this pay-and-chase environment attracted an overwhelming number of fraudsters to the programs. The OIG estimated that the SBA disbursed over $200 billion in potentially fraudulent COVID-19 EIDL loans, EIDL Targeted Advances, Supplemental Targeted Advances, and PPP loans. This means at least 17 percent of all COVID-19 EIDL and PPP funds were disbursed to potentially fraudulent actors. The OIG's collaboration with the SBA, the U.S. Secret Service, other federal agencies, and financial institutions has resulted in nearly $30 billion in COVID-19 EIDL and PPP funds being seized or returned to the SBA.

Recent studies dive deeper to examine specific questions around fraud in the PPP. Mills (2024) provides an overview of the evidence of fraud and discusses different types of fraud, such as fake businesses, manipulating payroll numbers, and lender fraud, as well as other problems, such a large national chains qualifying for and receiving loans, bad accounting, and verification limitations. Bailey, Brody, and Sokolowski (2022) carefully examined numerous PPP fraud cases to find out more about how they committed the fraud. The study finds that most of the cases falsified tax data to access program loans and inflated payroll numbers to obtain larger loan amounts. Applicants who sought large amounts applied using multiple companies and across multiple lenders, consistent with the use of multiple loans to avoid the scrutiny of a single large loan with a single lender. Griffin, Kruger, and Mahajan (2023) examined PPP loan fraud and the rise of fintech in providing these loans. They performed a big data analysis of loan features on the 11.5 million PPP loans and found that fintech loans were more than three times as likely to have had a primary indicator of misreporting information compared with traditional loans and more than six times as likely to have had a primary indicator that was confirmed by an additional indicator. More broadly, the study found that the number of PPP loans with an industry and county pair frequently exceeded the number of business establishments in the same industry-county pair in U.S. Census data. Finally, Mills (2024) has provided a discussion of the issues.

11 The Economic Recovery: The Next Three Years

In this chapter, I examine business activity and earnings starting in 2022, which is the second full year in the recovery, through the end of 2024, which is more than four and a half years after the extensive social distancing restrictions were implemented. COVID-19 has been referred to repeatedly as a once in a generation disruption to the economy, and, given the magnitude and breadth of the disruption, it is not clear how long a full recovery might take. New evidence on the recovery for small business owners is provided here.

COVID-19 Cases

The start of 2022 did not go well for fighting back on COVID-19. The number of new COVID-19 cases was not under control, or even under any sense of management. In the last full week in 2022 there were slightly fewer than 600,000 new cases. Figure 11.1 displays the number of new COVID-19 cases per week from the beginning of 2022 to the end of 2024. In the first full week of 2022, which ended on January 8, 2022, the country witnessed a jump to slightly fewer than one million new COVID-19 cases that week. January 2022 was a difficult month for hoping that COVID-19 would move to the rear-view mirror. The huge increase from the end of 2021 was unexpected and worrisome.

Fortunately, the high levels of new COVID-19 cases each week subsided quickly and sharply. Case numbers dropped to fewer than 500,000 for the week of February 5, 2022, and dropped further, to 311,000, for the week ending March 5, 2022. Case levels dropped further over the rest of

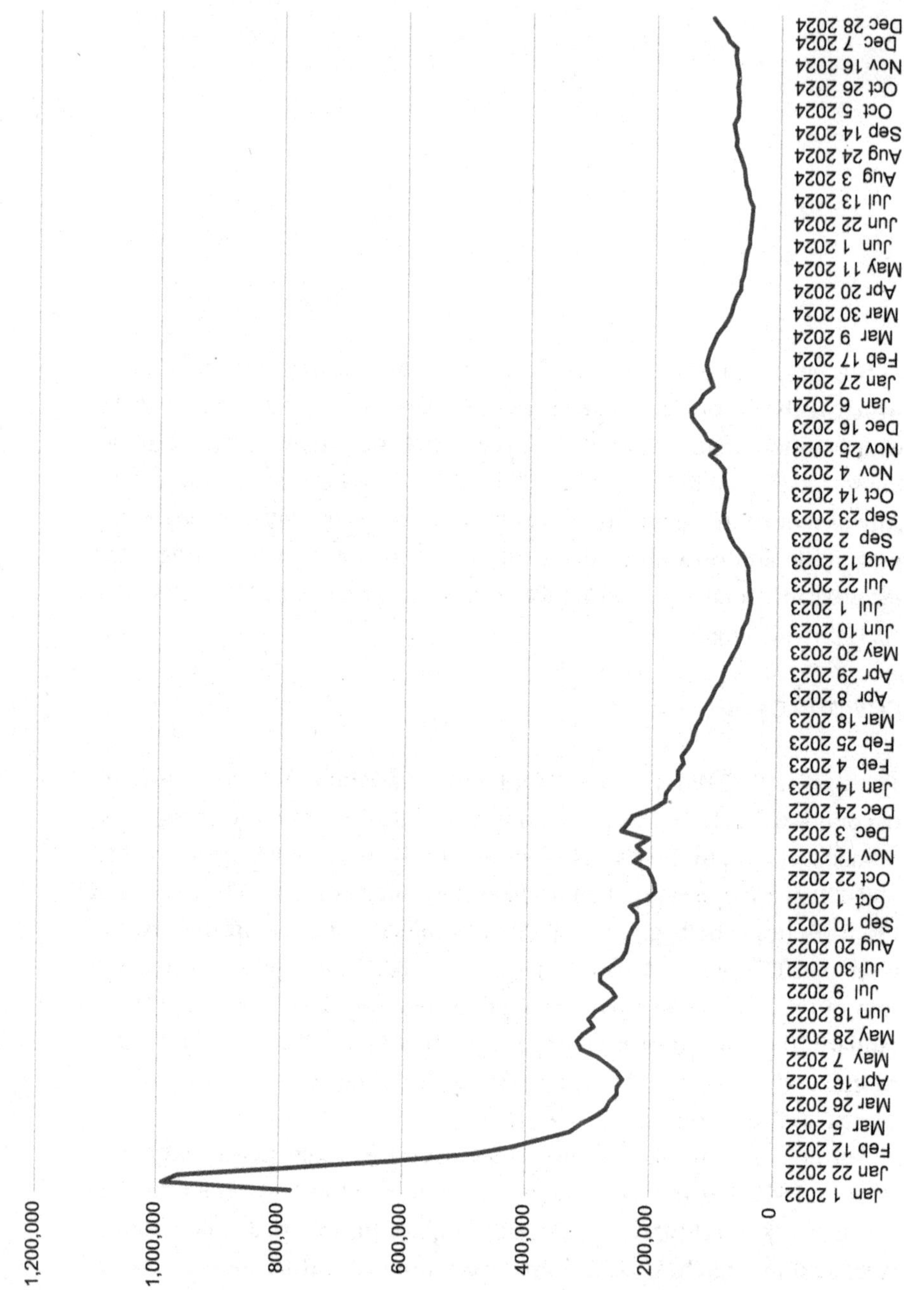

Figure 11.1
New COVID-19 cases in the United States per week for weeks ending January 1, 2022, to December 28, 2024.

2022, and the last couple of weeks of the year saw new case numbers below 200,000 per week.

Through most of 2023, COVID-19 new case numbers dropped steadily, reaching levels that were below 50,000 cases in most weeks in June and July 2023. Once again, however, COVID-19 case numbers started to rise. COVID-19 was stubborn and not ready to go away. The number of new cases per week reached a high that year of 141,000 for the last full week of 2023. In 2024, new COVID-19 cases repeated this general pattern of declining in the early part of the year through the summer and then increasing in the fall and early winter. The future will determine whether this pattern continues to repeat year after year. COVID-19 appears to be with us for some time.

Business Activity Starting in 2022

The beginning of 2022 marked perhaps a final turning point in the rocky recovery from COVID-19. Figure 11.2 displays monthly business activity levels through the end of 2024. Business activity increased for the next few months and experienced only a slight drop in the summer of 2022. Levels of business activity were higher in 2022 than prior to the pandemic. Every month of 2022 witnessed higher levels of business activity than the same month in 2019. For example, in July 2022 business activity was 4 percent higher than in July 2019. When averaged across all months during the year, business activity was 5 percent higher each month in 2022 than in the same month in 2019.

Business activity continued to increase in 2023 and 2024. The number of active business owners reached a peak in September 2024, at 17.1 million. The month-to-month comparisons between 2019 and 2024 indicate solid growth for every month. The average increase for all months from 2019 to 2024 was 6.5 percent. Business activity, at least when measured as total active business owners in the U.S. economy, has shown more than a full recovery and strong growth since the disruption caused by COVID-19 in the spring of 2020. The positive forces on entrepreneurship outweighed the opposing forces in the economic recovery. As noted in chapter 2, the a priori theoretical prediction of changes in business ownership activity in recessions or recoveries is not always clear.

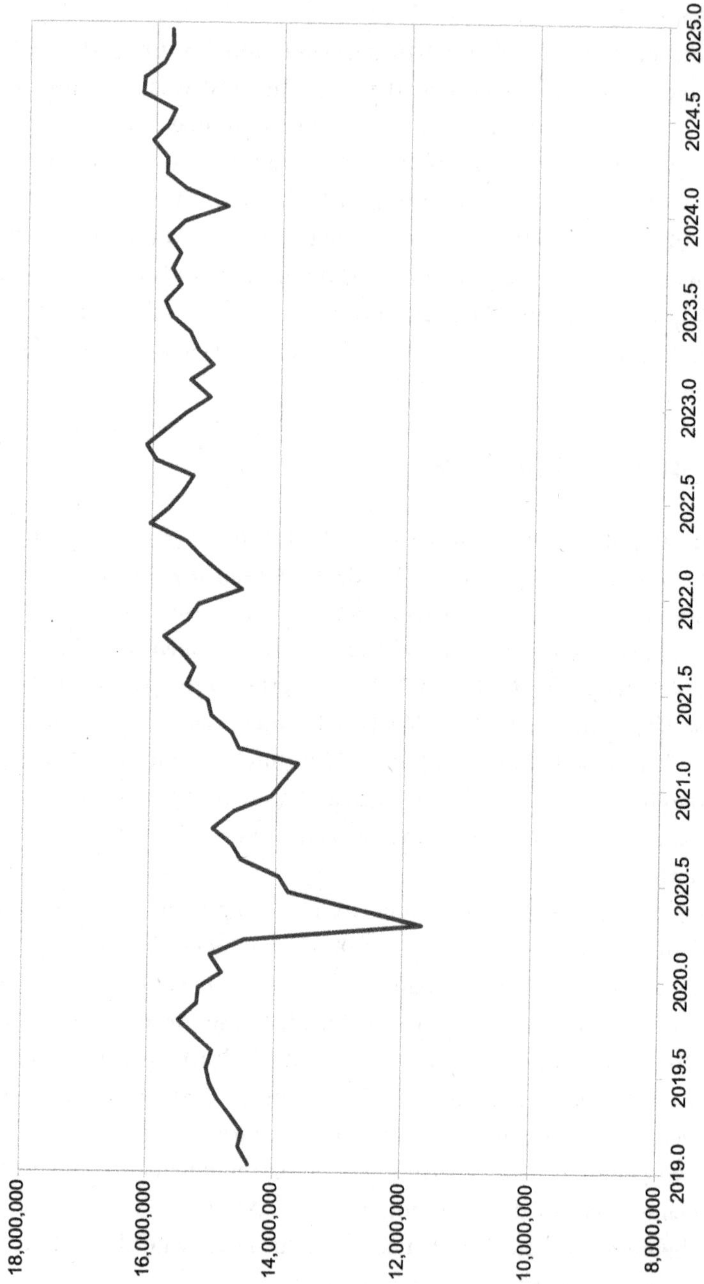

Figure 11.2
Number of active business owners in the United States, January 2019–December 2024.

Business Earnings Since 2022

The losses to business earnings were severe in the first year of the pandemic but rebounded in 2021. Did business earnings continue to rebound in 2022 and 2023?[1] COVID-19 case numbers were declining rapidly, vaccines and boosters were readily available, and social distancing restrictions and mask mandates were disappearing. Figure 11.3 displays trends in mean and mean log business earnings by calendar year through 2023.

The rebound in 2021 was just that, a rebound from the disruption caused by COVID-19 in 2020 and not the beginning of a longer upward trend in business earnings. If anything, using mean business earnings as the measure shows a slight decrease in 2022 and 2023. The mean value of business earnings was now roughly at 2019 levels. Inflation was relatively high in 2022, contributing to the lack of real earnings growth in the economic recovery from the pandemic. Using mean log business earnings as the measure produces a slightly less pessimistic picture as the trend is slightly upward. But the main conclusion is the same: Business earnings did not trend upward and at the end of 2023 were at, or slightly lower than, the level just prior to the start of the pandemic.

Industry Recoveries in 2022 and 2023

As noted in chapters 3 and 7, business earnings dropped for nearly all industries in the first year of the pandemic but then rebounded strongly for most industries in the following year, 2021. What happened to business earnings by industry in 2022 and 2023? Table 11.1 reports growth rates in mean business earnings from prepandemic levels (2019) to 2022 and 2023. Business earnings in Agriculture continued to grow since the start of the pandemic. In both 2022 and 2023, mean business earnings were much higher than in 2019. The stratospheric gains in Information continued in 2022 but finally cooled off in 2023. Mean business earnings in 2023 were only 11 percent higher than just prior to the start of the pandemic. Leisure and Hospitality still had not recovered fully from the early months of the pandemic. In both 2022 and 2023, mean business earnings were 18 percent below prepandemic levels. Wholesale and Retail Trade and Educational and Health Services had lower average business earnings in both years compared with 2019. For other major industry groups the

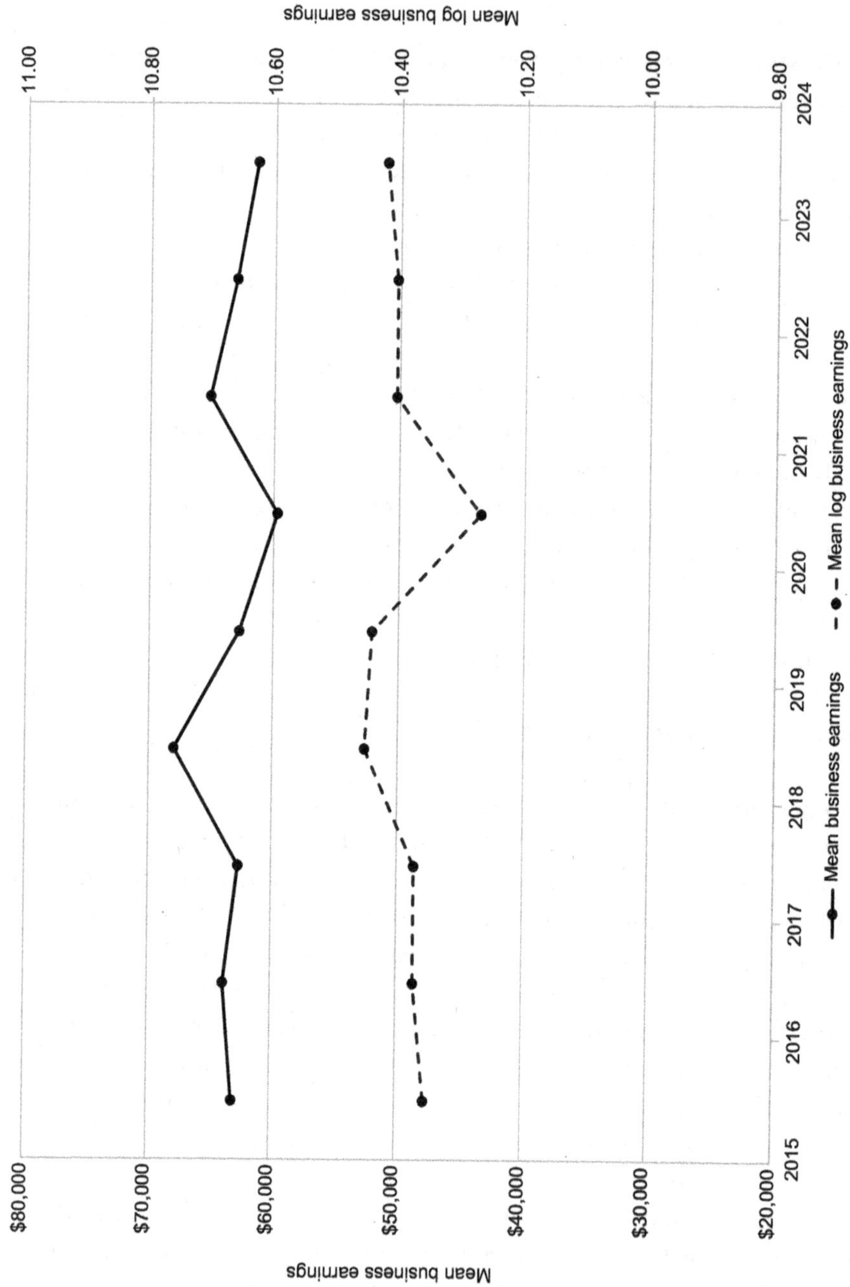

Figure 11.3
Business earnings trends, 2015–2023.

Table 11.1

Business Earnings Losses by Industry, 2019–2022 and 2019–2023

	Mean business earnings			
Industry	2019	Percent change, 2019–2022	Percent change, 2019–2023	Average *N*
Agriculture	$42,262	70	47	349
Construction	$50,512	6	2	1063
Manufacturing	$70,465	−12	5	196
Wholesale and Retail Trade	$66,539	−23	−4	518
Transportation	$51,185	11	−12	355
Information	$49,958	81	11	99
Financial Activities	$98,315	3	3	462
Professional and Business Services	$73,437	4	−6	1,216
Educational and Health Services	$71,215	−11	−4	578
Leisure and Hospitality	$60,032	−18	−18	423
Other Services	$40,154	−3	−2	587

Notes: Author's calculations from Current Population Survey (CPS) microdata, 2019–2023. All estimates use CPS-provided sample weights. The sample includes only individuals with longest-job-held work activity as self-employed business owner in the calendar year.

estimates vary somewhat as to how much business earnings had recovered or not recovered.

The Rate of New Business Activity and Necessity Share in the Recovery

I next examine patterns in new business activity and the necessity share of new business activity in the recovery period. The analysis expands on the results presented in chapter 3. Table 11.2 reports both measures from 219 to 2024. New business activity declined mostly steadily from its highest level in 2020 to 2024. In 2024, the new business activity rate was 0.33 percent, which is close to the five-year average prepandemic

Table 11.2
New Business Activity Rate and Necessity Share, 2019–2024

Year	New business activity rate (%)	Necessity share of new business activity (%)
2019	0.31	13.1
2020	0.38	30.3
2021	0.36	19.1
2022	0.37	11.7
2023	0.35	14.8
2024	0.33	17.7

Notes: Author's calculations from compiled monthly Current Population Survey microdata.

level of 0.32 percent. The rate of 0.33 percent in 2024 implies that each month, 330 out of 100,000 adults created a new business. As discussed in chapter 2, theoretically and empirically the new business activity rate is not necessarily pro-cyclical.

The necessity share of new business activity demonstrates a countercyclical pattern. It dropped from its peak of 30.3 percent in 2020 to 19.1 percent in 2021 and again to 11.7 percent in 2022. In 2023, the necessity share increased but approximated prepandemic levels, where the five-year prepandemic average was 14.5 percent. In 2024 there was an unexpected increase in the necessity share to 17.7 percent.

GDP Growth and Unemployment in 2022 and 2023

Did the broader economy continue to recover in 2022 through 2024? Table 11.3 reports GDP growth rates from the first quarter of 2022 through the last quarter of 2024. The GDP fell in the first quarter of 2022 but grew strongly at the end of the year. The year 2023 experienced positive growth in every quarter. GDP growth slowed somewhat in 2024 but was 3 percent or higher in two quarters of the year.

The unemployment rate dropped slightly at the beginning of 2022, ending the major decline from historical levels at the start of the pandemic. Figure 11.4 displays the national unemployment rate from January 2019 through December 2024. The unemployment rate declined slightly through the end of 2022, reaching an extremely low level of

Table 11.3
GDP Growth Rates from 2022 to 2024

Year	Quarter	GDP growth rate (%)
2022	1	−1.0
2022	2	0.3
2022	3	2.7
2022	4	3.4
2023	1	2.8
2023	2	2.4
2023	3	4.4
2023	4	3.2
2024	1	1.6
2024	2	3.0
2024	3	3.1
2024	4	2.3

Source: U.S. Bureau of Economic Analysis, National Income and Product Accounts, Percent Change from Preceding Period in Real Gross Domestic Product.

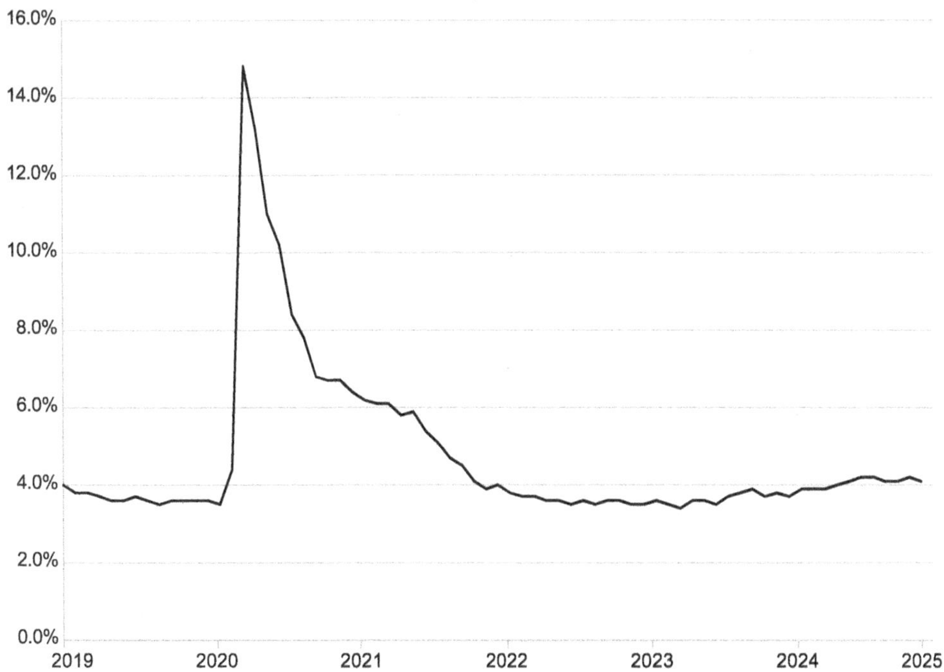

Figure 11.4
Unemployment rate, January 2019–December 2024.

3.5 percent in December of that year. The labor market was very strong that year with the unemployment rate under 4 percent for every month except January.

The unemployment rate remained extremely low throughout 2023. The unemployment rate was under 4 percent the entire year. It was not until 2024 that the unemployment rate crept above 4 percent again. As measured by the unemployment rate, the U.S. economy was strong during the entire time period from January 2022 to December 2024.

12 Was the Recovery Even for All Groups? Implications for Racial Inequality

February 2022 marked perhaps a final turning point after which small businesses were clearly on the road to recovery. Business activity increased for the next few months and experienced only a slight drop in the summer of 2022. Levels of business activity were higher than prior to the pandemic. In September 2022 there were 15.9 million active business owners, compared with 15.2 million in September 2019. Gross domestic product (GDP) was growing and the unemployment rate returned to the low levels that existed just prior to the pandemic. As seen in previous chapters, however, the experiences of small businesses can differ substantially by race.

Did business owners of all races experience similar rebounds in economic activity? Or did some groups struggle in the rebound from the beginning of 2022 to the end of 2024? This chapter builds on the findings in the previous chapter to explore these questions. The analysis answers the fundamental question of whether there was a grand-scale reopening of small businesses shared by racial groups or whether some groups experienced a sluggish economic recovery.

Business Activity by Race

Figure 12.1 displays the number of active business owners by race from the beginning of 2019 through the end of 2024. I focus on the period from January 2022 to December 2024. All minority groups experienced increases from the beginning of 2022 to the end of 2024 in the number of active business owners. The upward trends for Black, Latinx, and Asian business activity are clear during this period. The recovery from the depths of pandemic appears to be strong, at least as measured by business activity for each group.

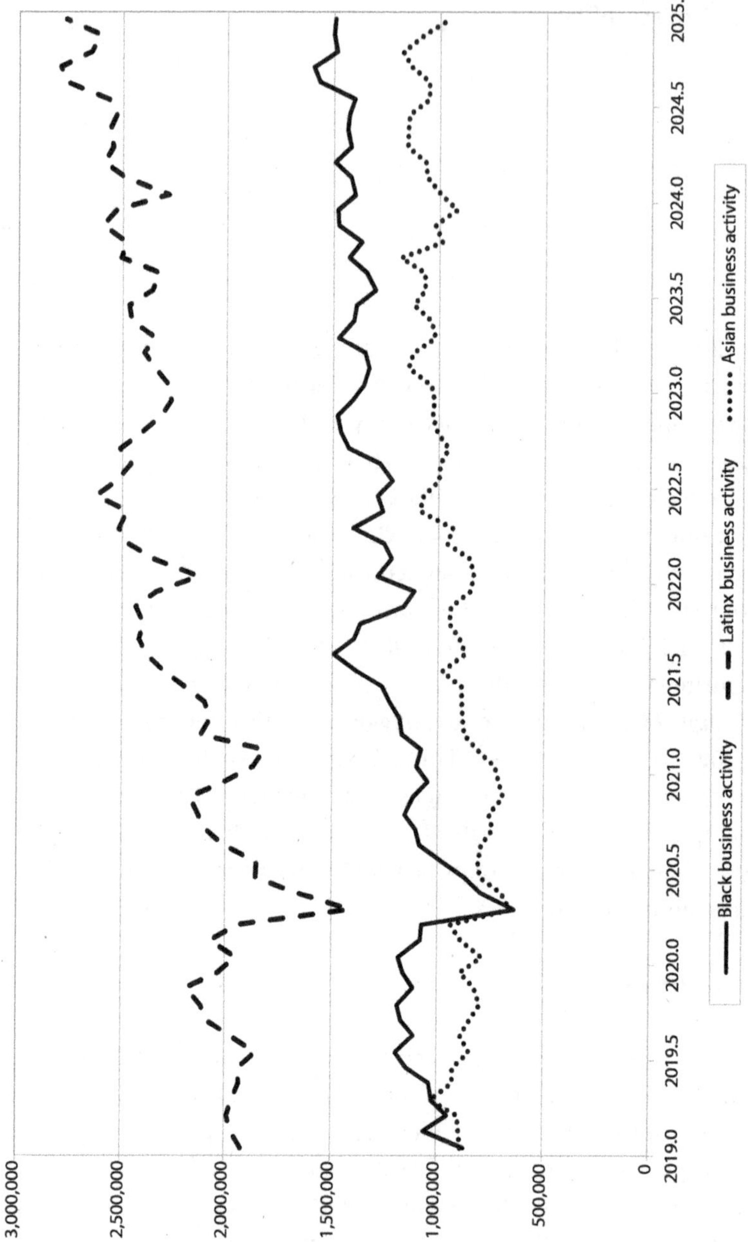

Figure 12.1
Number of active business owners by race, January 2019–December 2024.

Using the change from December 2021 to December 2024, I find that the number of active Black business owners increased by 34 percent. The number of active business owners who are Latinx grew by 19 percent, and the number of active business owners who are Asian grew by 12 percent. The figure indicates, however, month-to-month variation that partly owes to seasonality. Another way to gauge economic growth for each group is to compare annual averages in 2024 with those in 2021. By combining months, the seasonal variation can be smoothed out. From 2021 to 2024, the number of active Black business owners increased from 1.25 million to 1.47 million, representing an increase of 18 percent. The number of Latinx business owners increased from 2.2 million in 2021 to 2.6 million in 2024, which is similarly a growth rate of 18 percent. The percentage of active Asian business owners grew the most, 23 percent, from 2021 to 2024, increasing from 881,000 in 2021 to 108,400 in 2024.

Although not shown in figure 12.1, the number of active white business owners decreased slightly during this same period. From December 2021 to December 2024, the number of active white business owners decreased by 3 percent. There were 10.3 million white business owners in 2021 and 10.2 million in 2024, representing a slight decrease of 1 percent.

The findings of strong rebounds for all groups represent a major departure from the findings reported in chapter 4. The analysis there revealed that the number of working business owners plummeted from 15.0 million in February 2020 to 11.7 million in April 2020 but rebounded in the following months. The losses and rebounds, however, were felt differently by race. African American businesses experienced the largest losses, with 41 percent of active business owners eliminated. Latinx businesses also experienced major losses, with 32 percent of business owners halting activity between February and April 2020. Asian businesses experienced a loss of 26 percent in business activity in the first month of the pandemic and also experienced an especially slow initial rebound. By the end of 2024, all three groups had easily surpassed the February 2020 levels just prior to the pandemic or the respective 2019 annual average.

The drop in business activity from February to April 2020 for white business owners was smaller, at 17 percent. The rebound as measured from the February 2020 level or from the 2019 annual average indicates slight losses in the number of active white business owners from those levels to 2024.

Active Business Ownership Rates

Over a longer period of time, it is also useful to examine business activity by race while adjusting for potential growth in the size of the labor force for each group. The active business ownership rate is defined as the percentage of the labor force that is actively running a business. Figure 12.2 displays active business ownership rates for each racial group from the beginning of 2019 to the end of 2024. Active business ownership rates for each minority group show the same times-series pattern as the pattern for the number of active business owners: a large drop at the beginning of the pandemic, followed by a large rebound in the next few months, then longer-term growth. Growth in active business ownership rates during the economic recovery over the next few years is evident for all three groups.

Although some variability exists in month-to-month rates of business ownership, each group experienced a higher active business ownership rate in 2024 than in 2019. The annual average of monthly rates for the Black business ownership rate increased from 5.2 percent in 2019 to 6.6 percent in 2024. The Latinx business ownership rate increased from 7.7 to 8.9 percent, and the Asian business ownership rate increased from 7.8 to 8.0 percent. In contrast to these patterns, the white business ownership rate declined from 10.5 percent in 2019 to 10.3 percent in 2024. In general, shifting the focus from the number of active business owners to the active business ownership rate does not change the conclusions regarding longer-term trends in the economic recovery from the COVID-19 recession.

Another important finding revealed in the reported estimates of active business ownership rates is that the ordering of groups by business activity rates remained constant over time. The Black business ownership rate was the lowest throughout the time period. Even with a large increase in rates in the recovery from the pandemic, Black business ownership rates remained lower than the rates of other groups. Latinx and Asian business ownership rates were higher and roughly similar over the time period. The white business ownership rate was the highest throughout the time period.

Recovery in 2022 for the Subset of Employer Businesses by Race

Focusing on businesses with employees, there is additional evidence of growth in the number of Black-, Latinx-, and Asian-owned firms in the

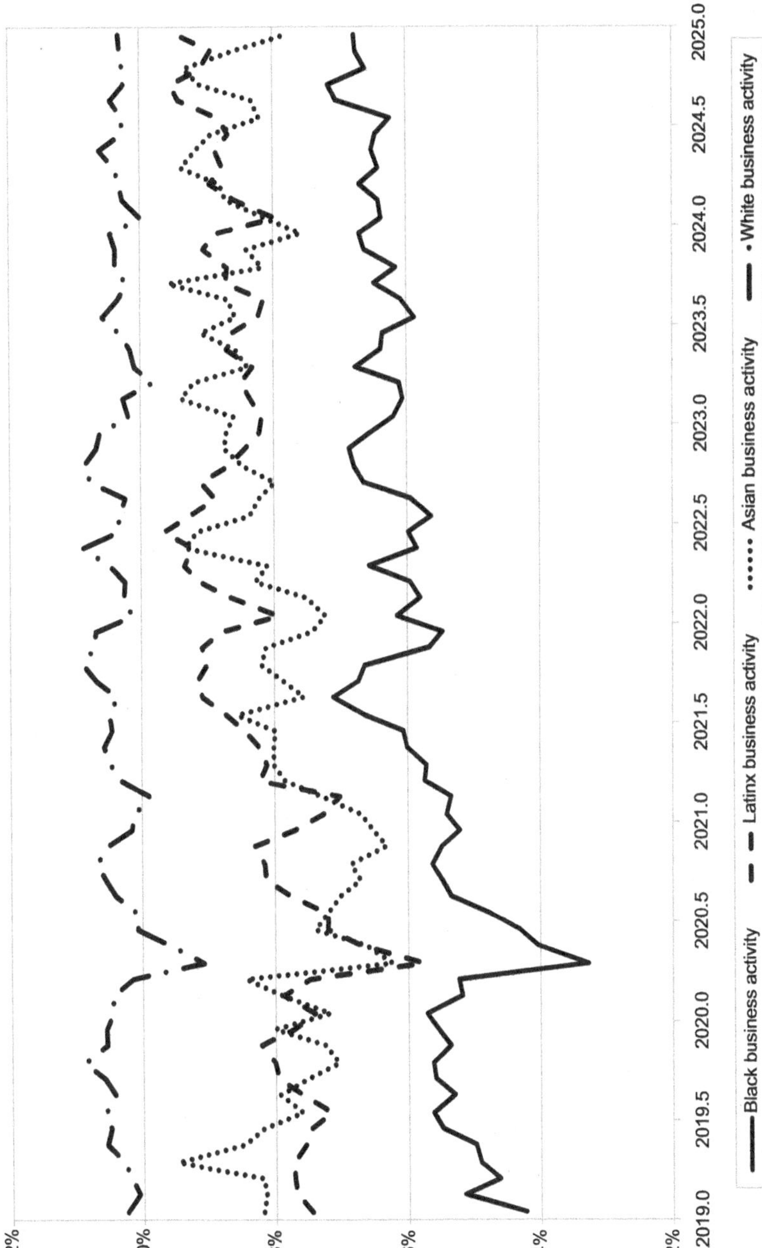

Figure 12.2
Active business ownership rates by race, January 2019–December 2024.

Table 12.1
Growth in the Number of Employer Businesses by Race: Percent Change from 2019 to 2020, 2021, and 2022

Racial/ethnic group	No. in 2019	Percent change from 2019 to: 2020	2021	2022
Total	5,771,292	0	2	2
Black	134,567	5	20	45
Latinx	346,836	8	17	34
Asian	581,200	5	11	12
White, non-Latinx	4,441,453	–1	–1	–3

Source: U.S. Census Bureau, Annual Business Surveys.

pandemic recovery. The U.S. Census Bureau has released information on employer businesses by race through 2022. Table 12.1 reports estimates of the number of employer businesses by race in 2019 and growth rates in the number of employer businesses by race from 2019 to 2020, 2021, and 2022.

The number of Black-owned employer firms increased by 20 percent from prepandemic levels. The growth rate was even higher through 2022, when it was 45 percent higher than in 2019. The recovery indicates strong growth for Black businesses with employees, which is consistent with the finding of strong growth in business activity.

Latinx businesses with employees also experienced strong growth early in the recovery. The number of employer businesses increased by 17 percent in 2021 and 34 percent in 2022 relative to prepandemic levels. Growth rates were less strong, but still strong, for Asian businesses with employees. Asian employer businesses grew by 12 percent from 2019 to 2022. In contrast to these patterns, the number of white employer businesses declined slightly in the early part of the recovery. From 2019 to 2022, white businesses with employees fell by 3 percent.

Business Earnings Patterns by Race

Business earnings fell strongly in the first year of the pandemic but rebounded strongly the next year. In 2022 and 2023, business earnings did not continue to grow as strongly as they did in 2021. Did these patterns differ by race?

Figure 12.3 displays mean log business earnings for each racial group from 2015 to 2023. Similar to the pattern for total business earnings examined in

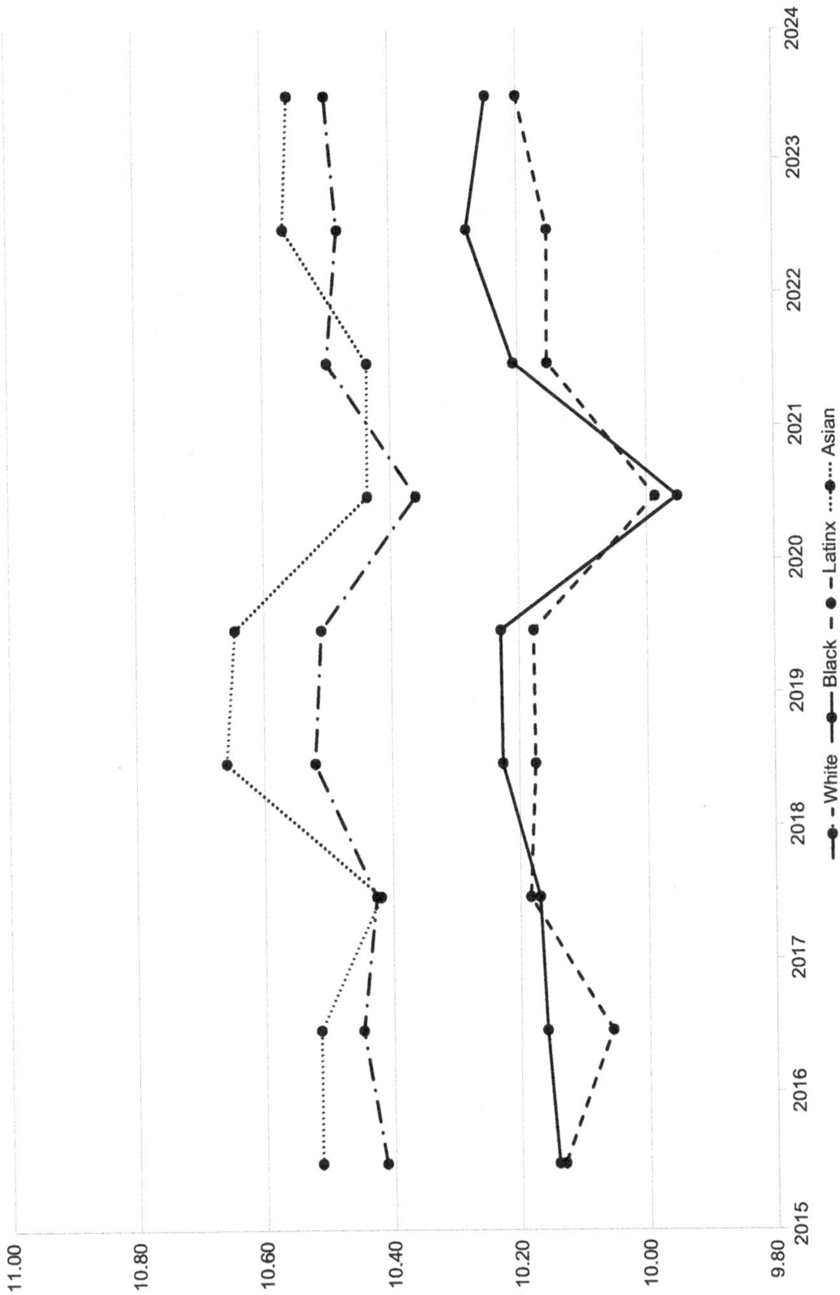

Figure 12.3
Mean log business earnings trends by race, 2015–2023.

chapter 11, the white business earnings trend was essentially flat after the initial rebound from COVID-19. From 2021 to 2023, there was no growth in average business earnings among white business owners.

In contrast, mean business earnings of Black business owners grew by roughly 4 percent from 2021 to 2023. Latinx business owners experienced a growth of roughly 5 percent in mean business earnings from 2021 to 2023. Asian business owners also experienced positive growth in mean business earnings. Their mean business earnings grew by the most, 12 percent, from 2021 to 2023.

Although business earnings growth was strong for Black and Latinx business owners, the figure underscores lasting inequality. Mean Black and Latinx business earnings are considerably lower than mean white and Asian business earnings over the entire time period. Just before the start of the pandemic, mean business earnings were roughly 28 percent lower for Black business owners and 33 percent lower for Latinx business owner relative to white business owners. Fast forward to 2023, and Black business earnings were 25 percent lower and Latinx business earnings were 30 percent lower than white business earnings, roughly. The trends in business earnings by race do not point to a major reduction in business earnings inequality in the years following the start of the pandemic.

Trends in Total Earnings Inequality

How do the trends in business earnings inequality compare with broader trends in earnings inequality by race? Using the same CPS data on earnings, I expand the sample to include all working individuals and examine total earnings, including both business earnings and earnings from wage and salary jobs. Figure 12.4 displays mean log total earnings by race from 2015 to 2023. A few patterns are evident. First, average total earnings for all workers dropped early in the pandemic and recovered strongly in 2020.

Second, the drop was not nearly as large as it was for mean business earnings for all groups. The finding is consistent with small business owners being especially hard-hit during the pandemic. Contributing to total earnings are large numbers of workers as large firms were much less affected by the shutdowns. Third, there was growth in total earnings for Asian and Black workers in the last two years but not for white or Latinx workers. Finally, racial patterns in total earnings are similar over the time period as

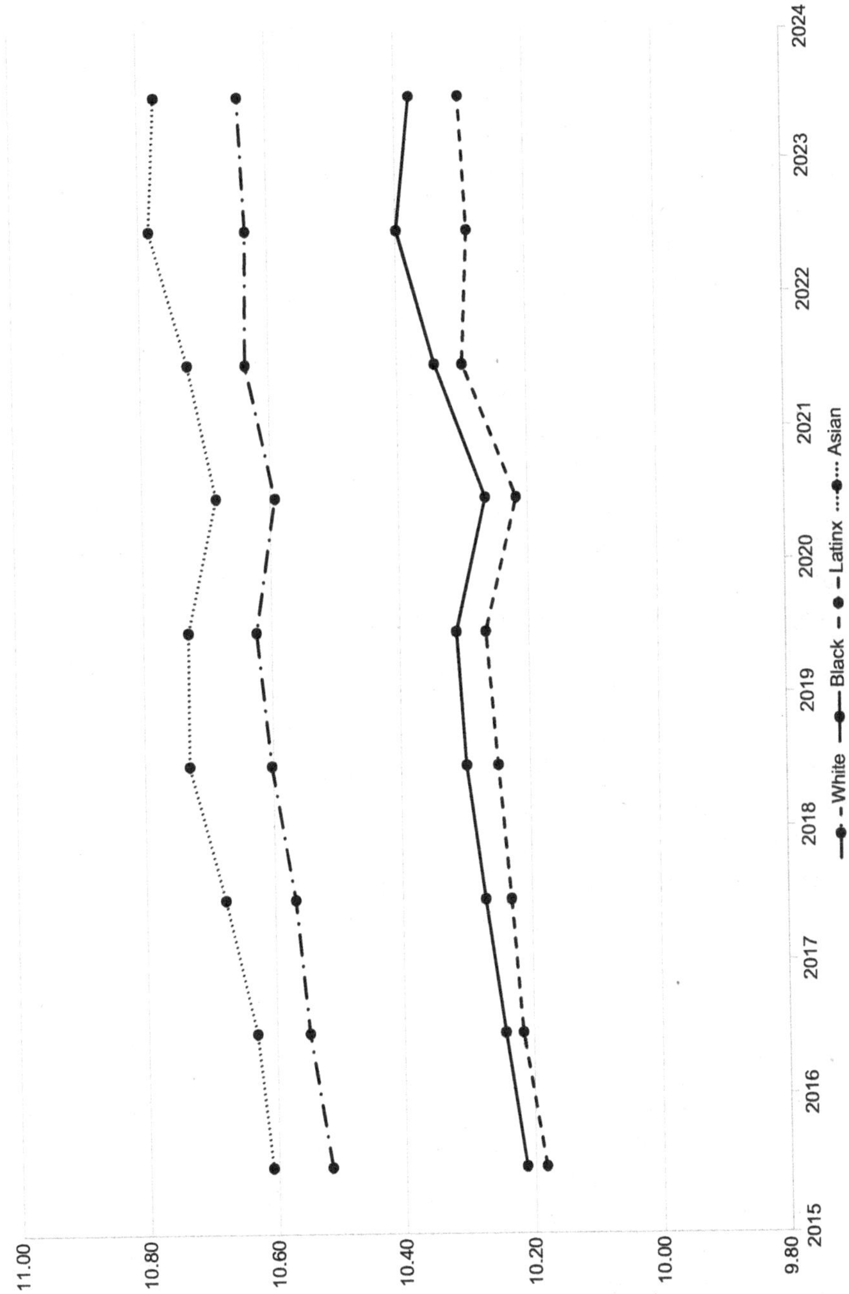

Figure 12.4
Mean log total earnings trends by race, 2015–2023.

for business earnings. Asian workers have the highest total earnings, followed by white workers. At lower levels, Black workers have slightly higher mean total earnings than Latinx workers. Inequality in total earnings is similar to inequality in business earnings.

Contributing to these different patterns are trends in wage and salary earnings by race. Workers who do not own a business and instead work for an employer constitute the other group of workers in the total earnings calculations. Figure 12.5 displays mean log wage and salary earnings by race from 2015 to 2023. The smaller losses in 2020 from COVID-19 are even more evident when focusing on the earnings of wage and salary workers only. Wage and salary workers had much smaller losses in earnings from COVID-19 than did small business owners for all racial groups.

The findings for business earnings, wage and salary earnings, and total earnings provide evidence on how difficult COVID-19 was for small business owners of color. The losses to business owners of color not only were extremely large at the beginning of the pandemic but also were much larger than for wage and salary workers. The losses from 2019 to 2020 were 3 percent for Black wage and salary workers, compared with 28 percent for Black business owners. For Latinx wage and salary workers the losses were 4 percent, compared with 19 percent for Latinx business owners. Asian wage and salary workers experienced losses of 4 percent, but Asian business owners experienced losses of 21 percent in the first year of the pandemic. For comparison, the mean earnings losses for white wage and salary workers and white business owners were 2 percent and 15 percent, respectively. Business owner losses during the pandemic clearly contributed to inequality in total earnings during this unprecedentedly large economic disruption.

Total Wealth Inequality

The CPS data do not include information on wealth. The main source of information on household wealth levels by major racial group is published by the U.S. Census Bureau. The underlying data come from the Survey of Income and Program Participation (SIPP). Table 12.2 reports median household wealth by race from 2019 to 2022. Median wealth for households in the total U.S. population increased from $118,200 just prior to the pandemic to $140,800 in 2020 and to $176,500 in 2022. Even after adjusting for inflation, median wealth levels increased by 18 percent from 2019 to

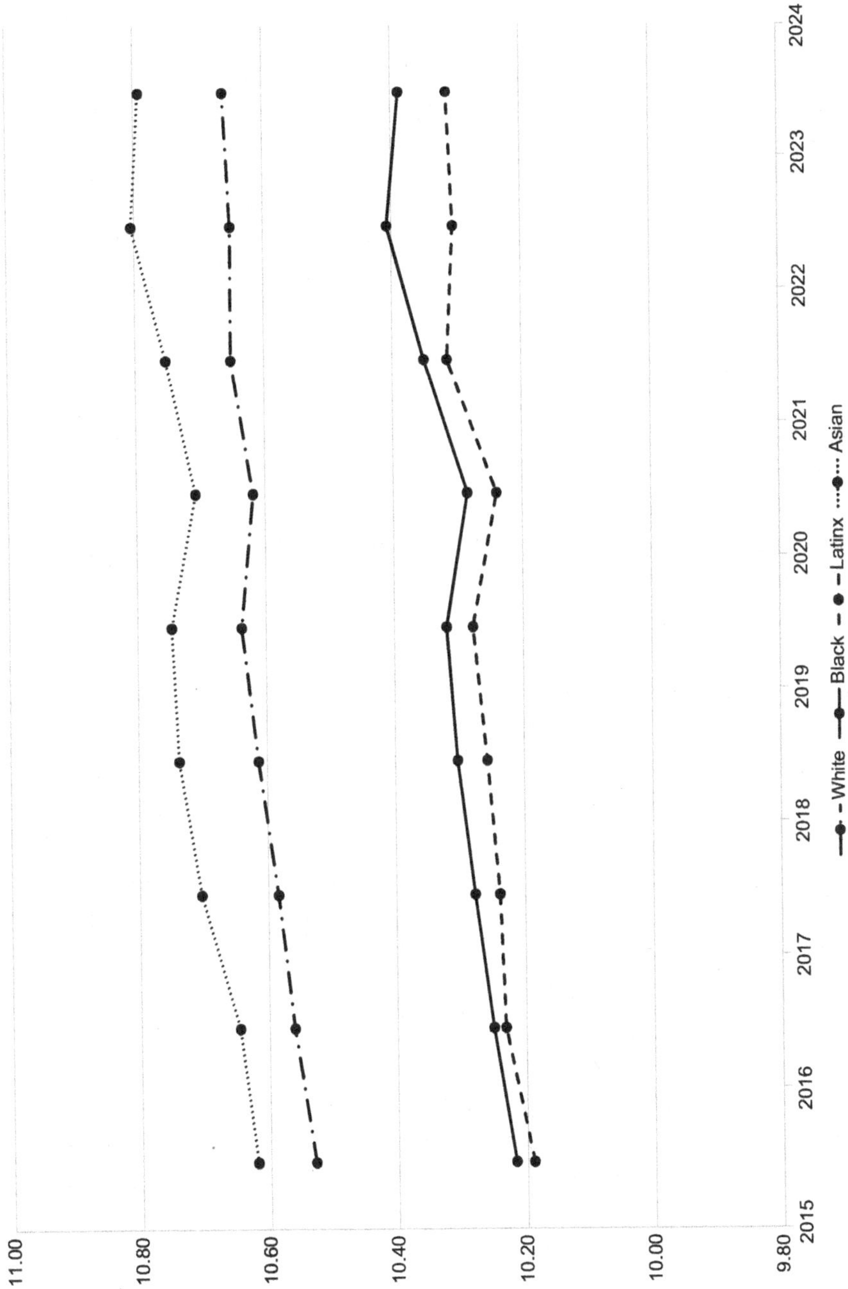

Figure 12.5
Mean log wage and salary earnings trends by race, 2015–2023.

Table 12.2
Median Household Net Worth by Race, 2019–2022

Racial/ethnic group	2019	2020	2021	2022
Total	$118,200	$140,800	$166,900	$176,500
White, non-Latinx	$187,300	$217,500	$250,400	$256,000
Black	$14,100	$18,430	$24,520	$31,250
Asian	$206,400	$264,800	$312,800	$383,800
Latinx	$31,700	$39,800	$48,720	$59,380

Source: U.S. Census Bureau, Wealth, Asset Ownership, & Debt of Households Detailed Tables, 2019–2022.

2020 and by 30 percent from 2019 to 2022. The housing market became increasingly expensive throughout most of the country during the pandemic, which contributed to increases in wealth.

Focusing on racial inequality in wealth, prior to the pandemic there were large inequities in wealth levels. The median level of wealth among Black households was $14,100 in 2019. The median wealth of white households of $187,300 was thirteen times larger than Black household median wealth. It was also $173,200 larger, and that gap in median wealth represented 47 percent of the U.S. total median level of wealth of $118,200. Latinx households also had a much lower level of median wealth, at $31,700. Median wealth for white households was 5.9 times or $155,600 larger than median wealth for Latinx households. In contrast to these two patterns, Asian household wealth was larger, at $206,400.

The evidence on whether wealth inequality increased after COVID-19 arrived is unclear and depends on the measure used. In terms of median wealth ratios, wealth inequality decreased from 2019 to 2022 for Black households and Latinx households. However, in terms of total dollar amounts, wealth inequality increased for both groups. Interestingly, when median wealth level by group is considered as a percentage of the total U.S. median wealth level, inequality decreased slightly for both Black and Latinx households. Asian levels of wealth clearly increased relative to white levels of wealth from pre-COVID-19 to post-COVID-19 years. In 2022, median wealth among Asian households grew to $383,800.

13 The Rise of Tech and the Loss of Retail: Industry Shifts

The findings presented in the previous two chapters demonstrate the strength of the rebound from the pandemic as measured by growth in business activity and the more tempered rebound as measured by growth in business earnings. The rebound was especially strong for business owners of color. White business owners, however, did not experience growth in business activity and earnings in the rebound period starting in 2021. Over this uneven recovery period, did the industry structure of small businesses change? Did industry compositions change by race of the business owner? This chapter explores whether the nature of business ownership changed during the economic recovery. The primary question is whether there was a major restructuring of the types of small businesses that existed before the pandemic started to five years later in the recovery.

COVID-19 was such a major disruption that it might have accelerated some trends and dramatically changed others. For example, well before the pandemic started, consumers were steadily moving their shopping patterns from in-person purchases to online purchases. In early 2020, COVID-19 necessitated a nearly full-scale shift to online shopping under the strict social distancing restrictions that were imposed. The shift to online shopping declined somewhat as customers returned to the in-person experience as restrictions were relaxed but to nowhere near the level existing prior to the start of the pandemic. Another consumer shift that started in the pandemic was increased demand for delivery of goods and even services in some cases. These long-term shifts in consumer behavior might have affected the industry structure of small businesses during the economic recovery.

Industry Structure of Business Owners

Was there a restructuring of the types of businesses that were owned from prepandemic times to postpandemic times? I start by examining how major industry groups grew from before the pandemic to three, four, and five years later in the recovery. I use the same Current Population Survey (CPS) data as were used in previous chapters to explore this question. The focus is on all business owners defined by their main job activity and that the owner is actively working. The number of active business owners primarily captures the number of active small business owners. Table 13.1 reports growth rates for major industries from 2019 to 2022, 2023, and 2024.

The Transportation industry experienced the strongest recovery from the pandemic. Transportation grew by 26 percent from prepandemic levels to 2024. The pandemic created a surge in demand for personal deliveries

Table 13.1
Business Owner Activity Growth by Industry

	Percent change in no. of active business owners		
Industry	2019 to 2022	2019 to 2023	2019 to 2024
Agriculture	−1	−4	−8
Construction	2	−3	1
Manufacturing	6	0	−7
Wholesale Trade	−17	−12	−13
Retail Trade	−6	1	−2
Transportation	23	19	26
Information	15	6	17
Financial Activities	15	14	13
Professional and Business Services	2	3	6
Educational Services	−16	−19	−17
Health Services	0	4	10
Arts, Leisure, and Hotels	14	15	14
Restaurants	5	7	11
Repair and Maintenance	8	1	6
Personal and Laundry Services	3	12	14
Total	4	4	6

Notes: Author's calculations from compiled monthly Current Population Survey microdata.

that was first a sequela of social distancing restrictions but then became part of what consumers wanted. Ride-sharing or ride-hailing apps such as Uber and Lyft, which were growing rapidly before the pandemic, also created new opportunities for self-employed business owners. In the CPS data, ride-sharing app drivers who also work at a job are considered business owners if they work more hours per week driving than they do for their employer. Thus part-time drivers who worked more hours in a wage and salary job are not classified as business owners here.

The Information industry also experienced strong growth from 2019 to recent years. As discussed in previous chapters, the Information sector grew rapidly during the pandemic. The massive shift from working in an office to working from home during the pandemic continued, and office work did not return fully to prepandemic levels. Demand for computers, internet connections, video cameras, software, and other technology fueled the growth in opportunities for business owners in this sector. The number of active business owners in the Information industry grew by 17 percent from 2019 to 2024.

Service industries such as found in the Financial Activities and Personal and Laundry Services sectors recovered strongly in the economic recovery. Industries that were hit hard by shutdowns early in the pandemic also recovered. The Arts, Leisure, and Hotels and Restaurants industries showed growth from prepandemic levels to the five-year anniversary of the start of the pandemic. In contrast to these patterns, small business owners in the Educational Services, Manufacturing, and Agriculture sectors experienced losses in business activity. For the total U.S. economy, business activity grew by 4 percent from 2019 levels through 2023 and by 6 percent from 2019 levels through 2024.

Racial Differences in Business Activity Growth

As noted in chapter 12, there was strong growth in the number of business owners of color from 2019 to 2022, 2023, and 2024. Annualizing numbers for each year, the growth rates from 2019 to 2024, for example, were 35 percent for Black business activity, 30 percent for Latinx business activity, and 22 percent for Asian business activity. In contrast, white business activity dropped by 3 percent from 2019 to 2024.

Table 13.2 reports the largest industry groups realizing growth from 2019 to 2023/2024 for Black, Latinx, and Asian business activity. The years 2023 and 2024 are combined to increase precision in estimates for each group. For Black business owners, the largest contribution to the overall growth came from the Professional and Business Services sector (which accounted for one quarter of the total). The next industry contributing the most to overall growth was Transportation, representing 18 percent of the total. Financial Activities accounted for 14 percent of the growth, and Personal and Laundry

Table 13.2
Top Industries for Business Activity Growth by Race, 2019 to 2023/2024 [Combined]: Share of Total Growth

Race/ethnicity and industry	Percent change, 2019 to 2023/2024
Black business activity	
Total growth (%)	32
Top industries:	Share of total growth (%)
Professional and Business Services	24
Transportation	18
Financial activities	14
Personal and Laundry Services	13
All other industries	31
Latinx business activity	
Total growth (%)	26
Top industries:	Share of total growth (%)
Professional and Business Services	23
Construction	22
Transportation	10
Personal and Laundry Services	8
All other industries	37
Asian business activity	
Total growth (%)	21
Top industries:	Share of total growth (%)
Restaurants	27
Financial Activities	25
Retail Trade	20
Transportation	17
All other industries	11

Notes: Author's calculations from compiled monthly Current Population Survey microdata.

Services for 13 percent. All other industries accounted for 31 percent of the total growth from 2019 to 2023/2024 for Black business activity.

For Latinx business owners, the two largest drivers of growth in business activity were the Professional and Business Services industry and the Construction industry. Professional and Business Services accounted for 23 percent of total growth and Construction accounted for 22 percent of total growth in business activity from prepandemic levels to the 2023/2024 average. The Transportation industry accounted for the next largest share, at 10 percent of the total. Personal and Laundry Services represented 8 percent of the total growth in the number of Latinx active business owners from 2019 to 2023/2024. Growth is concentrated in fewer industries for Latinx business owners. All other industries accounted for 37 percent of total growth in business activity.

Growth in the Restaurant industry accounted for 27 percent of the total growth among Asian business owners from prepandemic levels to 2023/2024. Financial Activities followed closely, representing 25 percent of overall growth. Asian business activity was also strong in the Retail Trade industry, representing one-fifth of total growth in Asian business activity. Transportation also captured a large share of total growth in business activity for Asian business owners. Growth in this industry accounted for 17 percent of total growth. Asian business activity growth was highly concentrated in these four industries. These industries captured 89 percent of the total growth for Asian businesses.

Across all minority groups, the Transportation industry was important for the strong rebound in business activity from the negative shock of COVID-19. Black, Latinx, and Asian business owners took advantage of the new opportunities in this industry. As shown in table 13.1, for the total economy, the Transportation industry experienced the strongest recovery from the pandemic of all major industry groups, growing 26 percent from 2019 to 2023/2024. The demand for personal deliveries and ride-sharing apps such as Uber and Lyft grew strongly in the pandemic and continued in the recovery of the next few years. Taxi and ride-sharing drivers are typically defined as self-employed business owners if this is their main work activity.

Another notable industry that created growth opportunities for Black and Latinx business owners was Professional and Business Services. This industry includes a wide range of different types of businesses and professions, among them lawyering, accountancy, and management. It also includes employment services, business support services, and travel agent services. Finally, it includes landscaping, building services, and waste management. Overall, the industry grew by only 3 percent from 2019 to 2023 and 6 percent from 2019 to 2024 (see table 13.1), but it accounted for nearly a quarter of the strong growth in business activity for both Black and Latinx business owners.

The Industry Structure of Employer Businesses

Using administrative data on business establishments with employees, I dive deeper into how the industry structure changed in the recovery from the pandemic. The most up-to-date information comes from administrative data from the U.S. Bureau of Labor Statistics Quarterly Census of Employment and Wages (QCEW). I examine industry growth rates by extracting and compiling raw data from BLS web pages. Data through the end of 2024 recently became available (release was on June 4, 2025). Unfortunately, no demographic information is available in these data. A major difference between these data and the CPS data used above is that the QCEW covers only employer businesses and does not include nonemployer businesses.

Figure 13.1 displays industry growth rates from 2019 through 2024 for business establishments with employees. The Information industry stands out, having a growth rate of 60 percent, which was nearly twenty percentage points higher than that of any other industry in the recovery and 41 percent higher than the total growth rate for all industries. The vast business opportunities in computers, the internet, and related technologies that were created because of COVID-19 and social distancing restrictions did not subside. To be sure, the Information industry was growing rapidly prior to COVID-19. Over the five-year period just prior to the start of the pandemic (2014–2019), the number of employer business establishments in the Information industry grew by 23 percent. But the five-year period after 2019 resulted in a 37 percent higher growth rate over the same amount of time. The pandemic has certainly resulted in structural changes to the economy that provide more opportunities for businesses in the technology sector.

Another industry that grew rapidly during the economic recovery was Management. The Management industry is defined as comprising (1) management of companies and enterprises, (2) managing offices of bank holding companies, and (3) corporate, subsidiary, and regional managing offices.

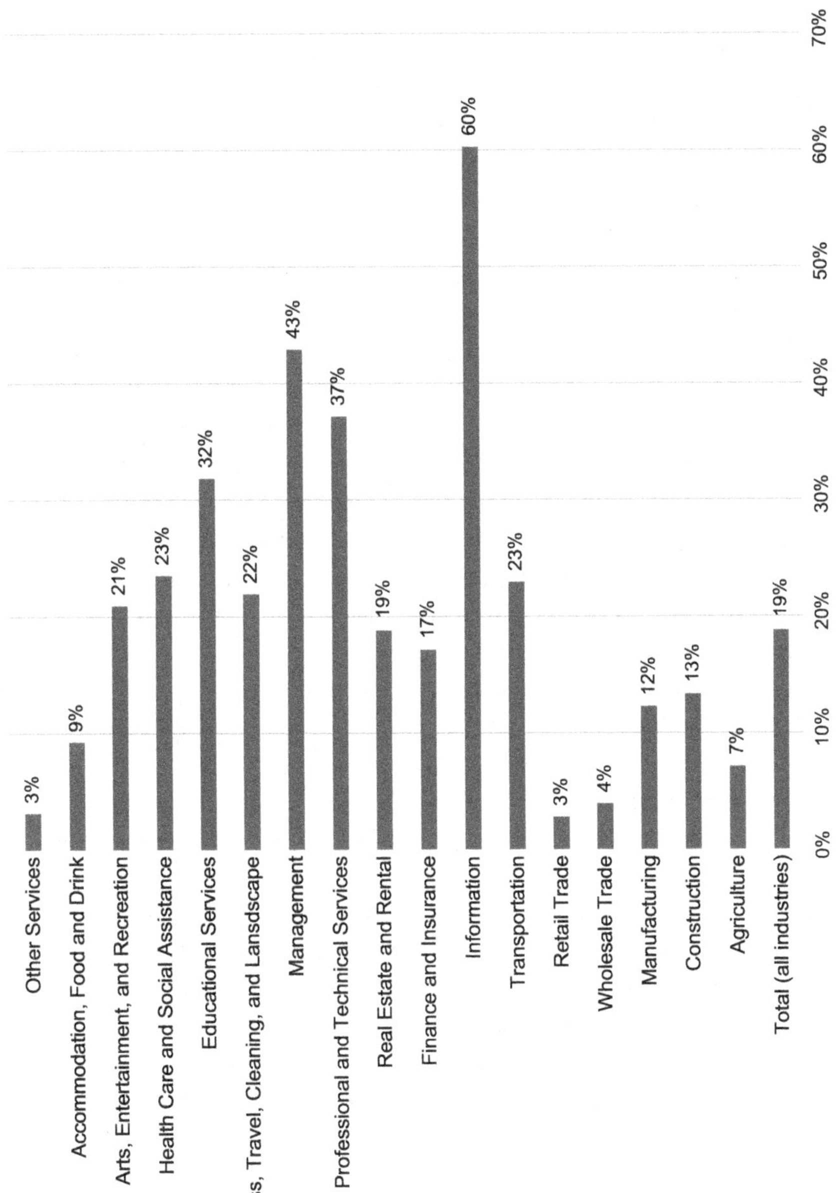

Figure 13.1
Industry growth rates in employer business establishments, 2019 to 2024.

Thus it is a catchall industry related to the management of businesses. The industry grew by 43 percent from 2019 to 2024, experiencing the second-highest growth rate over this period of time among reported industry groups.

The Professional and Technical Services industry had the next highest growth rate from 2019 to 2024. The industry grew by 37 percent over this period of time. Opportunities for high-skill businesses grew in the recovery. A related high-skill industry that also grew rapidly during the COVID-19 recovery was the Educational Services industry. The industry grew by 32 percent.

In contrast to rapid growth in these industries, several industries experienced much slower growth than the total growth rate of 19 percent for all industries combined. Notably, Retail Trade grew by only 3 percent and Wholesale Trade grew by only 4 percent from 2019 to 2024. The lack of growth in Retail Trade is noticeable as even today, many downtown areas continue to have empty, and in some cases boarded-up, storefronts. The change is noticeable. Many downtowns across the country have a hollowed-out feeling to them. It is not clear how long it will take for stores to return to these areas at the level prior to the pandemic, if they ever do. Consumers appear to have made a major shift toward the convenience of purchasing many goods online instead of visiting stores.

Similar to the struggles of stores and shops that make up the Retail Trade industry, businesses in the Accommodation, Food and Drink industry also struggled to recover from the social distancing restrictions, health concerns, and resulting changes in customer behavior during the pandemic. The Accommodation, Food and Drink industry grew by 9 percent from 2019 to 2024.

Two additional industries of note are Construction and Agriculture. Both experienced lower growth rates than the total growth rate for all industries combined. Construction grew by 13 percent from 2019 to 2024. Agriculture, which typically has steady growth and is generally recession proof, experienced relatively slow growth, at 7 percent. Looking back in time, both of these industries grew at roughly similar rates. From 2014 to 2019, Construction grew by 11 percent and Agriculture grew by 7 percent. Therefore, growth in Construction and Agriculture in the pandemic recovery does not appear to be out of sync with earlier levels of growth.

14 Conclusions and Implications

COVID-19 took the world by storm. Not only did it have a severe effect on the health of the world's population, it caused an economic disruption unlike anything ever seen before. The social distancing restrictions imposed to slow the spread of the novel coronavirus shut down or disrupted businesses in all sectors of the economy. Small businesses were especially hard-hit by mandated shutdowns and the fears of consumers, owners, and workers over catching the contagious virus in stores, restaurants, offices, warehouses, plants, and anywhere else people interacted face-to-face.

Small businesses had limited ability to adjust quickly to changes in regulations when the pandemic hit. Small businesses also did not necessarily have the financing needed to make those adjustments required to remain open for business. Customers might have had more health concerns over shopping at small businesses than at larger retailers even within the same store category. For example, customers might have felt less safe visiting small grocery stores than visiting large chain grocery stores. Similarly, customers might have been more concerned about purchasing food from small restaurants than from large chain restaurants. The shift of consumers toward online retailers and large retailers with an online presence during the pandemic also hurt small businesses, which relied primarily on brick-and-mortar sales to customers.

This book has traced the trajectory of the disease, the plight of small businesses, racial inequality, and broader measures of the U.S. economy from the very beginning of the pandemic through its five-year anniversary. These five years undoubtedly represent one of the most tumultuous periods in history for small businesses and the economy. I have drawn on several sources of the most up-to-date data, including novel datasets only recently released, across the timeline of the pandemic and the recovery period to provide a comprehensive, in-depth, and nuanced picture of what happened to small businesses and racial inequality in small businesses during the the pandemic and subsequent economic recovery.

One goal in writing this book was to provide a resource, and specifically an authoritative, comprehensive, and wide-ranging source of information, on how small businesses fared during the pandemic and the recovery from the pandemic-induced recession. In addition to covering overall patterns, the book has been concerned with the differential effects of the pandemic on small businesses by race of business owner and how small businesses fared differently by race during the recovery. All of the analyses used timely data from several different sources, including the universe of Paycheck Protection Program (PPP) loans, the latest microdata from the Bureau of Labor Statistics, and new data from the U.S. Census Bureau and Small Business Administration (SBA) on federal aid receipt and business survival and job destruction. I examined the effects of the more than $1 trillion in aid provided though the PPP and other programs to small businesses. The analysis covered the five-year anniversary of COVID-19 (i.e., from January 2020 to December 2024). This chapter summarizes the findings, discusses what lies ahead for small businesses, and identifies several areas for research.

The First Year of the Pandemic

The start of the pandemic was very destructive to small businesses. In the first month of the pandemic small business activity fell by 22 percent. In comparison, there was only a 5 percent drop in business activity during the Great Recession of 2008–2009, which lasted eighteen months. Losses were even larger for certain groups of the population: Black business activity dropped by a staggering 41 percent in the first month, Latinx business activity dropped by 32 percent, and Asian business activity dropped by 26 percent. Business activity in most major industries faced large reductions in April 2020. Small business owners in Construction, Restaurants, Hotels, Transportation, and Personal and Laundry Services were especially hard-hit. The concentrations of Black-, Latinx-, and Asian-owned businesses in industries hit hard by the pandemic contributed to the higher losses in business activity for these groups than the national average.

A partial rebound happened quickly but not evenly. The findings indicate that there was a partial rebound in May and an additional rebound in June. The number of active business owners bounced back by seven percentage points in May 2020 and by an additional five percentage points in June, resulting in ending at an 8 percent lower level from February to June 2020. Against the larger backdrop, GDP dropped by a record amount—30 percent—in the second quarter of 2020 but rebounded by a record amount in the third quarter. The national unemployment rate hit its long-term peak in April 2020, at 14.8 percent, but dropped rapidly in the next few months. The U.S. economy had never before experienced such a severe disruption that resulted in a large negative initial shock and fast partial rebound.

Although there was a partial rebound, the number of actively working Black business owners remained 26 percent lower in May 2020 than in February 2020 and 19 percent lower in June 2020 than in February 2020. The losses in Latinx business activity from COVID-19 continued into the second and third months after widespread shelter-in-place restrictions were imposed. The number of active Latinx business owners dropped by 19 percent from February to May 2020 and by 10 percent from February to June 2020. Asian business owners suffered continued losses: even with the rebounds in May and June, the number of Asian business owners who were actively running their businesses dropped by 21 percent and 10 percent, respectively, during those months.

The losses to business earnings were large in 2020. Pandemic-induced losses to business earnings in 2020 were 16–19 percent for all business owners. In percentage point terms, the losses might have been even higher except that the earnings data are available only for calendar year 2020, which includes months before social distancing restrictions were imposed and started having effects. There were disproportionate impacts by race: for example, Black business owners experienced larger negative impacts on business earnings, 12–14 percent, relative to white business owners. Using a novel pandemic-focused decomposition technique, I found that the industry concentrations of Black, Latinx, and Asian business owners placed each of these groups at a higher risk of experiencing disproportionate business earnings losses during the pandemic. The types of businesses that experienced the largest losses in business earnings in the pandemic were in the Leisure and Hospitality industries and in Wholesale and Retail Trade.

Several additional measures of business outcomes show large negative effects of COVID-19 early in the pandemic. For example, necessity entrepreneurship, which captures business starts out of unemployment, increased dramatically in 2020, much higher than during the Great Recession. Administrative data from California indicate that taxable sales dropped by 15.4 percent in the second quarter of 2020 relative to the second quarter of 2019. For comparison, taxable sales in California normally grow by 3–4 percent year over year. Losses to taxable sales were nearly 50 percent in major business types such as Clothing and Clothing Accessories Stores, Gasoline Stations, and Food Services and Drinking Places. The same administrative data from California show that the business closure rate increased substantially, from 3.7 percent in the second quarter of 2019 to 6.7 percent in the second quarter of 2020. Closure rates were much higher for small businesses than for large businesses during the pandemic, resulting in an increase in market concentration.

The rebound in business activity in May and June of 2020 generally continued through the remainder of 2020. Through the summer and into the fall, small businesses were opening again and customers were returning to shop at those small businesses. By August 2020 the number of active business owners was only 3 percent lower than it was one year earlier. Business activity continued to increase in September and October. Business activity hit its postpandemic peak in October for the year but still remained lower than in October 2019. The upward trend, however, stopped and reversed course. Because of the rapid increase in new COVID-19 cases in the late fall and early winter, social distancing restrictions and consumer fears ramped up. The number of active business owners actually fell in the next two months, ending the year down nearly one million from the October 2020 peak and down 1.1 million from December 2019.

Overall, business activity experienced a rocky road over 2020. At no time during the year was the recovery complete. Fears were high after COVID-19 cases increased sharply in the fall, disrupting holiday plans. Officials were urging restraint in travel across the country for the holidays to contain the spread of the disease. The surge in COVID-19 cases and increased fear in the fall and winter led to a retrenchment, with business activity levels ending 2020 7 percent lower than at the end of 2019. Mask mandates were widespread across the country at the end of 2020, and many people were reluctantly postponing plans until 2021, when vaccines were expected to become available to everyone.

In addition to the uneven effects of COVID-19 on business owners by race early in the pandemic, there were differential trends in business activity through the rest of 2020 by race. Black business activity showed a continual upward trend until hitting a peak in October but ended the year nearly 10 percent lower than 2019 levels. In contrast, Latinx business activity essentially fully recovered compared to 2019 levels. Asian business activity recovered the least, ending the year roughly 20 percent lower than in 2019.

The Turning Point in 2021

As vaccines started becoming available, there was optimism that 2021 would bring about some major changes for small businesses and the rest of the economy. Indeed, business activity increased fairly consistently over the year, and business earnings experienced a major rebound in 2021, although the rebound was inconsistent across industries. GDP growth was also strong in all four quarters of 2021, and the national unemployment rate reached a surprisingly low level of under 4 percent by the end of the year. COVID-19 cases, however, increased in the summer of 2021 and surprisingly ended the year higher than at the beginning of the year, even with the rollout of vaccines that year.

Latinx business owners experienced the strongest rebound and growth in activity over 2021. Latinx Americans ended 2020 with 2.0 million active business owners. By the end of 2021, the total had grown to 2.3 million active business owners. The growth rate of 16 percent in business activity over the year was quite strong. Black business activity also grew over 2021. There were 1.0 million active Black business owners at the end of 2020. Business activity grew to 1.1 million in December 2021, for a growth rate of 6 percent over the year. Compared with December 2019, however, Black business activity was still 4 percent lower. Additionally, the month-to-month time pattern reveals a potential dip in the last few months of the year. The patterns for Asian business activity show growth over the year. At the end of December 2021 there were 850,000 active Asian business owners. Asian business activity was up 19 percent relative to a year earlier but down 5 percent from December 2019. In comparison, white business activity ended 2021 at 10.5 million active business owners, which represents an increase of 5 percent from the end of 2020 but a decrease of 2 percent from the end of 2019. Of the groups, Latinx business owners were the only group that ended 2021 at a higher level of activity than just before the start of the pandemic.

With respect to effects on business earnings in 2021, Black business earnings mostly returned to prepandemic levels, and Latinx business earnings returned to prepandemic levels. Asian business earnings, however, did not rebound in 2021. In contrast to these patterns, there is some evidence that white business earnings were higher in 2021 than prepandemic levels.

The Economic Recovery over the Next Few Years

After the turning point in 2021, the recovery for small businesses and the broader economy became clearer, which aligned with improvement in slowing the spread of COVID-19. The number of new COVID-19 cases continued to drop from 2022 through the end of 2024, but not consistently. For example, there were 600,000 new cases per week in early 2022 but nearly one million new cases per week at the end of 2022. Case numbers then dropped to roughly 300,000 new cases per week in March 2022, and even further, to 200,000 new cases per week, by the end of 2022. In 2023, new case numbers dropped steadily, reaching levels that were generally below 50,000 new cases per week in the summer of 2023, but then reversed course, rising to 141,000 new cases for the last full week of 2023. The year 2024 witnessed a similar pattern of new COVID-19 cases declining in the early part of the year through the summer and then increasing in the fall and early winter.

The beginning of 2022 marked perhaps a final turning point in the rocky recovery from COVID-19 for small business activity. Business activity increased in the first few months of 2022 and experienced only a slight drop that summer. For every month of 2022, business activity was higher than for the same month in 2019. Averaging across all months during the year, business activity was 5 percent higher each month in 2022 than in the same month in 2019. Business activity continued to increase in both 2023 and 2024. The number of active business owners reached a peak in September 2024, at 17.1 million. The month-to-month comparisons between 2024 and 2019 indicate solid growth for every month. The average increase for all months from 2019 to 2024 was 6.5 percent. Business activity has clearly increased since the disruption created by COVID-19 in March and April 2020.

The rebound in business earnings in 2021 did not continue in 2022 and 2023. It was not the beginning of a longer upward trend in business earnings. Mean business earnings showed a slight decrease in 2022 and 2023, whereas mean log business earnings showed a slightly less pessimistic picture as the trend was slightly upward. But the main conclusion is the same: business earnings did not trend upward and were at, or slightly lower than, the level of earnings just prior to the start of the pandemic.

The broader economy continued to improve in 2022 through the end of 2024. GDP grew in nearly all quarters over the three-year period. The unemployment rate trended downward in 2022, reaching an extremely low level of 3.5 percent in December of that year. The labor market was very strong in 2022, with the unemployment rate under 4 percent for every month except January. The unemployment rate remained extremely low throughout 2023, and it was not until 2024 that the unemployment rate crept above the 4 percent level again. As measured by the unemployment rate, the U.S. economy was strong during this time period.

The gains over the past few years were generally felt similarly across different racial and ethnic groups. All minority groups experienced increases from the beginning of 2022 to the end of 2024 in the number of active business owners. The upward trends for Black, Latinx, and Asian business activity are clear during this period. The recovery from the depths of the pandemic appeared to be strong, at least as measured by business activity for each group. Comparing annual averages in 2024 to 2021, the number of active Black business owners increased from 1.25 million to 1.47 million, representing an increase of 18 percent. The number of Latinx business owners increased from 2.2 million in 2021 to 2.6 million in 2024, which is also a growth rate of 18 percent. The percentage of active Asian business owners grew at the fastest rate from 2021 to 2024 (23 percent), increasing from 881,000 in 2021 to 1,084,000 in 2024. In contrast, the number of active white business owners decreased slightly during the recovery period. There were 10.3 million white business owners in 2021 and 10.2 million in 2024, representing a slight decrease of 1 percent.

Focusing on the subset of businesses with employees, there is additional evidence of growth in the number of Black-, Latinx-, and Asian-owned firms in the recovery, at least through 2022. The number of Black-owned employer firms increased by 20 percent from prepandemic levels. The growth rate was even higher through 2022, 45 percent higher than in 2019. Latinx businesses with employees also experienced strong growth early in the recovery. The number of employer businesses increased by 17 percent in 2021 and 34 percent in 2022 relative to prepandemic levels. Growth rates were less strong, but still strong, for Asian businesses with employees. The number of Asian employer businesses grew by 12 percent from 2019 to 2022. In contrast to these patterns, the number of white employer businesses declined by 3 percent from 2019 to 2022.

With respect to racial patterns in business earnings, the white business earnings trend was essentially flat after the initial rebound from COVID-19 in 2021. In contrast, mean business earnings grew from 2021 to 2023 for Black business owners by roughly 4 percent. Latinx business owners experienced a growth of roughly 5 percent in mean business earnings from 2021 to 2023. Asian business owners experienced the strongest growth in business earnings, 12 percent, from 2021 to 2023.

Implications for Longer-Term Inequality

Disproportionate losses to business activity and earnings among business owners of color in the pandemic are concerning because of the potential to widen broader economic inequality. This widening would set back one of the long-term goals of fostering minority business development (e.g., Bradford 2003, 2014; Chatterji, Chay, and Fairlie 2014; Kroeger and Wright 2021). Another stated goal of the Minority Business Development Agency, which is part of the U.S. Department of Commerce, for example, is to "promote the growth and global competitiveness of Minority Business Enterprises (MBE) to unlock the country's full economic potential" (MBDA 2025).[1] The idea of "unlocking" economic potential or gains in economic efficiency by expanding opportunities for minority businesses is often overlooked (Fairlie and Robb 2008). Business formation has been associated with the creation of new industries, innovation, job creation, improvement in sector productivity, and economic growth (Reynolds 2005). If minority entrepreneurs face liquidity constraints, discrimination, or other barriers to creating new business or expanding current businesses, there will be efficiency losses in the economy. These efficiency losses may have been exacerbated during the pandemic. Barriers to entry, growth, and survival in the economic recovery are potentially costly to productivity and local job creation, especially as minorities represent a growing share of the population.

Losses to business activity may be especially damaging for job creation and economic stability in low-income and disadvantaged neighborhoods (Boston 1999, 2006; Stoll, Raphael, and Holzer 2001). Business activity losses are very important to the owner because of the impact on the owner's income, savings, and debt. There is evidence that disadvantaged business owners have more upward income mobility and experience faster earnings growth than disadvantaged wage and salary workers (Fairlie 2004; Holtz-Eakin, Rosen, and Weathers 2000).

Previous studies have identified wealth disparities, access to financial capital, discrimination in lending, other types of discrimination, human capital, family business background, social capital, and other factors as limiting minority business creation and success.[2] In a series of previously published papers and books, I used various datasets to study the causes of racial and ethnic disparities in business ownership, formation, and outcomes, focusing on the theoretical constraints that limit productivity and cause inefficiencies in the economy. These studies provide examples and collectively a summary of many of the key findings from this literature.

In a book published earlier with the MIT Press (Fairlie and Robb 2008), we drew on confidential, restricted-access business-level data from the U.S. Census Bureau to explore why Asian-owned firms have higher average performance in comparison with white-owned businesses and Black-owned firms have lower average performance. We found that access to financial capital is the largest factor limiting the success of Black-owned businesses and also the largest factor contributing to the outperformance (relative to white-owned businesses) of Asian-owned businesses, on average. Family business experience also plays a role in explaining differences in outcomes.

Focusing on business ownership and earnings disparities, I used Current Population Survey (CPS) and American Community Survey (ACS) data to examine potential barriers created by human capital, wealth, and demographic, geographic, and industry constraints for all major racial groups (Fairlie 2018). I found that low levels of wealth contribute to lower Black and Latinx business ownership rates and high levels of wealth contribute to higher Asian business ownership rates. Low levels of education contribute to the lower business income of Black and Latinx owners and high levels of education increase Asian business income. Focusing on Mexican American entrepreneurship, Fairlie and Woodruff (2010) studied why group levels are so low in the United States even though self-employment rates are extremely high in Mexico. We found that low levels of education and wealth explain the entire gap between Mexican immigrants and non-Latino whites in business formation rates; together with language proficiency, these factors explain nearly the entire gap in business income. Legal status represents an additional factor for low rates for Mexican immigrants.

In another book published with the MIT Press (Fairlie et al. 2023), we focused on the early stages of starting and running a business. As part of the broader analysis of startups we examined patterns and causes of racial disparities in startup ownership and employment. Using data from the 2007 Survey of Business Owners (SBO), we found that compared with the demographic composition of the U.S. labor force, Black, Latinx, and Native American workers are underrepresented in startup ownership and Asian workers are overrepresented. Black-, Latinx-, and Native American–owned startups hire fewer employees per startup in the initial year than do non-Latinx white-owned startups. Asian-owned startups hire more employees in the initial year than white-owned startups. We also found that undercapitalization and low levels of human capital are barriers faced by Black-, Latinx-, and Native American–owned startups that explain relatively low initial employment levels. Asian-owned startups have the highest level of startup capital, which is associated with the highest level of early-stage employment among startups owned by any major racial or ethnic group.

In more recent work focusing on startups (Fairlie, Robb, and Robinson 2022), we used confidential and restricted-access panel data from the 2004–2011 Kauffman Firm Survey to explore disparities in capital use between Black- and white-owned startups. We found that Black-owned startups start smaller and stay smaller over the entire first eight years of their existence. Black startups face more difficulty in raising external capital, especially external debt. We found that disparities in creditworthiness constrain Black entrepreneurs, but perceptions of treatment by banks also hold them back. Black entrepreneurs apply for loans less often than white entrepreneurs largely because they expect to be denied credit even when they have a good credit history and in settings where strong local banks favor new business development.

Economic Inequality: Total Earnings and Wealth

Long-term disparities in business ownership, earnings, and other business outcomes contribute to overall economic racial inequality. Chapter 11 examined whether there is any evidence that the larger losses in business activity and earnings at the beginning of the pandemic increased overall economic inequality more recently. The chapter analyzed trends in total earnings (i.e., not limited to business owners) using the same dataset in the pandemic and economic recovery. The analysis showed that losses to total earnings were not nearly as large as losses to business earnings for all groups. Although small business owners were hit especially hard during the pandemic, the losses did not result in an increase in racial inequality in total earnings losses from prepandemic levels to the growth period. For all groups, total earnings increased from 2019 to 2023, and total earnings grew by more for Black, Latinx, and Asian workers than for white workers.

Chapter 11 also examined trends in racial disparities in wealth using another source of data from the Census Bureau. Turning to wealth inequality, the answer depends on the measure used. In terms of median wealth ratios, wealth inequality decreased from 2019 to 2022 for Black households and Latinx households. However, in terms of total dollar amounts, wealth inequality increased for both groups. Interestingly, as a percentage of total U.S. median wealth level, inequality decreased slightly. Asian household levels of wealth increased relative to white levels of wealth from pre-COVID-19 to post-COVID-19 years for all measures. Unfortunately, the evidence is somewhat ambiguous with regard to longer-term effects on wealth inequality, but it does not appear as though the large losses at the beginning of the pandemic resulted in a large increase in inequality, possibly because of the strong recovery after the initial disruption in the first few months.

Future Research: The Pandemic, Recovery, and Racial Inequality

The causes of racial disparities in pandemic impacts and their consequences for long-term closures, job creation, and business earnings are complex. Whether these disparities have implications for longer-term racial inequality in business and economic success is an important question. A first step for future research would be to extend the analysis through more years. Extending the analysis presented in chapter 12 on total earnings and wealth inequality through the end of 2024 as the data become available would be helpful. More research is needed on whether differences in business earnings losses during the pandemic had longlasting effects on total earnings and wealth through losses to savings, increased debt, and employment or career disruption.

One area that requires further study is whether and how the pandemic changed access to financial capital. Did it change the underlying constraints that have traditionally limited access to capital for some groups, or did it open up new opportunities for financing startups and expansions? There was an earlier shift toward fintech, for example, that was accelerated because of COVID-19 (Mills 2024). Did the expansion of fintech in financing small businesses reduce some of the financial constraints faced by minority-owned businesses? Did the high rates of inflation and an increase in interest rates early in the recovery make loans too expensive for small businesses? Did banks become nervous about lending early in the pandemic and recovery because of uncertainty over how fast the economy would return to a full recovery?

In recent research using loan data for small businesses collected between January 2022 and June 2023, Bradford et al. (2025) found that after controlling for detailed firm risk factors, Asian American–owned firms paid 2.9 percentage points higher interest rates, Hispanic-owned firms paid 2.9 percentage points higher rates, and Black-owned firms paid 3.1 percentage points higher rates than white-owned firms for loans. They also found evidence that Black-owned firms pay higher interest rates in states with higher structural racism, and higher rates than their white counterparts at credit unions, fintech lenders, and nonbank finance companies. More research is needed on these important questions because of the importance of access to financial capital for small businesses and the finding that constraints on access are an underlying factor in inequality for business ownership, performance, and survival.

More research is also needed on whether disproportionate losses early in the pandemic had longlasting impacts on owners and led to disruptions for others, including their employees. Owing to data limitations, very little research has focused on permanent business closures during the pandemic and whether these differed by group. Survival rates among minority-owned businesses were lower than among nonminority-owned businesses, and an important unanswered question is whether there is a critical point early in the life cycle of a startup that determines success or not. A careful examination of the stage after startup in which minority startups were especially likely to fail during the pandemic would be useful. For example, was there a critical length of shutdown time during the pandemic after which any additional closure time turned into a permanent closure? Or perhaps temporary shutdowns might not capture the main underlying factor causing permanent closures and instead permanent closures might be primarily caused by continued months or years of reduced business earnings. Access to capital, even through the owner's savings or wealth, might also play an important role in preventing or delaying permanent closures. More research is needed on all of these questions.

A new data source from the Census Bureau should expand opportunities to study questions around business inequality during the pandemic and recovery period. The U.S. Census Bureau's Nonemployer Statistics by Demographics (NES-D) database uses existing surveys and administrative records at the U.S. Census Bureau on demographics to replace the loss of survey information that was previously collected for employer businesses.[3] The NES-D can be linked to the longitudinal information on survival, growth, and employment of startups in the Comprehensive Startup Panel (CSP) dataset created in the previous MIT Press book (Fairlie et al. 2023) to study new questions on racial inequality in business outcomes. The CSP tracks the universe of startups in the country since the 1994 startup cohort, following each startup for up to seven years.[4] In general, it has been difficult to find information on the race and ethnicity of business owners, and the NES-D, linked with other datasets such as the CSP, could help to fill that void.

Another promising area for future research takes advantage of the ability to merge the CSP with other Census Bureau datasets that provide detailed information on owner characteristics, including race and ethnicity. The ACS has information on home ownership and values, and the Survey of Income and Program Participation (SIPP) has additional information on ownership and values of detailed assets. The Annual Business Survey (ABS), which includes employer businesses, provides detailed information on demographics and financial status. In an exciting new research project, Robb and Diagne (2025) merged the CSP with the 2012

Survey of Business Owners (SBO) to study startups that began operations in 2011 or 2012 over the 2012–2019 period. They examined the transition from nonemployer to employer status, firm survival, and job creation by startups. The matched CSP-SBO sample includes more than 100,000 startup businesses tracked over their first seven years. Among the numerous results, they find that financial capital investment is a critical factor, with higher levels of investment among startups being correlated with the likelihood of a transition from nonemployer to employer status. Higher levels of financial capital investment are also associated with higher survival rates and employment growth. The study also found that Black-owned startups have lower rates of transitioning from nonemployer to employer status and lower survival rates. A fourth option is to link the Longitudinal Employer-Household Dynamics (LEHD) dataset to the CSP. The LEHD includes detailed information on work histories, such as prior earnings and employers.

Linking these data sources and others to the CSP could open up many new avenues for research on racial inequality in access to financial capital, human capital constraints, and detailed business outcomes. One possibility is to link several, or all, of these datasets to provide a comprehensive view that includes longitudinal information on detailed business outcomes, owner demographics, and owner's wealth, education, and labor market experiences. It could move the needle on understanding the underlying causes of racial inequality in business ownership and success, and possibly on how the pandemic changed or did not change the trajectory of trends in racial inequality in business outcomes.

In general, more research is needed on whether disproportionate business earnings losses are long-lasting. Because of data limitations, very little research has focused on permanent closures during the pandemic years and whether these differed by race and ethnicity. An important question is whether the continuing shift in consumer behavior toward online shopping and new developments in robots, AI, and automation will lead to permanent closures among small businesses and have disproportionate effects by race. A promising sign is that the number of active business owners has increased since prepandemic levels for Black, Latinx, Asian, and Native American business owners. New businesses might be filling in some of the storefronts emptied by COVID-19 and moving into nontraditional service areas (Simon 2024).

Paycheck Protection Program Loan Receipt, Closures, and Jobs

Many health experts and scientists have proclaimed that the question is not *whether* there will be another pandemic but *when* (e.g., CDC 2024; Feldscher 2024; Giddings 2025). The CDC warns that infectious disease threats from emerging pathogens and global outbreaks of dangerous viruses are increasing. In thinking about the next pandemic, was the $1 trillion spent by the federal government to help small businesses money well spent? Was the $800 billion spent on the largest program targeting small businesses, the PPP, worth it from a benefit-cost perspective? What were the benefits and costs of the PPP and other programs? Did they save small businesses and jobs in the long run, and limit economic disruptions? Or was there just a reallocation of resources in the economy that made no one better off in the long run?

In thinking about the big picture of broader federal spending in the pandemic, Cecilia Rouse, former chair of the Council of Economic Advisors (2021–2023), notes that the federal government went "big" on total spending in the pandemic and that the recoveries in the labor market and for the GDP were relatively fast, but that there was a spike in inflation (Rouse 2024). In the end, she notes that the full benefits and costs of federal spending in the pandemic will take some time to figure out. She concludes by stating that this was probably not "perfect" economic policymaking but for now appears to be "good" economic policymaking. More research is needed on these big policy questions.

The PPP evolved substantially over time. Chapter 10 analyzes a new data source that provides information on PPP loan receipt, survival, and job destruction among small businesses. The Business Dynamics Statistics of SBA COVID Response (BDS-SBA COVID) recipients database links data on the universe of employer businesses to data on the universe of PPP loans. The analysis of data that I compiled from tabulations from the BDS-SBA COVID data yields five main findings:

1. Small businesses receiving PPP loans were less likely to exit than small businesses not receiving PPP loans. Although this finding does not necessarily imply that PPP loan receipt caused the lower exit rate, it is consistent with a causal impact.
2. Exit rates were lower for small businesses receiving PPP loans earlier in the pandemic than later in the pandemic. Earlier receipt of PPP funds might have reduced exit rates among small businesses.

3. Exit rates were higher for small businesses not receiving PPP loans relative to small businesses receiving PPP loans for the two smaller employment size groups. Among firms with 1–9 employees, the establishment exit rate was 12.7 percent without PPP receipt, compared with 9.0 percent with PPP receipt. The differential in exit rates is even larger when early versus later PPP loan receipt are compared.
4. PPP loan receipt was associated with a job destruction rate of 11.3 percent. Job destruction was slightly lower among business establishments not receiving PPP funds. The job destruction rate was 10.9 percent.
5. The difference in job destruction rates between businesses receiving and those not receiving PPP loans is smaller when the analysis focuses on early receipt of PPP loans. Among small businesses receiving loans before April 24, 2020, the job destruction rate was 10.6 percent, compared with 10.9 percent for small businesses not receiving loans before April 24.

Whether the PPP helped small businesses survive and retain employees during the pandemic is an important but difficult question to answer. Although the comparisons made between businesses receiving loans and businesses not receiving loans provide a useful first step to better understand the effects of the PPP on small businesses, there are concerns over selection bias. The fundamental concern is that the businesses receiving loans might be the ones that could benefit the most from them (positive bias), or perhaps the businesses not receiving loans were the ones that were confident they could survive without them (negative bias). Selection bias is notoriously difficult to address in estimating the effects of government policies. Chapter 10 reviewed several studies that employed empirical strategies in an attempt to address these concerns in estimating the impacts of the PPP program on small business outcomes (Agarwal et al. 2024; Autor et al. 2022; Bartik, Cullen, Glaeser, et al. 2020; Chetty et al. 2024; Cole 2024; Granja et al. 2022; Hubbard and Strain 2020; Humphries, Neilson, and Ulyssea 2020; Staples and Krumel 2023). The studies generally found positive effects on survival and employment, but some studies found estimates of large costs per employee saved.

The findings from the analysis of BDS-SBA COVID data and previous studies of the effectiveness of pandemic aid to small businesses provide some insights into what happened during this tumultuous time, but much more remains to uncover. More research is clearly needed on the benefits of the PPP and other aid provided during the pandemic. How much did it save in terms of the value of reducing business closures, saving jobs, reducing unemployment insurance, reducing economic disruptions of families (through fewer defaults on mortgages or other loan payments), reducing welfare receipt, and ameliorating other potential costs? A step in this direction could be taken by linking additional Census Bureau datasets to the universe of PPP loans. For example, linking loan data to the new CSP dataset could be useful for studying job creation, survival, and other outcomes of startups during the pandemic and how early-stage patterns were changed or not changed by receiving or not receiving PPP funds.[5] Ninety-two percent of all PPP loans were forgiven (U.S. Census Bureau 2025). It would also be useful to analyze differences along this dimension.

PPP Loans and Race

For chapters 5 and 9, I compiled and analyzed PPP loan microdata to shed light on how the major changes the program went through over time affected the disbursement of funds to minority communities and small businesses across the country. The PPP microdata cover the universe of loans and provide information not only on the loans but also on the small businesses receiving those loans and the lenders providing them. To examine whether PPP funds were disbursed evenly to minority communities, thus benefiting the businesses and employees in those communities, I drew on data measuring the minority share of the population and total businesses in the analysis. The question is partly motivated by one of the stated goals of the original CARES Act, which was to prioritize serving "underserved markets" and businesses owned by "socially and economically disadvantaged individuals" (U.S. Congress 2020).

PPP funds were provided over three rounds that varied in total dollar amounts, number of loans, types of financial institutions providing the loans, whether employer or nonemployer businesses were emphasized, and first-draw versus second-draw loans. The first round of the PPP ran from April 3, 2020, to April 16, 2020 (i.e., the first two weeks of the program) and provided 1.7 million loans to small businesses for a total of $342 billion. The second round ran from April 17, 2020, to August 8, 2020, and provided 3.6 million loans to small businesses for a total of $183 billion. The PPP was rebooted in 2021 for a third round of funding, which provided 6.7 million loans to small businesses for a total of $278 billion. In total, 5,500 different financial institutions provided 11.8 million loans to small businesses for a total of $800 billion lent.

In addition to these differences across the three rounds of the PPP, the analysis of loan microdata revealed the following main findings:

1. The top-fifteen lists of financial institutions providing loans across the three rounds of the PPP changed markedly. The first round mostly involved large banks, owing to the rush to get funds out early in the pandemic. The second round involved more fintechs and CDFIs, and the third round involved an even wider range of financial institutions providing loans.
2. In the first round of the program, there was a negative relationship between the number of PPP loans per business and the minority share of the population or the minority share of businesses. PPP loans were not disbursed evenly to minority communities in the first two weeks of the program.
3. The relationship became positive in the second round of the PPP as a wider range of financial institutions became involved in providing loans and the devastating early impacts of COVID-19 on Black-, Latinx-, and Asian-owned businesses became better known from research (e.g., Fairlie 2020a).
4. In the rebooted program in 2021, there was a positive relationship between the number of loans per business and the minority share of the population or the minority share of total businesses. The finding is consistent with the emphasis on helping eligible borrowers in underserved and disadvantaged communities in this round of the PPP.
5. The positive relationship holds for first-draw loans and second-draw loans. There is some evidence of a weaker positive relationship for second-draw loans, which is consistent with the receipt of second-draw loans being conditional on receiving a first-draw loan (possibly from the first round of the PPP).
6. The 2021 program also targeted nonemployer businesses, and a positive relationship between PPP loan receipt and minority share is found for this subset of businesses.

PPP funding to minority communities evolved from a negative relationship in the first round to a strong positive relationship in the third round partly because applying for PPP loans very early in the pandemic favored businesses having long-established relationships with banks, which minority businesses were less likely to have (Mills and Battisto 2020). Minority-owned businesses also tend to be smaller than nonminority-owned businesses (Fairlie and Robb 2008; U.S. Census Bureau 2016), and smaller businesses often took longer to complete the required paperwork because of a lack of resources and experience. The findings from the new BDS-SBA COVID data indicate that the smallest small businesses tended to receive PPP funds later than midsize small businesses. The third round of the PPP included an exclusivity period to favor very small businesses in accessing funds. The program also shifted over time in the types of financial institutions that were involved, which resulted in more loans to minority-owned businesses (Fei and Yang 2021; Howell et al. 2021; Liu and Parilla 2020; Mills 2024). The 2021 program also provided a head start for applications through Community Development Financial Institutions (CDFIs). The analysis of top-fifteen lender rankings reveals the rising importance of fintechs and CDFIs over subsequent rounds of the PPP.

Differential PPP Loan Receipt and Survival by Race

Racial inequality in the receipt and effectiveness of federal aid in the pandemic represents a glaring hole in our knowledge of the immediate and long-term impacts of the pandemic. For example, the important question of whether Black, Latinx, and Asian businesses received PPP loans in proportion to their eligibility is essentially unknown. Minority communities did not receive a proportional amount of aid in the first round of the PPP but this turned around in the second and third rounds of the PPP. Attempts by previous studies to identify the owner's race of PPP receipt faced limitations. The new BDS-SBA COVID data do not provide information on the race of the owner.

The underlying problem is that information on owner's race and ethnicity is incomplete in the PPP loan data, with the vast majority of loans providing no information and the small percentage of loans with this information not representative of the universe of loans. As reviewed in chapter 5, previous studies used different approaches to impute missing race information on PPP loans. The approaches included predicting a business owner's race and ethnicity using information such as the owner's name and location, proxying with listed food types from Yelp listings, using state administrative data on restaurant licenses, or looking through corporate records, voter registrations, lien filings, and mortgage records (Chernenko and Scharfstein; Fei and Yang 2021; 2021; Howell et al. 2021). As discussed above, new and existing datasets available from the Census Bureau provide race information for business owners; these datasets include the NES-D, SBO, ABS, ASE, ACS, CPS, and SIPP. All of these datasets can potentially be linked to loan data in future research to shed light on the question.

Another criticism of the PPP is that no information was collected on applications for loans that were denied. This information is important for gauging demand and unmet need for these loans by minority businesses and in minority communities. There is a major difference in potential policy response between whether minority businesses needed these loans but faced barriers (e.g., lack of established bank relationships, lack of information about loans, the digital divide, or discrimination) and whether they did not need loans or needed smaller loans. An early study using matched-pair audit testing found that Black and white PPP applicants with similar credit characteristics applied to a lender in the same time period but were found to receive differential treatment in encouragement to apply for a loan, the products offered, and the information provided by the bank representative (Lederer et al. 2020). Using survey data from the Survey of Small Business Finances (SSBF), the U.S. Federal Reserve Banks (2021) found racial disparities in both applications for PPP loans and receipt of the full amount applied for in loans. Another worrisome discovery is that Garcia and Darity (2022) found evidence of benefits from not reporting race by Black-owned businesses on PPP loan applications early in the pandemic. More research is clearly needed on numbers of applications, requested amounts, and the success rate of those applications to government aid programs. It would be particularly interesting to use linked longitudinal data to examine which businesses and circumstances led to second-draw loans in 2021. Many minority businesses might have been reluctant to apply for PPP loans because of uncertainty over future revenues as a result of entering the pandemic in a weakened position. More research is needed on the dynamics of PPP receipt over the three rounds of funding. All of this information is important for creating programs to provide financial aid in future pandemics or crises that are equitable and to address information constraints and potential lending discrimination.

In sum, more research is clearly needed on whether the $800 billion PPP had any long-term effects on helping minority business owners survive the pandemic. The answer to whether unequal access to loans affected racial gaps in business outcomes such as survival, earnings, and employment is mostly unknown. Information on race and ethnicity in the loan data has been a major limitation for previous research, but linking administrative and survey data on business outcomes and race to the loan data holds promise for future research.

The Need for Real-Time Data on Business Activity

One lesson learned during the pandemic is the need for real-time data on business activity not only to measure outcomes but also to use for financial aid provision such as PPP loans. Both the former director of the SBA, Karen Mills, and the former head of the Council of Economic Advisors, Cecilia Rouse, have noted this concern. Specifically, Rouse (2024, 4) notes that a lesson learned from the pandemic is that "better calibrated economic policymaking will require much deeper investment in data and infrastructure." She notes this would have helped address problems with the PPP, including inefficiently delivered assistance, waste and poor targeting of funds, and outright fraud. In discussing pandemic aid for small businesses, Mills (2024, 123) argues that "the lack of a federal registry for small businesses . . . led to difficulties in quickly establishing who was, in fact, eligible for benefits," and that this registry would be beneficial for "a wide range of small business policymaking and programs."

Given the threat of another pandemic or crisis, there is a clear need for more real-time data on small businesses activity. The analysis in many chapters of this book takes advantage of a "near" real-time dataset to track business activity, the CPS microdata. The findings from these data, which are based on surveys to capture the unemployment rate by the BLS, were influential for policymaking and research during the pandemic. My first papers using these data to study racial inequality in business activity and unemployment were released very early in the pandemic (Fairlie 2020a; Couch, Fairlie, and Xu 2020a). The findings of both studies were released as NBER working papers in May 2020. The advantage of the monthly CPS data is that they were intended to provide a timely measure of the national unemployment rate, which is used extensively by policymakers, businesses, investors, workers, and many others. Fortunately, the BLS and the Census Bureau post the microdata for download very quickly after the monthly labor report is released. The BLS releases the Employment Situation Summary on the first Friday of each month at 8:30 a.m. Eastern time. The CPS, however, is the exception as most datasets provided by the federal government take much longer to be released.[6]

Real-Time Measures of Business Activity

At the beginning of the pandemic, several efforts were made to tap into nontraditional sources of "real-time" data collected by private companies for their business purposes. For example, Bartik, Bertrand, Feng, et al. (2020) used data from Homebase, a provider of clock-in, clock-out tracking software, and measured business shutdowns by firms stopping their reporting of clock events. Kurmann, Lale, and Ta (2021) also used Homebase data but augmented the information by additionally checking whether business owners updated their status in Google Places or stopped posting on Facebook. Rigobon et al. (2022) used data from Google Places in the retail and food service sectors and compared "scraped" data at two different points in time to identify business exits. Yelp (2020) used its online platform of business reviews to track business closures when owners updated their Yelp pages. Chetty et al. (2020) relied on Womply, which aggregates transaction and revenue data from several credit card processors. Firms that reported zero credit card revenues for three days in a row were counted as closures. A few studies used sources of information on foot traffic from mobile or cell phone location data to measure business activity. For example, Ong, Cheng, and Ong (2020) used data from SafeGraph to examine customer behavior at restaurants and retail locations in various Los Angeles neighborhoods from February through September 2020. De Vaan et al. (2021) also relied on foot traffic data from mobile applications provided by SafeGraph to identify business closures in service-oriented businesses. Mobile location data, such as that from SafeGraph, have now become widely used to study numerous questions around broader human mobility patterns but have been noted to suffer from some biases (Li et al. 2024).

These studies thereby focused on business sectors in which time clocking, the use of social media, the use of credit cards, or customer foot traffic are common. As noted in previous chapters, small businesses can be found in an extremely wide range of industries and structural forms and have widely varying customer bases. Although these nontraditional data sources can provide fast and important first impressions of changes in business activity, they are limited in their representativeness and ability to track business shutdowns, permanent closures, and job losses. There is a strong need for the federal government to use its vast resources to provide real-time tracking of business activity in future emergencies. The lack of real-time measures of business activity left the country in the dark at the very beginning of the pandemic, but it should not happen again. We have learned that there is a strong need for real-time tracking of business activity that can be useful for future crises.

But What About Permanent Business Closures?

A major gap in our knowledge of what happened in the pandemic is how it affected permanent closures of small businesses. COVID-19 led to a large drop in the number of businesses operating early in the pandemic, but surprisingly little is known as to whether these shutdowns were temporary or turned into permanent closures. Measuring permanent closures is a heavy lift with business-level data. Closures cannot easily be tracked with real-time data for three main reasons. First, panel or longitudinal data that follow the same businesses monthly, quarterly, or annually over a reasonable length of time are needed but are not readily available. Second, defining a permanent closure is very difficult and subject to much debate. In panel data, for example, do you look for one quarter of no business activity, one year of no business activity, two years of no business activity, or an even longer time frame? There is no correct answer to this question.[7] Third, real-time data can only track what is happening at the moment and cannot accurately forecast a permanent closure in all cases.

One approach taken early in the pandemic to analyze permanent business closures used panel data covering the universe of businesses filing sales taxes from the California Department of Tax and Fee Administration (CDTFA) (Fairlie et al. 2022). The analysis of CDTFA data revealed large increases in closure rates in the second quarter of 2020, which were substantially larger for small businesses than large businesses. The disproportionate closing of small businesses was also found to lead to a sharp concentration of market share among larger businesses in the pandemic.

Chapter 10 presented some results on PPP loan receipt and closure rates among small businesses from the new data source, the BDS-SBA COVID tables. A comparison of businesses receiving loans with those that did not provides suggestive evidence on the effects of the PPP on small business outcomes in the pandemic. Although the comparison is straightforward, exploring potential effects on closures requires the ability to follow businesses over time after the receipt of loans, to measure survival. The analysis of BDS-SBA COVID data indicates that in 2022, the exit rate for business establishments receiving PPP funds was 7.7 percent, whereas the exit rate for business establishments that did not receive PPP funds was 10.4 percent. Another finding from the analysis of these data in chapter 10 is that the exit rate was lower for small businesses receiving PPP loans earlier in the pandemic than for small businesses receiving PPP loans later in the pandemic. Although these findings do not necessarily imply that PPP loan receipt versus no receipt or earlier PPP loan receipt versus later receipt caused lower exit rates among small businesses, the findings are consistent with causal impacts on small business survival.

Building on this work, the CSP could provide a valuable source of data to study the impact of the pandemic and receipt of PPP funding on startup closure rates. The longitudinal nature of the CSP allows identifying whether closures are short term or long term. The CSP can be linked to the PPP loan data on both employer and nonemployer businesses, expanding the range of small businesses included in the analysis. The ability to link to nonemployer businesses could be important for better understanding the effects of the third round of the PPP in 2021, which emphasized providing pandemic relief aid to business owners without employees.

The Future for Small Businesses: Consumer Trends, Robots, AI, and Downtowns

The pandemic created an unprecedented disruption to the U.S. economy, but new opportunities and overall growth for small businesses have risen from the ashes in the postpandemic recovery. What lies ahead? Will recent upward trends in business activity continue or will they reverse? Shifting consumer behavior and the rapid ascent of robots and AI make it difficult to predict what will happen to small businesses over the next several years.

Recent Industry Shifts

A review of trends since the turning point in the pandemic might provide some insight into what will happen next. Some industries grew rapidly in the past few years and others grew slowly. The main takeaways from the analysis of the economic recovery from the pandemic in chapter 13 are the following:

1. For business owners, the Transportation industry experienced the strongest recovery from the pandemic, growing 26 percent from prepandemic levels to 2024. A surge in demand for personal deliveries occurred during the pandemic and continued over the past few years.
2. The Information industry also experienced strong growth from 2019 to 2024, at 17 percent. Growth was fueled by demand from consumers, workers, and businesses for technology.
3. Industries that were hard-hit by shutdowns early in the pandemic also recovered substantially. For example, the Arts, Leisure, and Hotels industry grew by 14 percent and the Restaurant industry grew by 11 percent from prepandemic levels to 2024.
4. Annualized growth rates from 2019 to 2024 for all industries combined were 35 percent for Black business activity, 30 percent for Latinx business activity, and 22 percent for Asian business activity. In contrast, white business activity dropped by 3 percent.
5. For Black business owners, growth in Professional and Business Services accounted for 24 percent, Transportation accounted for 18 percent, Financial Activities accounted for 14 percent, and Personal and Laundry Services accounted for 13 percent of total growth from 2019 to 2023/2024.
6. For Latinx business owners, growth in Professional and Business Services accounted for 23 percent of total growth and Construction accounted for 22 percent. The Transportation industry accounted for 10 percent, and Personal and Laundry Services accounted for 8 percent of total growth from 2019 to 2023/2024.
7. For Asian business owners, growth in the Restaurants sector accounted for 27 percent of total growth, Financial Activities accounted for 25 percent of overall growth, Retail Trade accounted for 20 percent, and Transportation accounted for 17 percent of total growth from 2019 to 2023/2024.
8. Switching to growth numbers for businesses with employees, the Information industry grew by 60 percent from 2019 to 2024. Additional

high-skill industries grew strongly from prepandemic levels to 2024: Management, Professional and Technical Services, and Educational Services grew by 43, 37, and 32 percent, respectively.

9. Industries experiencing relatively slow growth rates were Retail Trade (3 percent), Agriculture (7 percent), Wholesale Trade (4 percent), and Accommodation, Food and Drink (9 percent). From 2019 to 2024, the total growth rate for all industries was 19 percent.

An important question for future trends is whether the continuing shift in consumer behavior toward online shopping continues or changes course. The importance of consumers in helping small businesses recover was clear and was embraced by governments, large corporations, and grassroots organizations during the pandemic. For example, states promoted shopping locally, such as California's #ShopSafeShopLocal. American Express provided cardholders with information such as a local Shop Small Map to find eligible small businesses in local areas. It also provided incentives through statement credits to shop at these small businesses. Numerous cities across the country posted Buy Black business web pages listing local businesses owned by Black residents. Target devoted a section of its web page under "Categories" to allow consumers to find and purchase products from Black-owned businesses. Can these efforts and similar ones counteract consumer trends working against small businesses? Relatively slow growth over the past few years in the Retail Trade and Restaurants sectors, however, does not bode well for a reversal.

The Loss to Quality of Community

In addition to small businesses providing a way of making a living for owners and local jobs, they provide an important sense of community. The loss of shops and restaurants and the decline of many downtowns and local shopping districts across the country have created a vacuum in what used to be vibrant areas for commerce and socializing with others. Although there are many other ways in which people socialize, we learned during the pandemic that important social interactions occur in local stores, shops, and restaurants, as well as in offices and factories. Throughout history, individuals have derived more than economic value from visiting local markets to purchase food and other goods. Social interactions through going to these markets and chatting with the vendors, other customers, and workers have always been important for improving a sense of connectedness and well-being.

Although the economic recovery from the pandemic has been strong, the country appears to have arrived at an inflection point for the future of many downtown areas and shopping districts. Will more downtowns and neighborhood shopping districts look "hollowed out," such as places like Westwood Village, Los Angeles? Even with a very large university, UCLA, literally across the street, Westwood Village somehow has a large number of vacant storefronts. An informal count of missing retail spaces on the main thoroughfare indicates that roughly 40 percent of storefronts are empty. Similarly, Santa Cruz, California, which also has a large university, UC Santa Cruz, nearby and is also a major tourist destination because of its beaches, boardwalk, and redwood forests, also feels partially hollowed out. An informal count along its main thoroughfare indicates that roughly 30 percent of storefronts are empty. If neighborhood shopping districts or small city downtowns such as Westwood and Santa Cruz continue to struggle with so much going on for them, then how do other areas recover from a similar plight? To be sure, there are many downtown areas in smaller cities that are vibrant and do not share these problems.

What is the secret to bringing consumers back to small businesses in these locations? More research is needed to determine the complicated and distinct reasons why many local downtowns are continuing to struggle after the pandemic. The list of issues raised by numerous constituents is long: returning from COVID-19, online and other retail competition, high rents and rent increases, safety concerns, retail theft, zoning restrictions, visible homelessness, lack of parking, and other issues. Many of these issues are difficult to solve, but some might resolve themselves with increased consumer activity and business success.

Consumer Trends Are Important

The bottom line for many small businesses is whether customers will return to storefronts or continue to purchase an increasing number of goods online. Although small businesses often have an online presence to complement brick-and-mortar operations, they will always struggle when competing against larger retailers or online retailers. Larger retailers can take advantage of returns to scale with high sales volumes, which make possible both brick-and-mortar stores and an online presence. Online retailers can provide an expanded selection of goods and efficient delivery. To be sure, many small businesses have an online presence for customers, but it often represents only a small share of total sales, and they face stiff competition from larger online retailers.

Two advantages that small businesses with a physical presence have over online shopping are instant customer gratification and the opportunity for social interactions. Small businesses can provide an instant shopping experience and the ability to try on or personally examine products before buying, while shopping in stores can be combined with other activities such as dining at a restaurant or getting a haircut. But even online shopping has evolved to provide same-day delivery. Autonomous robots are delivering food now but likely will soon be delivering goods. In-home or on-site services are likely to continue to grow; these services already include auto repair, dog grooming, and personal care such as the provision of pedicures and haircuts. None of these shopping experiences, however, include the social opportunities provided by downtowns. Dining at a restaurant whose tables are filled with other patrons is not the same as eating alone at home. Downtown areas offer opportunities for pop-up stores, outdoor dining, pedestrian-only streets, special nights, farmers markets, art fairs, and many other activities that encourage social interactions to lure customers back. To attract customers, downtown areas and shopping districts also need to focus on making the spaces attractive, clean, and family-friendly.

Large businesses can play a role in helping small businesses continue to recover. National retailers can influence customer behavior by promoting small business supplier products through their web pages. Credit card issuers can provide information on small businesses and possibly provide incentives to shop at those businesses. Internet search engines can prioritize small businesses in local area searches instead of online retailers and big box stores. We also need more awareness and action regarding increasing the diversity of suppliers and producers. Consumers often value knowing whether their purchases of goods and services help disadvantaged businesses and their employees, but consumers and businesses need information to make these choices. Additionally, governments and large businesses can increase diversity in their suppliers.

A potential concern is that consumer confidence has not fully recovered in the recent economic recovery. The Index of Consumer Sentiment dropped from 2019 to 2020, and unlike other economic indicators it remained much lower in 2024 than before the pandemic.[8] In fact, it was lower in 2024 than in 2020 or 2021. General confidence on the part of consumers remains surprisingly low given the strength of the economic recovery. The future effects of these trends in consumer confidence on small businesses are unknown.

Robots, Automation, and AI

A few years before the pandemic started, I visited UC Berkeley and noticed a funny little rectangular "box" on wheels that had a small antenna. It was a robot driving around campus and the local downtown area. I looked more closely at the robot and discovered that it was delivering food to students, faculty, staff, and others. UCLA now also has many of these robots ("Starship" and "Cocos") delivering food on campus and in Westwood. I did not really think about the future implications of these autonomous robots at the time. They seemed more of a fun, engineering school–type experiment than part of a longer-term trend toward automated delivery services. But there has undoubtedly been an increase in the presence of automated delivery services over the past couple of years, which is likely to expand to more areas of the country.

More recently, I was watching the NBA playoffs and was captivated by a commercial that stated in an ominous tone, "The robots are coming." The commercial was for Waymo and the goal was to highlight the company's autonomous driving technology and its potential to change how people get around. At one point in the commercial a character even thanks Waymo after being dropped off at home. Robots that can vacuum houses have been around for a long time but have not completely replaced human cleaners, perhaps because of the complicated and varied nature of activities required.[9] Will this be the same for driving and delivery tasks? The expansion of robots and the automated delivery of goods and services are inevitable, but how much will robots replace and displace self-employed business opportunities for people?

The findings in chapter 13 revealed that the Transportation industry experienced the strongest recovery from the pandemic, with the number of active business owners growing by 26 percent from 2019 to 2024. The Transportation industry also was responsible for part of the growth, during the recovery, in the number of active business owners who are Black, Latinx, or Asian. The pandemic created a surge in demand for the personal delivery of food and other goods that was first necessitated by social distancing restrictions but then became part of what consumers wanted. Ride-sharing or ride-hailing apps such as Uber and Lyft, which were growing rapidly before the pandemic, also created new opportunities for self-employed business owners. As small robots deliver more food around campuses and downtown areas and as fully automated taxis drive people to their destinations, those growth opportunities for business owners might get displaced.

On the other hand, the Information industry and general technology use have been growing and are likely to continue to grow. The rapid expansion of the availability and use of AI could contribute to a continual small business recovery by helping with marketing, accounting, graphic design, the design and development of online customer interfaces, and other tasks. A recent report by the U.S. Census Bureau documents the rapid expansion of AI use by businesses (Bonney et al. 2024). Data from the Business Trends and Outlook Survey indicate that from September 2023 to February 2024, the share of employer firms using AI rose from 3.7 percent to 5.4 percent, and that this rate of use was expected to increase to 6.6 percent by early fall 2024. AI use is highest among large businesses but higher among very small businesses than among medium-size small businesses. Businesses report that the most common uses of AI are for marketing automation, support for virtual agents or chatbots, data analytics, and language analytics (e.g., natural language processing, text analytics, and speech recognition). For those businesses not using AI, the most common reported reason is because AI is not applicable for the business. The rapid evolution of AI, however, makes it difficult to predict how AI will be used by small businesses, even in the near future, and what the reasons will be for continuing to abstain from using the technology. Small businesses that can automate tasks using AI are likely to benefit the most from the rising trends in AI use, availability, and functionality.

Moving Forward

The unprecedented disruption to small businesses and the rest of the economy at the very beginning of the pandemic is clear: business activity, business earnings, GDP growth, employment, and many other economic measures showed record losses. Small businesses were hit especially hard by mandated social distancing restrictions and health concerns but they also rebounded quickly, partly owing to consumers being anxious to get out again and partly because of the massive amount of government aid that was provided to small businesses in 2020 and early 2021. We still do not have a complete picture of the costs and benefits of the roughly $1 trillion the federal government pumped into aid for small businesses in the pandemic, but it likely helped ease some of the potential losses.

Vaccines rolled out in 2021, which turned out to be a pivotal year for small businesses. The recovery from the pandemic, however, was not linear but instead sputtered along until a couple of years later. But by 2024 there were 850,000 more active business owners in the U.S. economy than there were in 2019. The growth in business activity in the recovery from the pandemic was driven by growth in Black-, Latinx-, and Asian-owned business activity, and would have been negative otherwise. These three groups had a combined increase of 1.2 million active business owners from 2019 to 2024, representing a growth rate of 30 percent.

The recovery has favored small businesses in some industries and hurt small businesses in other industries. Retail Trade, for example, has not fully recovered from the pandemic, as is visible in the struggles of many shopping districts and downtown areas across the country. The future direction of the economic recovery is unknown but consumer trends, robots, and AI will have a large influence on this future, and likely will have more influence than government policy, or at least government policy alone. Ultimately, to move forward and fully recover from the pandemic, we might need partnerships between local governments, chambers of commerce, and other organizations (e.g., universities, large employers, local institutions) to join forces in creating a conducive environment for small businesses to succeed and customers to visit those small businesses.

Predicting the rapidly changing small business landscape because of shifting consumer behavior, robots, and AI is difficult. The new findings presented here from a comprehensive analysis of the effects of the pandemic on small businesses and the economic recovery should be useful for policymakers, business leaders, and small business owners moving forward to address these emerging trends and help small businesses fully bounce back from the pandemic.

Notes

Chapter 1

1. Wee Sui-Lee and Donald G. McNeil Jr., "China Identifies New Virus Causing Pneumonialike Illness: Global Health," *New York Times,* January 8, 2020.

2. Wee Sui-Lee, "Japan and Thailand Confirm New Cases of Chinese Coronavirus," *New York Times,* January 15, 2020.

3. Javier C. Hernández, "China Reports New Cases of Mystery Virus, Raising Fears as Travel Season Begins," *New York Times,* January 20, 2020, A6.

4. Javier C. Hernández and Austin Ramzy, "China Confirms New Coronavirus Spreads from Humans to Humans," *New York Times,* January 20, 2020.

5. Roni Caryn Rabin, "First Patient with Wuhan Coronavirus Is Identified in the U.S.," *New York Times,* January 21, 2020.

6. Denise Grady, "Three U.S. Airports to Check Passengers for a Deadly Chinese Coronavirus," *New York Times,* January 17, 2020.

7. Melina Delkic, "Wuhan Coronavirus, Impeachment, Climate Change: Your Wednesday Briefing," *New York Times,* January 21, 2020.

8. Amy Quin and Vivian Wang, "Wuhan, Center of Coronavirus Outbreak, Is Being Cut Off by Chinese Authorities," *New York Times,* January 22, 2020.

9. Alexandra Stevens, "How China's Virus Outbreak Could Threaten the Global Economy," *New York Times,* January 23, 2020; Chris Buckley and Javier C. Hernández, "China Expands Virus Lockdown, Encircling 35 Million," *New York Times,* January 23, 2020.

10. "Toll From Outbreak Climbs in China as Infections Reach Europe and Australia," *New York Times,* January 24, 2020.

11. "More U.S. Coronavirus Cases Emerge, as China's Death Toll Rises," *New York Times.* January 26, 2020.

12. "More Than 7,700 Cases of Coronavirus Recorded Worldwide," *New York Times,* January 29, 2020.

13. Michael Corkery and Annie Karni, "Trump Administration Restricts Entry into U.S. from China, *New York Times,* January 31, 2020.

14. Denise Grady and Roni Caryn Rabin, "195 Quarantined in California After Fleeing Coronavirus Epicenter," *New York Times,* January 31, 2020.

15. Yuan Lee, "Emergency Measures Create Hurdles for Farmers and Small Businesses," *New York Times*, February 1, 2020, A.10.

16. Steven Lee Myers and Giulia Marchi. "Beijing in the Time of Coronavirus: No Traffic, Empty Parks and Fear: Beijing Dispatch," *New York Times,* February 3, 2020.

17. "C.D.C. Gives New Guidelines, New York to Close Restaurants and Schools and Italian Deaths Rise," *New York Times* (Online), March 15, 2020.

18. An exception is the comprehensive review presented in Couch (2025), which covers a wide range of topics on the impacts of COVID-19, including impacts on equality in health, education, and employment outcomes.

19. For example, the governor of California used the research to argue for support of three bills helping small businesses in the pandemic that were signed (AB 1577, SB 1447, and SB 115).

20. The NBER profiled my work in several ways, including in the *NBER Bulletin,* Reporter Article, Research Spotlight, Personal Research Summary, and a video.

Chapter 2

1. Delaware's list was accessed on March 22, 2020, at https://coronavirus.delaware.gov/resources-for-businesses/.

2. States varied in their policies regarding remote, hybrid, and in-person school learning and the timing of reopening schools, which might have indirectly affected the ability of business owners to operate their businesses. States such as California and New York tended to be strict about remote learning and generally reopened later or in a hybrid form, whereas states such as Florida and Texas pushed schools to reopen in the fall of 2020.

3. Early social distancing restrictions data were found at https://www.nytimes.com/interactive/2020/us/states-reopen-map-coronavirus.html.

4. Mask mandate data were found at https://www.nytimes.com/interactive/2020/us/states-reopen-map-coronavirus.html.

5. See the web page at https://www.sccgov.org/sites/phd/DiseaseInformation/novel-coronavirus/Pages/order-health-officer-031620.aspx.

6. See the web page at https://www.sccgov.org/sites/phd/DiseaseInformation/novel-coronavirus/Pages/order-health-officer-033120.aspx.

Chapter 3

1. Nonemployer businesses constitute 83 percent of businesses in the United States (26.5 million nonemployer businesses compared with 5.3 million employer businesses). Among startups, nonemployer startups constitute an even larger percentage (89 percent) of all startups (3.7 million nonemployer startups each year compared with 439,000 employer startups per year). See Fairlie et al. (2023) for details and more discussion.

2. Although farmers and other agricultural business owners might have continued to work during the pandemic, they might have experienced large losses in sales and revenues as a result of supply chain shutdowns from the closing of regular buyers, such as schools and restaurants.

3. Ride-sharing or ride-hailing drivers would be classified as business owners only if the number of hours worked driving was higher than the number of hours worked for other wage and salary jobs. This definition captures the idea of workers with many jobs having a primary job.

4. The "List of Delaware Business Categories That Are Essential and Non-Essential (March 22, 2020)" was available at https://coronavirus.delaware.gov/resources-for-businesses/ (accessed March 22, 2020).

5. A disadvantage of taking logs, however, is that business owners can have zero or negative earnings (unlike wage and salary earnings or hourly wages), and taking logs is not possible. To address this concern, all business earnings values less than $1,000 are set to $1,000 (i.e., censored) before taking logs. The implicit assumption is that earning any amount less than $1,000 per year from a business is the same as earning $0 per year from a business. Taking this approach removes the problem that a change from $100 to $50 in annual business earnings would be similar in log terms as a change from $100,000 to $50,000 in annual business earnings when the first change is inconsequential. Relative business earnings losses are not sensitive to using alternative cutoffs.

6. The evidence on the general relationship between recessions and entrepreneurship is surprisingly mixed, with many previous studies showing positive relationships, negative relationships, and zero relationships (Parker 2018).

7. The underlying CPS microdata that are used to measure the number of active business owners and business earnings can be matched month to month to measure new business activity or the flow into business ownership. They can also be used to measure the percent of that new business activity that comes out of necessity versus opportunity.

8. Estimates of annual new business activity rates would be approximately six to eight times higher. They are not twelve times higher than monthly rates because an individual could start and exit the business activity multiple times in the same year.

9. Data are available from the CDTFA at https://www.cdtfa.ca.gov/dataportal/dataset.htm?url=TaxSalesStatewide.

10. Womply aggregates data from several credit card processors to analyze for small businesses. The data are distributed across sectors for which credit card use is common and focus on small businesses, thus comprising a larger share of food services, professional services, and other services.

11. For example, to define a business closure in 2020Q2, the business must have had taxable sales in 2020Q1 but no taxable sales in 202Q2, 2020Q3, 2020Q4, or 2021Q1.

12. See Fairlie et al. (2022) for more information and trends through the third quarter of 2020.

13. Estimates are from the Bureau of Economic Analysis.

Chapter 4

1. See Bates (1997), Davila and Mora (2013), Fairlie and Robb (2008), and Parker (2018) for reviews of this literature.

2. The expression for the simulated change in the number of business owners for group j from February to April is:

$$\sum_{i=1}^{K} S_i^{US}(N_i^{j,\,Apr} - N_i^{j,\,Feb}),$$

where S_i^{US} is the share of all business owners represented by major industry i using the U.S. national industry distribution, and $N_i^{j,\,Month}$ is the number of business owners for group j, industry i, and the defined month.

3. The business earnings estimates reported here categorize race as any individual reporting that race on a "check all that apply" question. Thus individuals can belong to multiple race categories instead of mutually exclusive categories. When using the traditional single-race approach of categorizing individuals into each race group by including only individuals who report one race, the patterns are roughly similar.

4. Grouping all prepandemic years, median business earnings were roughly $44,000 for Asian business owners, $42,000 for white business owners, $30,000 for Black business owners, and $28,000 for Latinx business owners.

5. For the regressions, the sample consists of business owners (ages twenty to sixty-four) who worked in their business in the calendar year. Main control variables

include female sex, age, education, region, and central city status indicator variables. Coefficient estimates for these variables are not reported.

6. As noted above, individuals can report multiple races; however, only 6 percent of the Black and Asian samples reported multiple races.

7. None of the prepandemic year dummy variables interacted with race/ethnicity are statistically significant. In other words, there are no prepandemic "effects" of COVID-19 on racial inequality in business earnings.

8. Estimating a similar set of regression equations using active business ownership as the dependent variable, I find no effects of COVID-19 and no disproportionate effects of COVID-19 by race and ethnicity.

9. The Other Services category includes, for example, auto repair, barber shop, beauty salon, dry cleaning, and private household services.

10. See Hundley (2000), Zissimopoulos and Karoly (2007), and van der Sluis, van Praag, and Vijverberg (2005) for a few examples and Parker (2018) for an overall review of the literature.

11. Both measures were found at https://www.nytimes.com/interactive/2020/us/states-reopen-map-coronavirus.html.

12. The decomposition estimates are robust to alternative measures and specifications. These estimates are not sensitive to including or excluding region dummies or alternative measures of business restrictions, or to including these variables together or separately.

Chapter 5

1. The rounds of funding were part of larger packages of aid provided in the pandemic. These were (1) the March 27, 2020 CARES Act, (2) the April 24, 2020, Paycheck Protection Program and Health Care Enhancement Act, (3) the December 27, 2020, Consolidated Appropriations Act, and (4) the March 11, 2021, American Rescue Plan Act (Mills 2024).

2. PPP loan data can be downloaded from https://data.sba.gov/dataset/ppp-foia.

3. The microdata include information on the loan, lender, and small business receiving the loan. The name of the lender is provided, as are the geographic area, industry, business type, and jobs retained as self-reported by the business, as well as other information. Information on the race, gender, and veteran status of the owner, however, is incomplete.

4. The Federal Reserve lists JPMorgan Chase, Bank of America, Wells Fargo, Citibank, and US Bank as the five largest banks. See https://www.federalreserve.gov/releases/lbr/current/.

5. To show the general relationship between PPP receipt and minority population share, a quadratic regression at the zip code level is estimated and shown as the dashed line in figure 5.3.

Chapter 6

1. The losses conditioning on hours worked were also larger in May relative to February (19 percent for 15+ hours and 21 percent for 30+ hours). Both measures, however, show partial rebounds in May from April 2020. From nine to ten percentage points of the drops in active business owners were added back in May.

2. Further rebounds occurred in June, with losses to 15+ hours worked business activity at 11 percent and 30+ hours worked business activity at 13 percent. From February to May there was also a drop in total hours worked by business owners, but the drop was not as large, at 20 percent. From February to June total hours worked dropped by 12 percent.

Chapter 7

1. The FDA can use EUAs to provide access to medical products that may be effective in preventing, diagnosing, or treating a disease when facing public health emergencies. The known and potential benefits of the medical product must outweigh the known and potential risks of the product as determined by the FDA.

Chapter 8

1. Couch, Fairlie, and Xu (2023) find different patterns in racial gaps in unemployment rates over 2021. The Black-white unemployment gap did not immediately rise as much as for other groups but subsequently increased and was stubbornly higher through 2021Q3. The Latinx-white gap generally decreased after peaking in May 2020 to prepandemic levels by 2021Q4 but experienced a unique "hiccup" in early 2021. The Asian-white gap peaked later (in June 2020), was high in 2020Q3 (the "stall"), and remained positive through 2021Q4.

Chapter 9

1. The dashed lines in figure 9.2 are from quadratic regressions at the county level.

2. The NES data include all business entities that have annual receipts of at least $1,000; file IRS tax forms for sole proprietorships (Form 1040, Schedule C), partnerships (Form 1065), or corporations (the Form 1120 series); and have no paid employees. These data include all consultants, side businesses, hobby businesses, part-time contract or gig work, and other small-scale business activity as long as it

produces $1,000 or more in annual revenues, which were generally ineligible for PPP loans. Based on this very inclusive definition, there are roughly 26.8 million nonemployer business entities in the United States.

Chapter 10

1. See also Beem and Stinson (2025) for more information.

2. Although the PPP was generally limited to businesses with fewer than five hundred employees, there were exceptions for certain industries.

3. As noted in Beem and Stinson (2025), when a firm received PPP funding, there were no rules regarding how that funding was distributed across its separate establishments, and thus the new data record all of the firm's establishments as having received funding.

4. The RRF program does not have the same timing element as PPP and so there is only one recipient category. However, for these programs, data on applicants who were denied loans are also available. Hence tables for these programs report program status in three bins: applicant recipients, applicant nonrecipients, and nonapplicant nonrecipients. Importantly, this last group includes both businesses that never applied to one of these programs and businesses that applied but did not use an EIN that matched to an employer record in the Census Bureau's Business Register.

Chapter 11

1. Data for 2024 calendar year were not available at the time of writing this book.

Chapter 14

1. The MBDA was created in 1969 as part of the U.S. Department of Commerce and made a permanent agency in 2021 (https://www.mbda.gov/about).

2. For broader discussions and reviews of this literature, see Bates (1997, 2011), Davila and Mora (2013), Fairlie and Robb (2008), and Parker (2018).

3. The NES-D utilizes administrative records from the Business Register, tax data, the Decennial Census, the ACS, and Department of Veteran Affairs (VA) data to provide detailed demographic information (Luque et al. 2019). The SBO collected information on nonemployers but was replaced by the Annual Survey of Entrepreneurs (ASE) and, more recently, by the Annual Business Survey (ABS). In moving to the ASE and ABS, however, nonemployers were excluded.

4. The CSP data and the ability to match to other data sources are available at Federal Statistical Research Data Centers (FSRDCs) across the country (Fairlie et al. 2023).

The CSP can be accessed through a data package. The data package consists of the ILBD, the LBD, and SAS code that links the ILBD and LBD, identifies startups, and includes all startups starting in 1994 or later. The provided SAS code can be run to create the startup panel dataset, which will be ready for analysis.

5. The BDS-SBA COVID data include only small employer businesses, but a focus of the 2021 PPP was to provide loans to nonemployer business owners. One goal of the CSP is to track the universe of both nonemployer and employer startups.

6. Another exception is provided by the Census Bureau's Business Formation Statistics (BFS). The BFS tracks potential business formations based on the universe of administrative applications for an employer identification number (EIN). Monthly BFS data are released approximately eleven to twelve days after the end of the month. However, as noted in chapter 3, the data track EIN applications, many of which never actually become businesses, generate any revenue, or hire any employees.

7. The U.S. Census Bureau (2022) and the U.S. Bureau of Labor Statistics (2024) measure business or establishment closures using administrative panel data and defining closure over a one-year window. The Census Bureau's Business Dynamics Series (BDS) measures closures by establishments that have positive employment in the first quarter of the initial year and zero employment in the first quarter of the subsequent year. The BLS publishes information from the Business Employer Dynamics (BED) on annual survival rates for establishments with employees and reports the total number of closures each quarter.

8. See the website at https://www.sca.isr.umich.edu/tables.html.

9. Automated machines or robots have also existed for many years in manufacturing and warehousing for assembly and material handling. Agriculture is experiencing an increase in the use of automation that includes AI, sensors, and drones to increase crop yields. The impact of these changes is more direct on employees of larger businesses but could indirectly affect small business owners.

References

Agarwal, Sumit, Brent W. Ambrose, Luis A. Lopez, and Xue Xiao. 2024. "Did the Paycheck Protection Program Help Small Businesses? Evidence from Commercial Mortgage-Backed Securities." *American Economic Journal: Economic Policy* 16, no. 3: 95–132.

Alekseev, Georgij, Safaa Amer, Manasa Gopal, Theresa Kuchler, John W. Schneider, Johannes Stroebel, and Nils Wernerfelt. 2023. "The Effects of COVID-19 on US Small Businesses: Evidence from Owners, Managers, and Employees." *Management Science* 69, no. 1: 7–24.

Amuedo-Dorantes, Catalina, Cristina Borra, and Chunbei Wang. 2024. "Asian Entrepreneurship in the Coronavirus Era." *Journal of Population Economics* 37, no. 1: 22.

Asturias, Jose, Emin Dinlersoz, John Haltiwanger, and Rebecca Hutchinson. 2021. "Business Applications as Economic Indicators." U.S. Census Bureau, Center for Economic Studies.

Atkins, Rachel, Lisa Cook, and Robert Seamans. 2022a. "Discrimination in Lending? Evidence from the Paycheck Protection Program." *Small Business Economics* 1:1–23.

Atkins, Rachel, Lisa D. Cook, and Robert Seamans. 2022b. "Using Technology to Tackle Discrimination in Lending: The Role of FinTechs in the Paycheck Protection Program." *AER Papers and Proceedings* 112:296–98.

Autor, David, David Cho, Leland D. Crane, Mita Goldar, Byron Lutz, Joshua Montes, William B. Peterman, David Ratner, Daniel Villar, and Ahu Yildirmaz. 2022. "An Evaluation of the Paycheck Protection Program Using Administrative Payroll Microdata." *Journal of Public Economics* 211:104664.

Bailey, Cristina, Richard Brody, and Matias Sokolowski. 2022. "Fraudulent Loans and the United States Paycheck Protection Program." *Journal of Financial Crime* 29, no. 2: 519–532.

Bartik, Alexander W., Marianne Bertrand, Zoe Cullen, Edward L. Glaeser, Michael Luca, and Christopher Stanton. 2020. "The Impact of COVID-19 on Small Business

Outcomes and Expectations." *Proceedings of the National Academy of Sciences* 117, no. 30: 17656–17666.

Bartik, Alexander W., Marianne Bertrand, Lin Feng, Jesse Rothstein, and Matthew Unrath. 2020. "Measuring the Labor Market at the Onset of the COVID-19 Crisis. *Brookings Papers on Economic Activity*, Summer 2020.

Bartik, Alexander W., Zoe B. Cullen, Edward L. Glaeser, Michael Luca, Christopher T. Stanton, and Adi Sunderam. 2020. "The Targeting and Impact of Paycheck Protection Program Loans to Small Businesses." NBER Working Paper no. 27623. Cambridge, MA: National Bureau of Economic Research.

Bates, Timothy. 1997. *Race, Self-Employment & Upward Mobility: An Illusive American Dream* Washington, DC: Woodrow Wilson Center Press; Baltimore: Johns Hopkins University Press.

Bates, Timothy. 2011 "Minority Entrepreneurship." *Foundations and Trends® in Entrepreneurship* 7, no. 3–4: 151–311.

Bayard, Kimberly, Emin Dinlersoz, Timothy Dunne, John Haltiwanger, Javier Miranda, and John Stevens. 2018. "Early-Stage Business Formation: An Analysis of Applications for Employer Identification Numbers." NBER Working Paper no. 24364. Cambridge, MA: National Bureau of Economic Research.

Beem, Richard, and Martha Stinson. 2025. "Measuring the Business Dynamics of Firms that Received Pandemic Relief Funding: Findings from a New Experimental BDS Data Product." CES 25–05. U.S. Census Bureau, Center for Economic Studies, January 2025

Berry, Christopher R., Anthony Fowler, Tamara Glazer, Samantha Handel-Meyer, and Alec MacMillen. 2021. "Evaluating the Effects of Shelter-in-Place Policies During the COVID-19 Pandemic." *Proceedings of the National Academy of Sciences* 118, no. 15: e2019706118.

Bloom, Nicholas, Robert S. Fletcher, and Ethan Yeh. 2021. "The Impact of COVID-19 on US Firms." NBER Working Paper no. 28314. Cambridge, MA: National Bureau of Economic Research.

Bohn, Sarah, Marisol Cuellar Mejia, and Julien Lafortune. 2020. *The Economic Toll of COVID-19 on Small Business*. San Francisco: Public Policy Institute of California.

Bonney, Kathryn, Cory Breaux, Cathy Buffington, Emin Dinlersoz, Lucia S. Foster, Nathan Goldschlag, John C. Haltiwanger, Zachary Kroff, and Keith Savage. 2024. "Tracking Firm Use of AI in Real Time: A Snapshot from the Business Trends and Outlook Survey." NBER Working Paper no. 32319. Cambridge, MA: National Bureau of Economic Research.

Boston, Thomas D. 1999. "Generating Jobs Through African American Business Development." In *Readings in Black Political Economy*, ed. J. Whitehead and C. Harris. Dubuque, IA: Kendall-Hunt.

Boston, Thomas D. 2006. "The Role of Black-Owned Businesses in Black Community Development." In *Jobs and Economic Development in Minority Communities: Realities, Challenges, and Innovation*, ed. Paul Ong. Philadelphia: Temple University Press.

Bradford, William D. 2003. "The Wealth Dynamics of Entrepreneurship for Black and White Families in the U.S." *Review of Income and Wealth* 49, no. 1: 89–116.

Bradford, William D. 2014. "The "Myth" That Black Entrepreneurship Can Reduce the Gap in Wealth Between Black and White Families." *Economic Development Quarterly* 28, no. 3: 254–269.

Bradford, William D., Chunbei Wang, Magnus Lofstrom, and Michael Verchot. 2025. "(Mis)Pricing in Loans to Businesses Owned by People of Color." IZA Discussion Paper no. 17730.

Busby, Ron. 2020. "Testimony of Ron Busby on behalf of the U.S. Black Chambers, Inc. before the U.S. Senate Committee on Small Business & Entrepreneurship," Capital Access for Minority Small Businesses: COVID-19 Resources for an Equitable and Sustainable Recovery Hearing, U.S. Senate, July 23.

Cardin, Ben. 2022. "Independent Report Reaffirms Cardin Policies Increased Equity in Paycheck Protection Program." U.S. Senate Committee on Small Business & Entrepreneurship, Washington, DC, January 28.

Centers for Disease Control and Prevention. 2021. "COVID-19 Vaccine Breakthrough Infections Reported to CDC—United States, January 1–April 30, 2021." *Morbidity and Mortality Weekly Report* 70, no. 21: 792–793.

Centers for Disease Control and Prevention. 2024. "Preparing for the Next Pandemic: Lessons Learned and the Path Forward," Congressional Testimony before the Select Subcommittee on the Coronavirus Pandemic, Committee on Oversight and Accountability, U.S. House of Representatives (statement of Henry Walke, CDC Office of Readiness and Response), November 14.

Chatterji, Aaron K., Kenneth Y. Chay, and Robert W. Fairlie. 2014. "The Impact of City Contracting Set-asides on Black Self-Employment and Employment." *Journal of Labor Economics* 32, no. 3: 507–561.

Chernenko, Sergey and David S. Scharfstein. 2021. "Racial Disparities in the Paycheck Protection Program." SSRN Working Paper 3907575.

Chetty, R., J. N. Friedman, N. Hendren, M. Stepner, and Opportunity Insights Team. 2020. "The Economic Impacts of COVID-19: Evidence from a New Public Database Built Using Private Sector Data." NBER Working Paper no. 27431. Cambridge, MA: National Bureau of Economic Research.

Chetty, Raj, John N. Friedman, Michael Stepner, and Opportunity Insights Team. 2024. "The Economic Impacts of COVID-19: Evidence from a New Public Database Built Using Private Sector Data." *Quarterly Journal of Economics* 139, no. 2: 829–889.

Cole, Allison. 2024. "The Impact of the Paycheck Protection Program on (Really) Small Businesses." Arizona State University Working Paper.

Couch, Kenneth A. 2025. "Inequality and COVID-19." In *Handbook on Inequality and COVID-19*, 1–13. Cheltenham, Gloucestershire: Edward Elgar Publishing.

Couch, Kenneth A., Robert W. Fairlie, and Huanan Xu. 2020a. "The Impacts of COVID-19 on Minority Unemployment: First Evidence from April 2020 CPS Microdata." NBER Working Paper no. 27246. Cambridge, MA: National Bureau of Economic Research.

Couch, Kenneth A., Robert W. Fairlie, and Huanan Xu. 2020b. "Early Evidence of the Impacts of COVID-19 on Minority Unemployment." *Journal of Public Economics* 192:104287.

Couch, Kenneth A., Robert W. Fairlie, and Huanan Xu. 2023. "Racial Disparities in Unemployment During the COVID-19 Pandemic and Recovery: The 'Stubborn,' the 'Hiccup,' and the 'Stall.'" *Economic Inquiry* 61, no. 3: 480–495.

Cowan, Benjamin W. 2020. "Short-Run Effects of COVID-19 on US Worker Transitions." NBER Working Paper no. 27315. Cambridge, MA: National Bureau of Economic Research.

Dave, Dhaval, Andrew I. Friedson, Kyutaro Matsuzawa, and Joseph J. Sabia. 2021. "When Do Shelter-in-Place Orders Fight COVID-19 Best? Policy Heterogeneity Across States and Adoption Time." *Economic Inquiry* 59, no. 1: 29–52.

Davila, Alberto, and Marie Mora. 2013. *Hispanic Entrepreneurs in the 2000s: An Economic Profile and Policy Implications*. Stanford, CA: Stanford University Press.

Decker, R. A., and J. Haltiwanger. 2023. "Surging Business Formation in the Pandemic: Causes and Consequences?" *Brookings Papers on Economic Activity* 2023, no. 2: 249–316.

Desai, Sameeksha, and Jessica Looze. 2020. "Business Owner Perceptions of COVID-19 Effects on the Business: Preliminary Findings." Trends in Entrepreneurship 10. Kansas City: Ewing Marion Kauffman Foundation.

De Vaan, Mathijs, Saqib Mumtaz, Abhishek Nagaraj, and Sameer B. Srivastava. 2021. "Social Learning in the COVID-19 Pandemic: Community Establishments' Closure Decisions Follow Those of Nearby Chain Establishments." *Management Science* 67, no. 7: 4446–4454.

Erel, Isil, and Jack Liebersohn. 2020. "Does FinTech Substitute for Banks? Evidence from the Paycheck Protection Program." NBER Working Paper no. 27659. Cambridge, MA: National Bureau of Economic Research.

Evans, Connie. 2020. "Testimony of Connie Evans on behalf of the Association for Enterprise Opportunity before the U.S. Senate Committee on Small Business & Entrepreneurship," Perspectives from Main Street: COVID-19's Impact on Small Business, June 3.

Evans, David S., and Jovanovic, Boyan. 1989. "An Estimated Model of Entrepreneurial Choice Under Liquidity Constraints." *Journal of Political Economy* 97, no. 4: 808–827.

Fairlie, Robert W. 2004. "Does Business Ownership Provide a Source of Upward Mobility for Blacks and Hispanics?" In *Public Policy and the Economics of Entrepreneurship*, ed. Doug Holtz-Eakin and Harvey S. Rosen. Cambridge, MA: MIT Press.

Fairlie, Robert W. 2013. "Entrepreneurship, Economic Conditions, and the Great Recession." *Journal of Economics & Management Strategy* 22, no. 2: 207–231.

Fairlie, Robert. 2014. The Kauffman Index of Entrepreneurial Activity: 1996–2013. Kansas City: Ewing Marion Kauffman Foundation.

Fairlie, Robert. 2018. "Racial Inequality in Business Ownership and Income." *Oxford Review of Economic Policy* 34, no. 4: 597–614.

Fairlie, Robert W. 2020a. "The Impact of Covid-19 on Small Business Owners: Evidence of Early-Stage Losses from the April 2020 Current Population Survey." NBER Working Paper no. 27309. Cambridge, MA: National Bureau of Economic Research, May.

Fairlie, Robert. 2020b. "The Impact of COVID-19 on Small Business Owners: Evidence from the First Three Months After Widespread Social-Distancing Restrictions." *Journal of Economics & Management Strategy* 29, no. 4: 727–740.

Fairlie, Robert. 2021a. "The State of the Small Business Economy in the Pandemic." Testimony before the U.S. House of Representatives Committee on Small Business, February 4.

Fairlie, Robert. 2021b. "The Impacts of COVID-19 on Small Business Owners." Testimony before the California State Assembly Committee on Jobs, Economic Development, and the Economy, February 23.

Fairlie, Robert. 2022. "The $800 billion Paycheck Protection Program and the Impacts of COVID-19 on Small Businesses in the United States." Testimony in the hearing, "An Empirical Review of the Paycheck Protection Program," U.S. House of Representatives Committee on Small Business, Subcommittee on Oversight, Investigations, and Regulations, March 16.

Fairlie, Robert. 2024. "The Impacts of COVID-19 on Racial Inequality in Business Earnings." *Journal of Policy Analysis and Management* 43, no. 1: 258–288.

Fairlie, Robert W., and Aaron K. Chatterji. 2013. "High-Technology Entrepreneurship in Silicon Valley." *Journal of Economics & Management Strategy* 22, no. 2: 365–389.

Fairlie, Robert W., and Frank M. Fossen. 2019. "Defining Opportunity versus Necessity Entrepreneurship: Two Components of Business Creation." NBER Working Paper no. 26377. Cambridge, MA: National Bureau of Economic Research.

Fairlie, Robert, and Frank Fossen. 2021. "Did the $660 Billion Paycheck Protection Program and $220 Billion Economic Injury Disaster Loan Program Get Disbursed to Minority Communities in the Early Stages of COVID-19?" NBER Working Paper no. 28321. Cambridge, MA: National Bureau of Economic Research.

Fairlie, Robert, and Frank Fossen. 2022a. "Did the Paycheck Protection Program and Economic Injury Disaster Loan Program Get Disbursed to Minority Communities in the Early Stages of COVID-19?" *Small Business Economics* 58, no. 2: 829–842.

Fairlie, Robert, and Frank M. Fossen. 2022b. "The Early Impacts of the COVID-19 Pandemic on Business Sales." *Small Business Economics* 58, no. 5: 1853–1864.

Fairlie, Robert, and Frank Fossen. 2022c. "The 2021 Paycheck Protection Program Reboot: Loan Disbursement to Employer and Nonemployer Businesses in Minority Communities." NBER Working Paper no. 29732. Cambridge, MA: National Bureau of Economic Research.

Fairlie, Robert, and Frank M. Fossen. 2022d. "The 2021 Paycheck Protection Program Reboot: Loan Disbursement to Employer and Nonemployer Businesses in Minority Communities." *American Economic Review Papers & Proceedings* 112:287–291.

Fairlie, Robert, Frank Fossen, Reid Johnsen, and Gentian Droboniku. 2022. "Were Small Businesses More Likely to Permanently Close in the Pandemic?" NBER Working Paper no. 30285. Cambridge, MA: National Bureau of Economic Research.

Fairlie, Robert W., Dean Karlan, and Jonathan Zinman. 2015. "Behind the GATE Experiment: Evidence on Effects of and Rationales for Subsidized Entrepreneurship Training." *American Economic Journal: Economic Policy* 7, no. 2: 125–61.

Fairlie, Robert W., Zachary Kroff, Javier Miranda, and Nikolas Zolas. 2023. *The Promise and Peril of Entrepreneurship: Job Creation and Survival among US Startups*. Cambridge, MA: MIT Press.

Fairlie, Robert W., and Alicia M. Robb. 2008. *Race and Entrepreneurial Success: Black-, Asian-, and White-Owned Businesses in the United States*. Cambridge, MA: MIT Press.

Fairlie, Robert, Alicia Robb, and David T. Robinson. 2022. "Black and White: Access to Capital Among Minority-Owned Start-ups." *Management Science* 68, no. 4: 2377–2400.

Fairlie, Robert, and Christopher M. Woodruff. 2010. "Mexican-American Entrepreneurship." *BE Journal of Economic Analysis & Policy* 10, no. 1.

Farrell, Diana, Chris Wheat, and Chi Mac. 2020. *Small Business Financial Outcomes During the Onset of COVID-19*. Institute report. New York: JPMorgan Chase & Co.

Fei, Celine Yue, and Keer Yang. 2021. "Fintech and Racial Barriers in Small Business Lending," University of North Carolina at Chapel Hill Working Paper.

Feldscher, Karen. 2024. "The Next Pandemic: Not If, But When." Harvard University School of Public Health, September 12.

Fowler, J. H., S. J. Hill, R. Levin, and N. Obradovich. 2020. The Effect of Stay-at-Home Orders on COVID-19 Infections in the United States. *medRXiv,* May 12.

García, Raffi E., and William A. Darity Jr. 2022. "Self-Reporting Race in Small Business Loans: A Game-Theoretic Analysis of Evidence from PPP Loans in Durham, NC." *AEA Papers and Proceedings* 112:299–302.

Giddings, Andy. 2025. "Another Pandemic Inevitable, Virologist Warns." *BBC News,* March 23.

Granja, João, Christos Makridis, Constantine Yannelis, and Eric Zwick. 2022. "Did the Paycheck Protection Program Hit the Target?" *Journal of Financial Economics* 145, no. 3: 725–761.

Griffin, John M., Samuel Kruger, and Prateek Mahajan. 2023. "Did FinTech Lenders Facilitate PPP Fraud?" *Journal of Finance* 78, no. 3: 1777–1827.

Grotto, Jason, Zachary R. Mider, and Cedric Sam. 2020. "White America Got a Head Start on Small-Business Virus Relief." Bloomberg, July 30, 2020.

Headd, Brian. 2021. *Business Ownership Demographics.* U.S. Small Business Administration, Office of Advocacy, March.

Hipple, Steven F., and Laurel A. Hammond. 2016. "Self-Employment in the United States." U.S. Bureau of Labor Statistics.

Holtz-Eakin, Douglas, Harvey S. Rosen, and Robert Weathers. 2000. "Horatio Alger Meets the Mobility Tables." *Small Business Economics* 14:243–274.

Howell, Sabrina T., Theresa Kuchler, David Snitkof, Johannes Stroebel, and Jun Wong. 2021. "Racial Disparities in Access to Small Business Credit: Evidence from the Paycheck Protection Program." NBERWorking Paper no. 29364. Cambridge, MA: National Bureau of Economic Research.

Hsiang, Solomon, Daniel Allen, Sébastien Annan-Phan, Kendon Bell, Ian Bolliger, Trinetta Chong, Hannah Druckenmiller, et al. 2020. "The Effect of Large-Scale Anti-Contagion Policies on the COVID-19 Pandemic." *Nature* 584, no. 7820: 262–267.

Huang, Justin T., Masha Krupenkin, David Rothschild, and Julia Lee Cunningham. 2023. "The Cost of Anti-Asian Racism During the COVID-19 Pandemic." *Nature Human Behaviour* 7, no. 5: 682–695.

Hubbard, R. Glenn, and Michael R. Strain. 2020. "Has the Paycheck Protection Program Succeeded?" *Brookings Papers on Economic Activity* 2020, no. 3: 335–390.

Humphries, John Eric, Christopher A. Neilson, and Gabriel Ulyssea. 2020. "Information Frictions and Access to the Paycheck Protection Program." *Journal of Public Economics* 190:104244.

Hundley, Greg. 2000. "Male/Female Earnings Differences in Self-Employment: The Effects of Marriage, Children, and the Household Division of Labor." *ILR Review* 54, no. 1: 95–114.

Kim, Olivia S., Jonathan A. Parker, and Antoinette Schoar. 2020. "Revenue Collapses and the Consumption of Small Business Owners in the Early Stages of the COVID-19 Pandemic." NBER Working Paper no. 28151. Cambridge, MA: National Bureau of Economic Research.

Kroeger, Teresa, and Graham Wright. 2021. "Entrepreneurship and the Racial Wealth Gap: The Impact of Entrepreneurial Success or Failure on the Wealth Mobility of Black and White Families." *Journal of Economics, Race, and Policy* 4:183–195.

Kurmann, Andre, Etienne Lale, and Lien Ta. 2021. "The Impact of Covid-19 on US Employment and Hours: Real-Time Estimates with Homebase Data." Working paper. https://drive.google.com/file/d/1KNpXO_9mLvtj2Yd2JQlz1tB12rs8mV0t/view.

Lederer, Anneliese, Sara Oros, Sterling Bone, Glenn Christensen, and Jerome Williams. 2020. "Lending Discrimination Within the Paycheck Protection Program." Washington, DC: National Community Reinvestment Coalition.

Levine, Ross, and Yona Rubinstein. 2017. "Smart and Illicit: Who Becomes an Entrepreneur and Do They Earn More?" *Quarterly Journal of Economics* 132, no. 2: 963–1018.

Lewis, Dyani. 2022. "What Scientists Have Learnt from COVID Lockdowns." *Nature* 609, no. 7926: 236–239.

Li, Zhenlong, Huan Ning, Fengrui Jing, and M. Naser Lessani. 2024. "Understanding the Bias of Mobile Location Data Across Spatial Scales and Over Time: A Comprehensive Analysis of SafeGraph data in the United States." *Plos one* 19, no. 1: e0294430.

Liu, Sifan, and Joseph Parilla. 2020. "New Data Shows Small Businesses in Communities of Color Had Unequal Access to Federal COVID-19 Relief." Brookings Institution.

Luque, Adela., Rhenuka Bhaskar, James Noon, Kevin Rinz, and Victoria Udalova. 2019. "Nonemployer Statistics by Demographics (NES-D): Using Administrative and Census Records Data in Business Statistics." U.S. Census Bureau Working Paper no. 19-01.

Minority Business Development Agency. 2025. "About." www.mbda.gov.

Mills, Karen G. 2024. *Fintech, Small Business & the American Dream: How Technology Is Transforming Lending and Shaping a New Era of Small Business Opportunity,* 2nd ed. Cham: Palgrave Macmillan.

Mills, Claire Kramer, and Jessica Battisto. 2020. "Double Jeopardy: COVID-19's Concentrated Health and Wealth Effects in Black Communities." Federal Reserve Bank of New York.

Mills, Claire Kramer, Jessica Battisto, Mels de Zeeuw, Scott Lieberman, and Ann Marie Wiersch. 2020. *Small Business Credit Survey*. Federal Reserve Bank.

Montenovo, Laura, Xuan Jiang, Felipe L. Rojas, Ian M. Schmutte, Kosali I. Simon, Bruce A. Weinberg, and Coady Wing. 2020. "Determinants of Disparities in Covid-19 Job Losses." NBER Working Paper no. 27132. Cambridge, MA: National Bureau of Economic Research.

National Public Radio. 2020. "Coronavirus: All 50 States Report Cases; South America Has Nearly 1,000 Cases." March 17, 2020,

Ong, Paul, Alycia Cheng, and Jonathan Ong. 2021. "Asian American Businesses: The Impacts of Anti-Asian Racism: Survey of Asian American Businesses." UCLA Asian American Studies Report Brief.

Parker, Simon C. 2018. *The Economics of Entrepreneurship*. Cambridge: Cambridge University Press.

Reynolds, Paul. 2005. *Entrepreneurship in the US: The Future Is Now*. Springer.

Rigobon, Daniel E., Thibaut Duprey, Artur Kotlicki, Philip Schnattinger, Soheil Baharian, and Thomas R. Hurd. 2022. "Business Closures and (Re) Openings in Real-Time Using Google Places: Proof of Concept." *Journal of Risk and Financial Management* 15, no. 4: 183.

Robb, Alicia, and Adji Fatou Diagne. 2025. "Startup Dynamics: Transitioning from Nonemployer Firms to Employer Firms, Survival, and Job Creation." U.S. Census Bureau Center for Economic Studies Discussion Paper 25–26.

Rouse, Cecilia. 2024. "Lessons for Economists from the Pandemic." *Reporter*, no. 3 (October). Cambridge, MA: National Bureau of Economic Research.

Simon, Ruth. 2024. "Latinos Are Starting U.S. Businesses at a Torrid Pace." *Wall Street Journal*, March 26, 2024.

Stanford Latino Entrepreneurship Initiative. 2020. *The Impact of COVID-19 on Latino-Owned Business*. Stanford, CA: Stanford Latino Entrepreneurship Initiative.

Stangler, Dane. 2009. *The Economic Future Just Happened*. Kansas City: Ewing Marion Kauffman Foundation.

Staples, Aaron J., and Thomas P. Krumel Jr. 2023. "The Paycheck Protection Program and Small Business Performance: Evidence from Craft Breweries." *Small Business Economics* 61, no. 3: 931–956.

Stoll, Michael A., Steven Raphael, and Harry J. Holzer. 2001. "Why Are Black Employers More Likely Than White Employers to Hire Blacks?" Madison: University of Wisconsin, Institute for Research on Poverty.

U.S. Bureau of Labor Statistics. 2020. *Labor Force Statistics from the Current Population Survey*.

U.S. Bureau of Labor Statistics. 2024. "Business Employment Dynamics, Establishment Age and Survival Data: Table 7. Survival of Private Sector Establishments by Opening Year." https://www.bls.gov/bdm/us_age_naics_00_table7.txt.

U.S. Census Bureau. 2016. *Survey of Business Owners (SBO)—Survey Results: 2012*.

U.S. Census Bureau. 2020. "Small Business Pulse Survey." https://portal.census.gov/pulse/data/.

U.S. Census Bureau. 2021. "Census Bureau Announces Changes for 2020 American Community Survey 1-Year Estimates." Press release, July 29. https://www.census.gov/newsroom/press-releases/2021/changes-2020-acs-1-year.html.

U.S. Census Bureau. 2022. "2022 Business Dynamics Statistics Data Tables." https://www.census.gov/data/tables/time-series/econ/bds/bds-tables.html.

U.S. Census Bureau. 2025. "Business Dynamics Statistics of Businesses that Received SBA COVID Response Funds (BDS-SBA COVID Response)." https://www.census.gov/data/experimental-data-products/bds-sba-covid.html.

U.S. Congress. 2020. "Coronavirus Aid, Relief, and Economic Security Act." https://www.congress.gov/116/bills/hr748/BILLS-116hr748enr.pdf.

U.S. Department of Justice. 2024. "COVID-19 Fraud Enforcement Task Force 2024 Report." U.S. Department of Justice, Council of the Inspectors General on Integrity and Efficiency.

U.S. Federal Reserve Banks. 2021. "2021 Report on Firms Owned by People of Color: Based on the 2020 Small Business Credit Survey." *Small Business Credit Survey*. Federal Reserve Banks.

U.S. Government Accounting Office. 2023. "COVID Relief: Fraud Schemes and Indicators in SBA Pandemic Programs." Report GAO-23–105331.

U.S. Senate. 2020. "Cardin, Cantwell, Schumer, Booker, Cortez Masto & Harris Introduce Legislation to Invest in Minority-Owned Businesses." U.S. Senate Committee on Small Business & Entrepreneurship.

U.S. Small Business Administration. 2020a. "Disaster Assistance Update: Nationwide EIDL Loans, November 23, 2020" (table). www.sba.gov/sites/default/files/2021-02/EIDL%20COVID-19%20Loan%2011.23.20-508_0.pdf.

U.S. Small Business Administration. 2020b. "Disaster Assistance Update EIDL Advance July15, 2020." www.sba.gov/sites/default/files/2021-02/EIDL%20COVID-19%20Advance%207.15.20-508.pdf.

U.S. Small Business Administration. 2020c. "Paycheck Protection Program (PPP) Report: Approvals Through 08/08/2020." https://www.sba.gov/sites/sbagov/files/2021-09/PPP_Report%20-%202020-08-10-508.pdf.

U.S. Small Business Administration. 2021a. "Fact Sheet: Changes to Paycheck Protection Program by Biden-Harris Administration Increase Equitable Access to Relief." https://www.sba.gov/article/2021/mar/09/fact-sheet-changes-paycheck-protection-program-biden-harris-administration-increase-equitable-access.

U.S. Small Business Administration. 2021b. "Paycheck Protection Program (PPP) Report: Approvals Through 05/31/2021."

U.S. Small Business Administration. 2022a. "Disaster Assistance Update Nationwide COVID EIDL, Targeted EIDL Advances, Supplemental Targeted Advances." April 28.

U.S. Small Business Administration. 2022b. *Shuttered Venue Operators Grant Public Report.* Office of Disaster Assistance, July 5.

U.S. Small Business Administration, Office of Inspector General. 2023. "COVID-19 Pandemic EIDL and PPP Loan Fraud Landscape." www.sba.gov/sites/default/files/2023-06/SBA%20OIG%20Report%2023-09.pdf.

van der Sluis, J., M. van Praag, and W. Vijverberg. 2005. "Education and Entrepreneurship in Industrialized Countries: A Meta-analysis." *World Bank Economic Review* 19, no. 2: 225–261.

Wang, Chunbei. 2019. "Tightened Immigration Policies and the Self-Employment Dynamics of Mexican Immigrants." *Journal of Policy Analysis and Management* 38, no. 4: 944–977.

Wagner, Aaron B., Elaine L. Hill, Sean E. Ryan, Ziteng Sun, Grace Deng, Sourbh Bhadane, Victor Hernandez Martinez, et al. 2020. "Social Distancing Merely Stabilized COVID-19 in the United States." *Stat* 9, no. 1: e302.

Wilmoth, Daniel. 2020. *Black Business Owners Hit Hard by Pandemic.* U.S. Small Business Administration, Office of Advocacy Report, August.

Wilmoth, Daniel. 2021. *The Effects of the COVID-19 Pandemic on Small Businesses.* U.S. Small Business Administration, Office of Advocacy Issue Brief no. 16.

Yelp. 2020. "Yelp: Local Economic Impact Report." https://www.yelpeconomicaverage.com/business-closures-update-sep-2020.

Zissimopoulos, Julie M., and Lynn A. Karoly. 2007. "Transitions to Self-Employment at Older Ages: The Role of Wealth, Health, Health Insurance and Other Factors." *Labour Economics* 14, no. 2: 269–295.

Index

Publisher contact:
The MIT Press
Massachusetts Institute of Technology
77 Massachusetts Avenue, Cambridge, MA 02139
mitpress.mit.edu

EU Authorised Representative:
Easy Access System Europe, Mustamäe tee 50,
10621 Tallinn, Estonia
gpsr.requests@easproject.com

Printed by Integrated Books International,
United States of America